For those whom I have not met
Who have gone before,
Where the trees meet the sky
Waiting,
My brothers, I am coming.

But that the dread of something after death,
The undiscovered country from whose bourne
No traveller returns, puzzles the will,
And makes us rather bear those ills we have
Than fly to others that we know not of?

Shakespeare
Hamlet

Contents

INTRODUCTION — 1

820 PETOSKEY AVENUE — 7

The Summer
Cursum Perficio
The Winter
The Glaciers
The Land
The Night
The Town
Whitney's Tavern
The Sailboats
The Petunia Festival
The Venetian Festival
Traverse City
Leelanau
The Dinner Party
Overture in E-Flat Major
The East Jordan Road

LIGHT, DANCING ON WATER — 59

The White Shadow
The Possum
The Birds
The Red and The Blue
The Wild Ducks
The Great Blue Herons
The Red-Tailed Hawk
The Wild Turkeys
The Trilliums
The Monarch Butterflies
The Butterfly and His Wings
The Deer Hunter

6101 NORTH SHERIDAN ROAD   89

Chariots of Fire
The Land That Time Forgot
The 400 Blows
The Razor's Edge
Vivit Post Funera Virtus
The Gift of the Magi

THE BEAVER ISLAND BOAT FERRY   117

The Campfire
The Kindness of Strangers
The Sacred Grove
The Field of the Cloth of Gold
The Secret Garden
Freude, Schöner Götterfunken
The Heel-Stone
La Belle Au Bois Dormant
Brighid
The Cairn
The Blue Grotto
The Way of All Flesh

GHOSTS OF BOYNE CITY   153

Footsteps on the Ceiling
The Night Watch
La Règle Du Jeu

BARTON BRILEY AND THE NEW MOON   169

The Hundred-Acre Wood
The Elder Children
The Farm Pavillions
The Artist in His Studio
The Northern Country
When the Moon Was High
Potage Crème Des Champignons
Scotch And The Single Man

A BLOODY GOOD TIME AT THE BAR 189

Petoskey
Only Wise Men Know....
The Potteries
Portrait of the Artist as a Young Man
Cava
Chandler's
The Lives Of Others
The Last Supper
If You Could Read My Mind, Love
The Lightning Storm

UNDER THE MILKY WAY TONIGHT 223

The Seed
The Labyrinth
The Music
The Musicians
The Festivals
The Word
The Flower Children
The Lilies of the Field
Rose-Lipped Maidens; Lightfoot Lads
Some Like It Hot
The Lotus Eaters
The Walrus and the Carpenter
Under The Milky Way Tonight

WHERE THE WILD THINGS ARE 273

And What Rough Beast...?
Obelisk
The Long Way Home
The Bodyguard
Service with a Smile
The Christian Brother
The Michigan Dog-Man
The Stone Garden
The Angel of the Lord

ET LA POMME LUI DIT, MERCI   305

And Round That Early-Laurelled Head
Aftermath: The Poems for Jane

THE ITINERANT TRAVELLER   317

You've Got to Be Carefully Taught
The Winter's Tale
A View from the Bridge
The Evening Star
The Voice
The Nativity
The Nativity: A Poem
The Hummingbird
Et In Arcadia Ego
The Morning Star

A DEATH IN THE FAMILY   345

In Aslan's Country
Landscape, With Figures
Frei lebt, wer sterben Kann

THE LADY OF SHALOTT   363

The Moments of Happiness
Leave Right Now
Trio in E-Flat Major
Adjö Min Vän

AFTERWORD

NOTES

The Undiscovered Country

Special Edition

Where I shall find thee, in our fragrant garden,
'neath the nodding bluebells, shall be our shelter.

Introduction

I have taken it upon myself to write a chapter of my life, from a place I once thought should be my home; the programme of it was neither long nor short. As in all things divinely ordained, it was of its own length, woven, measured, and cut as the Fates demanded. It began and ended through means I did not imagine and did not foresee, for they were hidden from my view, like a road rising over the crest of pale-shadowed hills.

Time and its cousin, distance, have focussed their gaze upon this episode in differing views; in some, the glass is sharply attuned to each grain of sand, and in others, it is but a shadowy blur; the images are faint, and the colours muted. The eye is pressed firmly to the camera, but perceives these aspects mechanically; the light, falling upon our faces, which we see naturally, is reflected otherwise through its lens.

It will remain therefore, for the reader to assess this episode, whether to be quickly savoured as a morsel of sugared icing, a crumb from a slice of rich cake, or a more precious commodity, a dark, fragrant truffle, freshly dug from the roots of a spreading oak.

My own response I have not determined, for its presence in my life, and its progression within its framework did not occur immediately, but before I came to that place, and thus, long after. I have often wondered if it is the *caesura*, the pause in the music, removed from the composition, which clarifies and unites the whole. Perhaps the clarification has occurred through the vehicle of a broken eggshell and some scraps of beef, dropped into the boiling consommé, and thus rendered clear and sparkling, a shining, golden bowl reflecting God's own light.

Why this period was destined, I cannot say, for I know all things work together for the glory of God. His purpose is still unknown; He has not yet revealed it. One day, I shall see it spread before me, as though I were flying above the earth and the shape of it presented below, for my delight and my aedification; it shall be a broad facsimile of the English countryside, in its geometric beauty of fields and hedges, its variations, and shades of green. When I look upon it in its complete form, then I shall say, *yes*.

Now, I understand. This is how it was meant to be, and so it has been fashioned, and shaped, with light areas, and dark ones, in their proper position and sequence, and many other colours in the spaces between.

Perhaps I should prefer this pattern to resemble the Land of Counterpane; to appear as a vast, comfortable quilt worked with pieces of many colours and shapes. There will be squares of cloth almost threadbare, of worn, blue, and white-striped cotton, and other squares of finest silk velvet, fit for a prince. Some will be faded, with no discernible colour or pattern; others shall be richly embroidered, with fine gold threads. Some colours will appear bright and sunny, others darker or faded, and some will have disappeared altogether. They will have been removed, erased, for they are reminders of things best left forgotten; there is too much blood and dirt upon them to possess any value. They are torn and fragmented, for they bear numerous scars, and so the quilt must be mended, and the damages removed.

The stitchings will vary, for the edges of our lives must have their bindings; it is by the dimension of a thing that we can best comprehend its construction. Were the pieces not joined together, the entire jumble of these scraps should resemble the coloured bits and spangles found within an elegant kaleidoscope; I have not yet learned to turn the dial to reveal the correct pattern, for there are many variations. The sparkling fragments combine, forming different, startling, mosaics of colour and design, each worthy of contemplation and analysis; each turn reveals another enhancement, a composition of the whole, and we can fashion it to our will.

Which of these will form the correct alignment, which gives the most complete portrait, for they are all beautiful; yet each in its own sphere is incomplete, its finale unknown.

Regardez, devant vous
Il y a des pétales, sur la toile blanche
Tenez-même, dans vos mains
Pour leur beauté, qu'est tombée
Et leur parfum, comme une voile blanche
Dans l'air s'attarde maintenant
Vous ne pouvez pas le tenir
Pourtant, là, il s'accroche, et reste.

820 Petoskey Avenue

South of the Straits of Mackinac, which divide Upper and Lower Michigan, but which also join three of the Great Lakes, Huron, Michigan, and Superior, the land spreads gently and broadly; it curves to the east, into Lake Huron, and to the west, it reaches down along Lake Michigan. As the shores extend themselves, they form the Lower Peninsula, and this area, from the Mackinac Bridge to Traverse City, is known as northern Michigan. I once lived there, in Charlevoix, where I had a small house on the curving saddle of land separating Lake Michigan and Lake Charlevoix. My house was positioned on the Lake Charlevoix side, on a gently sloping lawn above the water.

In the winter mornings, when the trees were bare, it was possible to see the lake, glittering and grey, from my bedroom; in the summer, the view was masked by green leaves.

I did not regret the lack of a long, framed vista; the substance of it was always there; I felt it, and I heard it, at times, in the clear, still evenings. It was, and remained, a presence always felt beyond the edge of the trees; it was the focus of one's life, *centrum mundi*.

The summer light, slowly rising, cast overlapping shadows, in many layers of bright, clear green, upon the windows of my house. It was a moment I often longed to capture with oils, but my efforts were not a great success. When I took the paint, quivering on my brush, to the blank canvas, the colours muddied and ran together; they were dull and lifeless upon the square surface, and made only a poor facsimile.

To the west of my house, there rose a towering mass of cottonwood trees, a summit of heavy, aged heads. They marked the lines of the golf course, and the beginning of the water; they reminded me, in the golden, burning autumns, of Lothlórien, the Dream-flower; Laurelindórenan, the Valley of the Singing Gold.

To the east, the edges of my lawns were bordered by thick stands of oak and hickory trees; beyond that, the forest rose up, where the land slopes away, falling gently to Lake Charlevoix. There were houses there, and beyond there were other residential areas, but I had no access to them; the roads did not connect behind my house but went around it, skirting the golf links and the hotel.

On the north side, there was no view; the Petoskey Road ran directly across the high, sloping ground, and the lawn was bare, and speckled with patches of tough grass. Only the garage was visible from the road; even the front door was concealed. It was not a pretty landscape, but I did not spend time there; it was the public face of my house, and I remained behind it. There were high trees beyond the road, for they are a common border to all vistas in northern Michigan, the remnants of the great pine forests that stood for centuries. Across the road, on a bare lawn, vintage automobiles, with signs advertising their sale, would be parked by various persons; sometimes I would go look at them, and imagine how I might refurbish them, to their original appearance.

Nevertheless, it was to the south that I turned my directions, when I was in my house; it was the focus and the centre of my vision at all times. Towards the lake, away from the street, I had a wide strip of narrow garden bordered with yellow pine trees and thick, cedar hedges; the grass grew lush and green in the summers, and there were wildflowers along the edges in many colours of white, yellow, and lavender.

My house was not large, yet neither was it small; it was, as a certain young woman might have said, just *right*. I welcomed many guests there, and it was always pleasant to receive them all: friends, family, and fools. There was a big, high-ceilinged space, with the kitchen and the sitting room combined, and my bedroom, which had a large bath. There was a guest room, and a smaller room, which I used as my office. All these were connected by a long, wide corridor, surfaced in golden oak, with white, painted walls.

One felt utterly at ease in the seclusion, as though one were in a cozy, book-lined room, high up in a silent tower, or by a deep, mossy riverbank, shaded by spreading, flowering trees and glimmering here and there with buttercups. Here, one might do or say anything, for all outcomes were possible; even the most absurd conceptions might be realised, or brought to fruition in some artful fashion.

I have often imagined this room, when I have looked upon my life there, and conceived different schemes of interior decoration I might have employed; it was not furnished to my taste. I should not do it up in the same manner, however; my life has changed, and my tastes have evolved; they are stripped of excrescence, refined, and purified; a single, perfect vase such as Josiah Wedgwood might have made, and then shattered the casting mould upon the floor. Perhaps, at times, I have imagined that my tastes have evolved even further, from the Portland Vase to the Neptune, a continuing process of cleansing, as though the desert sands were stripping the surface smooth with their fine particles, revealing features of proportion, form, and colour.

When I first moved into the house, it was finished in white throughout, with only the shining floors to add colour and depth. Yet I was able to impress upon it the stamp and the shape of my personality, with my books, my rugs, and my curtains; I had no other furniture, save a few chairs from my old apartment. There were some patterned stuffs, relicts of old projects, salvaged from the dustbin, and fashioned into pillows, blankets, and loose covers; they were the colours of old, faded blue denim, dark Indian reds, and a sort of beige, which is sometimes called camel, or biscuit. It was the colour of the leather upholstery of a very old Series III X-type sedan, in the days when they were still hand-fashioned in Coventry and therefore of a quality to be admired, and possibly envied. Various small objects of crystal and brass were positioned about the shelves and the tables; these had belonged to my mother, she had brought them from India, and from England. Many of them had been wedding-presents, but my mother had asked me to take them; she knew they would be safe, in my care.

My small collection of model Jaguar sedan cars and drophead coupés was arranged on the bookcase; they were mostly red, but I had one XK120 in the classic British colour, dark racing green. I had an old creamware bowl mounted with rams' heads, which held apples on the dining table; it was always kept full and my guests would help themselves. On the drinks table, I kept my good glasses and several bottles, for my guests always brought wine for our meals, and we enjoyed our apéritifs in the evenings, before, and after dinner. My friends kept me well supplied with brandies and cognacs; I was once given a very old, dusty bottle of *marc*, which I enjoyed, alone, under the full moon, sitting on the porch looking over the garden. I was rarely alone there, however; there were animals and birds, on their own, swift passages, to enliven the edges of our evenings; they were fitting embroidery to our conversations, and often interrupted them. The lady, and her unicorn in the walled garden, might have felt at ease beneath its roof; the wild animals welcomed me equally there.

It was always pleasant, regardless of the weather, to sit outside on the deep porch, looking towards the water. There was no view of it in the summer, no captured vista of the Boyne hills, such as might have been translated there as at Ryōan-ji, and which adds value and meaning; it is a product of a refined, trained discipline in the gardener's art. Were it to have been so constructed, perhaps it might have featured in a publication; the enhancement of the view would have then made the garden seem even larger. What views held there were bound only by the sky, a thin, shimmering sheet of palest blue silk hung upon the air, delicate and quivering, with the faintest wash of green where it descended into the trees.

It was the trees, however, which gave scope and vision to the garden, for their heights reared far to the east and to the west, and formed a backdrop, which I did not possess but made glad use of. By their mass and their shape, they defined the edges, and formed a place in that world, which expanded it, and thus stitched it into the life of the town.

My porch was very wide and deep; it wrapped around three sides of the house, with a large, projecting bay, where one might be comfortable in the shade. I once thought of furnishing it as an outdoor room, with sofas and chairs, cushions, and many flowering plants; a friend showed me her own porch, which she had hung with gaily-striped fabrics. The light, in the evenings, was softened through the cloth, as though it were a fragment of faded, stained glass, from an old church in the country.

I enjoyed sitting on my porch, alone in the quiet mornings before the world came to life. The sun was a golden haze above the green-black trees, and the birds were not yet awake. Sometimes, I would glimpse my neighbours on the street below; out for a morning stroll with their dogs. Because of the land, and its slope, they could not see me; I could only barely view them through the shrubbery. Many evenings, a doe and her fawns would step daintily across the lawn, following the trail down to the lake. I often wondered at their ease across the grass, realising only later that the path had been there long before. Often, they would pass close by the porch; I felt I might reach out my hand to them. They took no notice of me, but walked past as though I did not exist. I did not wish to startle them; their presence was a gift, and a welcome one; yet I was the intruder.

The light, dancing upon the water, would glitter and flash, and always awaken me earlier than I had intended. The rising sun would shyly peep through the French doors of my bedroom, filling it with that soft, white light which is found only in the north. During the winter, the sun rose very late, in a pale red glow far to the south; the air was brisk and cold, yet I did not feel the chill, wrapped in my warm blankets. It was strange to me, used to the harshness of the Midwest, to come upon the tranquility of the Michigan winter, although I cannot say the same for its roads.

The Summer

The summers in northern Michigan are very short, but the days are long and warm, and the nights very cool; in the autumns, it can be very cold when one is dining outdoors, as I often did, on my porch. The white cloth would be laid, and smoothed flat, held down by beach rocks; they are called Petoskey Stones, and are a feature of the region. The stones are not very big, about the size of one's fist, or even smaller; their surfaces are a honeycomb of fossils and indentations, in a soft colour, like a beige travertine. They are easy to hold in the hand; they are warm, and cool all together; one wonders what journeys the stone has taken, to arrive at that place and that time, to be lifted into the air, that it might grace your palm.

The air in northern Michigan is dry, drier than in other parts of the state, even Grand Rapids, and thus possessed of a comfort not found elsewhere. It is a soft, caressing embrace, even in the heat; it cannot harm you, and it is clean, alive with the scent of the water, and the pine-trees, and the high, blue glaciers of the tundra. It will affect you like an alcohol, you will have become intoxicated upon the air, but it is not air; it is a distillation of light, washed with the high snows and filtered through the golden meadows. One is alert and awakened, and hears the sound of the grass as the air moves upon it.

When the wind rises in the afternoon, it brings over the great blue lakes the tang of the fish, and the deep waters.

The clouds of the northern country are ever changing, rising up in the northwest like giant puffs of cotton wool as they peek over the tops of the pine-trees, then drift slowly over the bay, and disperse eastwards, to the central massifs of Gaylord and Vanderbilt. When the weather changes, the winds, rushing off Lake Superior, gust hard against these sudden heights, the clouds are carried before it, like sheep chased by a yapping dog. In the gentle summer evenings, however, they spread slowly across the western skies, in many gold and purple layers, before drifting away. At times they are almost motionless, hanging perfectly still in the golden sky as the day fades, but when you turn your head, they will have moved on.

There is calm to the northern sunset; the sun slowly falls into the west, and the summer days are long and full-measured, a warm, golden twilight lingers into the night. Often I have remained outdoors very late with my book, without need of a lantern.

Cursum Perficio

Along the drive from Charlevoix to Petoskey, there is a section of road skirting closely along the shore; there is a little park here. The rocks spread themselves among the dune-grasses; they resemble clumps of hard, brown sugar, dimpled with pits and crevices. Here, the waves are stilled; they do not swell along the shoreline but remain calm; it is very peaceful. The lake-gulls perch on the rocks in the mornings, when the sun is lifting its head above the Petoskey hills. The light is a warm, blushing pink, suffused with gold, spreading across the horizon as the day begins.

Returning home in the evenings, I often stopped at the little park, to watch the sun slowly sink into the calm, flat waters. The light would turn to gold, gently rippling across the surface, deepening to a dark blue across the north, and brightening to a silver-white along the horizon. The sun was a sinking, fading ball of red fire, motionless in a lavender mist; it was not in a hurry; it knew its effect and took its time about it.

I was never alone at the little park; there were other people who appreciated the view, who would watch the sunset, sitting on the wide, flat rocks, with the lake-gulls fluttering around them.

I once stopped at the little park, and saw two lights hanging in the evening sky as I drove home one summer day.

Far over the water, they shone brightly together, almost touching, two perfect white orbs hanging motionless above the sun. They remained there for a time, and I was reminded of the meeting of Tarva and Alambil, the Lord of Victory and the Lady of Peace, performing their *pas de deux* in the stars, ignorant of those witnesses below. Who is the greater, I wondered, or the more complete: the actors in such a performance as this, or the audience invited to assemble around them?

The Winter

The snow in northern Michigan is unlike the lower Midwest; it is drier, and thus lighter, than what I have seen elsewhere. On the ski hills, it falls as a fine, delicate powder, which lifts one's skies almost effortlessly. In the towns, it falls heavily and quickly, and lingers long into the spring.

Snow does not bring hardship, for it generates revenue. I did not have to wait for the ploughs; indeed, they were almost there before the snow. In the night, I would hear the blades scraping the Petoskey Road, and I would call a man to plough my drive, so that I might get out in the morning. He always came early, and cleared the path to my garage; he was an efficient and cheerful worker. I had friends who lived further out, in the farm country; they equipped their own trucks with big, curving blades that pushed the snow into towering piles of hard, white rock-shaped lumps. The snow would be formed into great mounds, like tumbled mountains, in the carparks; they were very large, an alpine landscape in miniature. One could imagine a short film made of these piles, using toy figurines, lost in a vast, frozen wasteland, on the screen. The mountains of snow lasted into the spring and often revealed, as they slowly dissolved, odd bits of paper, leaves, and moss that had been gathered up with them, colourful scraps that lingered on the black pavements until the spring rains washed them away.

The Glaciers

The great glaciers of Michigan, as they retreated to the north ten thousand years ago, left behind fragments of earth, and trees, rocks, and plants, as they withdrew from the land. In the spring, as the farmers plough the long, flat acres, I have seen them stopping suddenly, as a chunk of weathered granite emerged from the soil, dusty pink, blue or green in the sunlight, which it had not seen for aeons. How long has it remained hidden in the earth, moving slowly upwards, towards the light, only to be hauled away into a pile beneath the trees?

The granite boulders and rocks are seen across the country landscape; there are many barns and houses built with granite foundations, in all the colours of the rainbow. Over time, they have weathered; their shades have softened to a uniform, smooth grey, but their original colours can be seen, upon closer inspection. I have often wondered if there might be wide veins of granite far below the surface, in deep greens, blues, or brilliant pinks that might have been quarried. They could be fashioned into many things, and generate an income for the people of the farm country.

I once thought it might be of interest to carve a date into these lumps of stone, as they were brought to the surface, a remark of the ploughing and the harvest, so soon to come after.

My suggestion came to naught in the end; I was not there in the spring, when the bright blades sliced into the cold earth. My friends on the farm called me, to tell me of the rocks they had unearthed as they went out to the fields. They had found granite boulders in colours of pink, blue and a whitish-grey, even a blackened colour that suggested a fire many years past. From Montmorency, another friend told me of rocks flecked with gold, they were iron pyrite, he said, but very beautiful; I should come see them. No, I said, I cannot, I am not there, and I am not here.

The Land

The fields of northern Michigan are found mostly in the broad, wide plateau stretching and rippling, like a hand-planed surface, from the Cadillac range to the Mancelona escarpment, and from there northeast to Gaylord and Elmira. From the air, they form an irregular checkerboard, within the Manistee and Huron forests, where the fields have been cleared. They are not flat like the plains of Indiana and Illinois, which are a billiard table, widening all around you to the horizon, and which excite you in their vastness. There, the land stretches far away from you on all sides; there is no edge to it, and the small, blue trees in the fields are like little balls of fluff on a green-stitched blanket. The sky disappears at its edge, simply falling away, and you cannot comprehend its termination; you are travelling beneath a vast dome of palest blue, ringed with soft, grey clouds.

In northern Michigan, however, the vista is contained; the edges are defined. There are blue-shadowed hills to the east and the sudden emptiness beyond the forest, to the west; one looks to see, and wonder what lies beyond them, for there are dragons and other fantastical monsters in the wilderness, that we do not always see, or imagine.

As you come into Grand Rapids and north to Cadillac, the land mounts up; a series of broad plateaus, arranged in concentric rings, each a wide, flat strip of green, edged by tumbled slopes.

One passes through these plateaus as one drives north: Kalkaska, Mancelona, and Elmira. One's view turns and rotates towards the sky; it becomes the perspective, defined by the long rows of white pine trees. North of Elmira, the land begins to fall towards the water, a series of long, wide slopes, rising, and tumbling again. The road falls, and rises again; you are coming home.

One draws closer to the water; it is a magnet, pulling your car forward, the rotation of the earth cannot be sufficient impulse. One can feel its proximity; the clouds over Mackinac tower up high into the sky; the lake is near. Far off to the north and west, there is a sudden, gleaming white edge above the trees; the lake is near. Then, as one crests the last hill, one sees it: the wide, stretching waters of Little Traverse Bay, of deep sapphire blue sprinkled with white bits of confetti; one has arrived, this is the northern country, at last, at last.

The Night

In the northern country, the darkness of night is different from the darkness of the city; it is a different colour altogether. In Chicago, the sky does not turn black, or even a deep blue; it remains suffused with the deep amber glare of the streetlights. Only in the morning does the light change, to a deeper shade of blue washed with copper, which slowly begins to fade, far to the east; at the edge of the water, a new day is approaching. There are stars to be seen, of course, but very few, and very dim. If the wind is from a certain direction, then one can also see a string of airplanes, suspended motionless in a long, straight row, reaching far into the distance, over Indiana, and the Michigan coastline beyond. As the planes align themselves to approach O'Hare field, they are directed over the lake, lights hanging on an invisible wire. At my dinner parties in Chicago, it became a game for my guests, to count the number of planes visible over the lake. My table was set parallel to the window, so that each might appreciate the view, and comment upon it; it was always beautiful at night, when the lake was calm and smooth, and the dim glow of the lights across Lake Michigan marked the edge of the sky, as the moon rose, round and red, from its depths.

However, in the farm country, there are no streetlights, and the skies are black when there is no moon. The houses are few, and lit by small lamps; there are no lights on the road. When one drives at night, it is with care, it is not easy to spot the whitetail deer, until they pass in front of you. Here walk the cougar, and the black wolf; the wolverine has been spotted in the Upper Peninsula. The coyotes howl at the autumn moon, and you hear their call; you long to join them on their hunts, to answer their voices, as they echo through the darkness. They are running tonight, they are hungry, and you may join them, if you will, and share in their feast.

In the night, it is possible, beneath the heavens, to feel that one is become a part of them, a unity of body and spirit magnified and expanded by your presence. The stars cast their pale, silver light upon the grass, and the woods are dark masses of shadow at the edges of the shimmering grey fields. Objects take on other shapes and forms from what we have known, together mysterious and alluring. Beyond the trees, one hears footsteps; there are other creatures passing through the forest, but they are hidden from your view; you do not see them. Across the silver grass comes a dark, bounding shape; it reveals itself to be a dog, friendly and panting as you feed him, then he is off again, to chase squirrels in the flowerbeds.

There is the sound of laughter, a golden beam of light spills from an open doorway, and with a word, a gesture, and a friendly greeting, you are once again with friends, and no longer alone in the world; a door has opened into another realm.

The Town

The town of Charlevoix is organised around two main thoroughfares, one leading south to Traverse City, and, in the opposite direction, leading northeast to Petoskey. The other leads south to East Jordan, and beyond that, to Mancelona, Antrim, and Kalkaska; one joins the main road to Cadillac, and Grand Rapids, from there. Both of these wrap gently, and with many curves, around Lake Charlevoix and its harbour, Round Lake, which connects to Lake Michigan through the Pine River. There is a fine park in the centre of town along Bridge Street, and the boat-docks are here, extending along the shoreline on the south; the ferryboats to Beaver Island dock nearby.

    Bridge Street is beautifully shaded with many large, old trees; they spread their dark branches across the road and provide a promenade. There are many stores and cafés along its length, and they all command fine views over the water; it is possible, at times, to look far down the length of Lake Charlevoix, if the light is good. In the summer, the local farmers set up their stalls of fruit, vegetables and pies, and in their season, the cherries and peaches, followed by the apples, and the autumn vegetables. The apple festival takes place in October, long after the summer people have left, but it is a vibrant, bustling event, full of the celebration of the fruit and the harvest.

Whitney's Tavern

Facing Round Lake, across the park, is Whitney's Tavern, with a small bar downstairs, and a long bar upstairs, on the roof. The locals use the small bar, it is perfectly sized for them; the long bar is open in the season, when the tourists come, and the summer people; it is very popular; the food and the drinks are very good.

Here, on a bright warm day, it is possible to eat icy-fresh oysters, still quivering in their shells on a bed of crushed ice, sweating alongside cold, marinated vegetables. There is a light, dry white wine, in thin, thin glasses with transparent stems, floating over the tablecloths. Outside, the sailboats sway and dart like errant birds; there are motorboats scampering over the waves like playful puppies. The wind is full of the smell of the light and the water, and the catch brought in that morning; I had good fish there, and it was a source of some pride for the tavern, for it was well prepared, simply and quickly, as fish should be.

I have only had better fish in France, I think, in its simplicity of preparation, and after that, in San Francisco; in Charlevoix, it was filleted with a sharp knife, while you waited, and then sautéed with sweet butter and wine, and presented on a very hot plate, with dill, in the Swedish fashion. Once, I ordered my trout *à la meunière*, and it was a true delight to me, for it came to the table properly made, sautéed in brown butter and lemon, not fried in a hot bath of oil, as I had usually experienced it. When I thanked the chef, as I was leaving, he smiled at my gratitude; the simplicity of the dish was natural to him, he did not make a pretense of it.

They served good drinks at the tavern; the bartenders were very friendly. When I once enjoyed there a superb Chenin Blanc with a dish of chicken and mushrooms, I realised to the full the courtesy of Edward VII, who once said to Escoffier after a banquet, "The Chateau d'Yquem…was excellent."

The Sailboats

In the summer, the sailboats are drawn up to the docks, and here are arranged many different types, mostly single-hulled, although I have seen catamarans on the water; there are sloops, cutters, ketches, and schooners, all attired in their own fashion. The hulls are usually painted white, with many different coloured stripes, and sometimes with very humourous names; there is one very large sailboat with a bright yellow hull, like the colour of a wasp; it is very conspicuous. They resemble nothing so much as proper society ladies at a ball in full rigging, dowagers, and princesses, speaking a language of their own.

    They will share it with you, for a price, and the assault upon your fortunes will not be a terrible one, but you will have paid, nonetheless. What you receive in return is a matter of personal interest; there is always something to be given, and taken, on the boats, and many exchanges are possible.

    At anchor, floating gently, the masts march down both sides of the docks in orderly procession, wrapped in their blue sleeves, one stands in a sunlit clearing in a nautical grove. Out on the water, however, the white canvas gleams brightly, and they come racing past; the water does not hold them, they are not creatures of this world. They are not a thing of nature, for they are entirely artificial, yet designed and built to respond to the forces of wind, air, and water: an object of great beauty and joy, a synthesis of art and machine, a strange chimaera, indeed.

    I have not yet decided whether a finely rigged sailboat is more like a bird or a fish, when it leaps through the water, and the spray glitters as you lean into it. The air rushes at you, and the light is blinding in a thousand sparks upon the water; the waves splash over the bow as you dip down, and then you are lifted high again, upon the rim of the world, higher and higher.

    You grasp the line firmly in your hands, your shoes grip the deck, all else is forgotten in the rush, the joy, and the speed; you are one with the boat, and the voices that call go unheard. The captain beckons from the wheel, and you acknowledge his voice, but you do not heed it. At this moment, you are not a human creature, but a bronzed-green sea-god, emerging from the deep; the boat has lifted you upon its prow like a dripping trophy; you have been raised above the water, and you look down upon it. Are you a fish, gasping at the air with canvas fins, or a bird swooping low over the waves with canvas wings? What sort of creature have you become, that you have been fashioned thus, neither of the one world nor the other; you are suspended, for the moment, between the two.

    It is very amusing, in the summer, to witness the bridge rising over the Pine River to allow the boats through, the law of the sea governs all. The boats hurry swiftly out; there is an air of excitement, of a bright, sun-filled day ahead; one is slightly jealous, as one sits at the bridge and peers at the boats, through the raised vertical gratings. They are lifted high into the air, a pair of slender gates, which salute the departures. In the evenings, the boats return slowly, calmly, happily; it has been a good day, and the sailors are sunburned; their shoulders gleam red in the fading light. The women wear dark glasses, large floppy hats, and yellow floral bikinis; they are smiling and holding drinks as they glide past. The captain allows you the wheel; you steer carefully as you approach the rocks lining the river; he takes the wheel from you again, but you stay with him, to admire his skill as he guides the boat through the water; you are both tired. He holds his arm next to yours, and they are not the same colour; he is a statue of bronze, but your skin is copper. The glasses clink with ice, and the tonic fizzes; there are fresh limes for the gin. He lets you wear his cap; for a moment, you have exchanged places, and you are now in command. Later, you will surrender your office, but for now, the boat is yours.

The Beaver Island ferries make many trips out to the island, and return from it, during the summer; in all the time I lived in Charlevoix, I never learned the timetable; I had to look it up at the ferryboat offices along the dock. There are two passenger ferries, the larger carries trucks: I have often taken it. The smaller ferry does not take cars, only people, and it can be very pleasant but cold to ride on the foredeck, with only the bow before you. The wind rushes at you in the early morning, and you sip scalding-hot coffee from your thermos; somewhere, amongst your belongings, there is a blue knapsack with a bottle in it. The larger ferry is more spacious, with a long upper deck, and wide, fixed seats at the tables; it is very pleasant to sit here, and watch the water gliding past in a wide, flat sheet of perfect, pleated blue.

  The morning passage of the boats was a great frustration for me, it would coincide, invariably, with my daily routine; I would spend many minutes waiting. The sun would be a wash of pink against grey clouds, the water would be a dark steel-coloured black, with only the barest hint of blue; the gulls would flutter overhead like animated bits of paper, white, grey, red, and yellow. Jane's engine would idle softly, and I would yawn and stretch, and make furious noises, then calm would come upon me, and I would find a café for breakfast; I needed coffee, eggs, and bacon, toast, and good marmalade.

The Petunia Festival

The festivals, advancing the calendar, mark the seasons in northern Michigan; they proceed in order, uninterrupted by any vagaries of weather. In Charlevoix, each spring, the Petunia Festival is held, where many hundreds of pink, white, and lavender-purple blooms are planted alongside Petoskey Avenue, and all the way into town. It is not, perhaps, as celebrated as the Venetian Festival in July or the Apple Festival in October, but it is a harbinger, and an important one; the summer season has begun.

The plantings actually began at my drive, on both sides of the road; my house was a long way out from the centre of town, and it was a pleasant conceit to think it had been planned this way, for my benefit. It was a surprise to me, soon after I had arrived, to find the bedding plants set out, at the edge of my lawns. I did not plant them, however; someone else came, and put them in the ground for me. I did not witness their planting, nor did I ever meet the gardeners; I should have wished to thank them, for it cannot have been an easy job.

Along both sides of the road, a narrow strip of soil is prepared, which extends along Bridge Street, and terminates at the other end of town; it is a length of nearly two full miles. Many hundreds of petunias are planted every year; they do not survive the cold winters, but thrive in the heat of summer.

Petunias are an odd creation; I am not certain if I like them. They are a very pretty summer flower, and spill out of baskets and bowls in a pleasing fashion; they have many colours. My favourite is a very deep purple, almost an eggplant, like a bruise on a boxer's cheek. In certain lights, it can appear almost blue, or even a rich, deep black colour. There are also many striped varieties, in pink, blue, red, and white. In the white, summer air of northern Michigan, the pink and striped colours seem best; the red varieties are better in Chicago, where the golden-misted light tints them in the mornings; they are very beautiful there.

Despite my affinity for white flowers, I do not care for the same in the petunia; they hold no value for me. Unlike the white narcissus, which is a rare winter treat, or the white iris, which is not found in nature; it is, instead, an earthy, fleshy colour; there is no delicacy, no infusion of light, no depth. The petals lie heavily in your hand; they have no life, no mystery. The surface is like a white cast-off skin of pale leather, an ungainly carapace.

Voltaire once spoke of the superfluous as a necessity, and there is truth in this, one finds it at Sissinghurst. The white gardens there have captivated me, with their arrangements by colour, shape, and texture; it is a reflection of the sensitivity and eye of their owners. It was a surprise to me to witness such profusion of blooms, of a single colour, in an enclosed space, and to exclaim in the joy of it; I had not thought such discipline could succeed; it is a triumph of rigour and steadfastness, and the sure, certain eye of its gardeners. It is easier, I suppose, to fill a room with many colours, reds, blues, and yellows, this I have done, and the effects of it have been very beautiful.

My own training in the designer's art has been an evolutionary process, it was not a formal discipline; my own background has been architecture. It may be said that the greatest architects have been the best designers; one need only look at the *oeuvres* of Mies, Frank, or even Charles for such confirmation. They designed the building and developed its structure; they designed the furniture and the fittings for its interior rooms. Today, their pieces command high prices at the auction houses, and are displayed in museums; they have inspired me, in many projects. I have designed my own furniture, and my clients have always enjoyed and applauded my efforts; they have been very beautiful.

When one is first exposed to those ideals of beauty and creativity that exist in the world, one longs to encompass the whole, and to embrace it within one's bosom. It is a new world; one has progressed beyond the horizon of one's own vision and has begun to realise the perspective of others; it is a thrilling experience.

One learns, through one's own method, to eradicate, to smooth out the wrinkles and disruptions, to eliminate the ugly, the unnecessary, and the vulgar. Where, like Nancy Lancaster, I should have once filled a room with many beautiful things and done so successfully, now I am content to focus on one, or possibly two, exquisitely made objects, lending definition and purpose to the space; all else is garnish. The journey from Oxfordshire to Weimar, via Barcelona, has been accomplished, with perhaps a greater distance than one has actually travelled, or flown by the crows' reckoning; there have been many steps, detours and meanders along its route.

One must discipline oneself; nothing may be overlooked. All must be brought within the perspective of the design, its concept, and its realisation. No detail is too small, for it is often the forgotten element, the straw upon the camel's back, which detracts from the beauty of the whole, and diminishes its value; it deflects the eye, and lessens appreciation.

In the Zen approach to design, inherent in its practise, it is common to leave one item unfinished, or unvarnished, cracked or broken: a deliberate error or flaw, in the realm of an otherwise perfect accomplishment. This is, I think, a gesture of great humility and respect; it is an acknowledgement of the limits of Man, in his attempts to look upon the face of God, and to glory in His perfection.

The Venetian Festival

The Venetian Festival is the highlight of the Charlevoix summer; the population swells to nearly fifty-thousand persons, all of whom congregate downtown, in the lakefront park. The streets become impassable with traffic, and crossing the Pine River becomes a journey requiring great patience. Once, I waited at the bridge for the boats to float slowly past, only to see it rise twice, again, before I could drive upon it. I made many calls to friends while I waited there; their responses were not sympathetic.

There are people everywhere, walking along the sidewalks, and hurrying across the street, while you wait for the light to change; if you are at the bridge, they will often walk past you. I have had many conversations with friends in this fashion, sitting motionless in Jane while the bridge was raised, and leaning out the windows. It is impossible to manoeuvre anywhere, in the morning, after luncheon, and long after dinner; more than once, I have committed a traffic violation unnoticed, to get home in a reasonable time. The police did not stop me, or care; they had their hands full with the crowds that swarmed everywhere, like the foam splashed upon the slippery rocks.

Thursday of Venetian Week is the official start of the celebrations, and the crowds gather thickly along the shores of Round Lake; there are many tents erected in the park. One tent serves only beer, another only wine; there is a special tent for vodka-based drinks. The crowds are enormous, a scrum of human bodies ebbing and flowing across the grass, like a vast herd of plump, cackling geese.

Our party, a large one, found its way to the upstairs bar, on the roof of the old tavern, where we could sit in some comfort and enjoy the spectacle, both below our window and in the crowd around us. The deck was full; the crowd at once immutable and amorphous; it changed shape, swelling and collapsing, as newcomers were added, and people came and went to the long bar for drinks. The noise was tremendous, like the crashing of rain upon a metal roof; one could not hear a word spoken, but merely nodded one's head in agreement. It was hoped that some dubious arrangement had not been coordinated by doing so.

It is an enjoyable and enviable position to be the sole male escort to a group of pretty women. One is enveloped within an intimate setting, a cloister of lace and silk, removed from the outside world, yet still highly visible, and therefore desirable. One is surrounded by them, and talking with them, while the other men in the bar stare hungrily. They straighten their neckties and hitch up their trousers when they are ready to make their overtures; the older ones will stiffen their spines, visibly. Occasionally, one of them will summon up sufficient nerve to speak to the ladies, but will not make further progress; the safety of the group holds them within its fortress, and if the man is unknown, he is not welcomed.

Once he has been dismissed, his carriage and demeanour are dissected, verbally, by everyone in the party; it is an enjoyable pastime, and fills the conversational gaps.

One evening at the bar, there stood a very thin, very strange young man dressed completely in black, wearing a black suède cowboy hat, uniquely foreign in that nautical atmosphere, who spoke to no one. He was not unattractive, but the lines of his face suggested a strange *ennui* in the thronging press. With some jollity, we took it in turn to approach him, inviting him to join us, but he would not be persuaded and stood alone, hemmed in by the crowd.

We watched, as he remained there, speaking to no one; he made no effort to join the fun; no one spoke to him. From time to time, he would withdraw large sums from the teller in the corner, and then disappear downstairs to the second floor; he would then reappear, empty of cash and making his way once again to the bar.

The ladies, having become very curious, now became very insistent; I was thus deputed to find out more, and so totted up some liquid courage to follow him, when he next went downstairs. He entered the men's lavatory and with some trepidation, I followed, for it was very crowded.

The young man had disappeared into one of the stalls; I saw his dusty, black boots under the door and wondered at his need for privacy after such a public display. Another stall door opened, and a man stepped out, someone I had not seen before, who walked quickly past me; he was putting his jacket on. The man looked at me, but I did not say anything; I turned on the taps and began to wash my hands. I heard the click of a latch, and the next stall door opened. The young man emerged, but did not wash his hands; he stood perfectly still. The other man left; I did not see him again, I thought he looked familiar.

It occurred to me the young man might be armed; the right to own weapons is not impeded in Michigan, as it is in Chicago. I dared not look at him. He seemed to sway a little, but said nothing; I washed my hands. As I finished, I turned for a cloth, and he put his hand out. For a brief instant, I thought he might touch me, and I backed away, towards the door.

He gripped the edge of the counter tightly, as though he might fall. I thought he might have been ill, or drunk.

"May I assist?" I asked.

He did not answer, but looked into the mirror, and I followed his gaze. His eyes were wide and staring, I could see many thin, red lines scarring his pupils.

"May I assist?" I asked him again.

Again, he did not answer, but remained looking into the mirror. Then slowly, very slowly, he turned his head, his eyes looking directly into mine.

"Please," he said.

His face was very white, he had no colour; his hat was dusty and creased, when I looked at it closely. He did not speak again, but turned to the mirror; I left him, staring, and silent.

The ladies waiting upstairs were full of questions, which I could not answer. Later that evening, we saw the flashing red and blue lights of a police cruiser as the young man was led away in handcuffs, and driven away. We did not see him again, but there were scattered reports of his presence in the town later that summer.

Traverse City

When I lived in northern Michigan, it was a great pleasure to visit friends near or far; the drive was never long, and there was always the pleasurable anticipation of a good dinner, and good company, at its terminus. I have often thought that a drive, before dinner, was more beautiful than the drive home. After nightfall, there are strange things along the roads and in the trees; their shapes are not easily defined or understood.

The drive from Charlevoix to Traverse City presents very beautiful scenery along its length, like many other drives in Michigan; it is admired through the year. It is along the lakeshore that the great vistas open up before you, as the road rises, curves, and falls along its passage.

One is aware of the water, and the sparkle of the steel-blue waves sequined with white foam, as they break along the shore. Far to the west, as you are driving, there is land; you cannot see it, a pale line of darkened blue at the horizon. The lake stretches out alongside you, like a satin ribbon on the hem of a rouched skirt. One is aware of the sky; it arches over you like a vast, white dome, washed with faint streaks of blue; it cannot be measured, but there is a dimension to it. Far to the west, it comes to an edge where it meets the water, and the land beyond; it is the definition of your passage.

As the road rises, the lake comes into view beyond the lines of trees and the spreading farms; in that moment, as you crest the hill, it glitters far and wide. There are large, dark shapes upon the water; huge, antediluvian whales, which progress slowly upon the horizon. They are islands or peninsulas, no one seems to know which, and when the road rises again, they have disappeared, and perhaps they really are strange, living creatures after all. Against the sky, there are smaller shapes: freighters and cargo ships steaming slowly to the north. When the road falls, as the hill slopes down into a glen, the lake disappears from view, and is lost once more.

As you come into Traverse City, the land flattens out and widens, the lake is present; it is a thin line of grey-blue across the expanse of the road, and you are able to navigate around it. One is aware of the water here; it is the base denominator of the landscape, and all directions are based upon it. The main thoroughfare, Front Street, runs parallel to it, as do the city parks; they extend for many blocks across its width, and the trees do not impede the vista.

Traverse City lies at the southern tip of the Grand Traverse Bay, a long, vertical expanse of water thrust deep into the map of Michigan; it is divided in the centre by the Mission Peninsula, into the East and West Arms, like the broad fingers of a blue hand. From the East Arm, one can drive north along the shore, passing through Elk Rapids, Torch Lake, and Eastport, before coming to Charlevoix; the road branches out to Kalkaska and around Elk Lake to Bellaire. From the West Arm, the Leelanau Peninsula reaches north to Suttons Bay and Northport; there are many vineyards here, and summer cottages. In the centre of the West Arm lies Lake Leelanau, a long sliver of water, its basin carved out by the glaciers. Further west, across the peninsula, are the Sleeping Bear Dunes and the nearby islands that are part of the reserve.

Leelanau

Leelanau is an Ojibwe name; it is supposed to mean, "delight of life." It is a very beautiful place, heavily forested and hilly, with long, flat slopes reaching down to the water. There are wines produced here, clear and light, sparkling with the pure, clean water and the high, bright heat of summer. In the autumn, the light is golden as it falls across the land, and the late-harvest grapes seem to burst with it. There are many vineyards here, some are owned by famous people; I did not know them. I often stopped along the road, to admire the vistas as the sun descended into the trees; the colours of the leaves changed to gold. Even the earth and the rooted vines took on its hue; all was washed with a deep, glowing golden light, and shimmering, gentle greens. The light fell in unexpected places through the golden darkness, touching upon a beech tree; it flamed like a beacon. Everything was perfectly still; I could not speak. Had I been struck, just then, by a short, sharp dagger, I should have made no response; I was immobile, transfixed. The light held the world in its grasp, a gleaming crystal paralysis, and then it was gone; the sun had slipped behind the trees, the light faded, and the world took on its usual colours once more. The earth was soft and brown, and the trees were darkened green; even the vines were no longer golden, but dull, burnished bronze in the twilight.

The Dinner Party

My friend Stephanie, a classmate from Notre Dame, had a summer cottage on Lake Leelanau; she invited me to dinner one evening. I had not seen her for many years, and it was delightful to dine with her, her husband and her children. We had met once before in Petoskey, and now were celebrating the end of the summer, before they returned to their winter home in Florida.

It is a great kindness to be received into a house; you are expected, and the air is cool and comfortable; there is good wine on the table, and the smiles that greet you are warm and genuine; you are with friends. There is the smell of good cooking in the kitchen; a fine dish is being prepared for your meal, and you are grateful to your hosts for their efforts; they are happy to see you. The wine flows in the glasses, it catches the light as it is poured from the bottles; there are candles flickering, and the light upon the terrace is blue and green; the sun is sinking behind the trees.

Stephanie's house was cool and comfortable, relaxed and friendly, beneath tall maple trees. Here, one lived almost out-of-doors in the summers, but the nights were cold with the lake breezes. The land was very flat and close to the water; from the terrace to the dock, there were only a few steps; the reflection of it flickered across our faces. Looking across the lake, one could see houses on the far bank, rising up wooded slopes, with docks and gazebos along the shore; already, many of them had been closed up for the season.

After dinner, we went out on the boat; the water was clear, clear to the bottom; there was fine, golden sand beneath the surface, and the crayfish darted about. They were a very dark bronze colour; it was easy to see them. The skies were burnished with gold, and then the light changed: the colour of it was gold and green, the colour of pine needles at dusk, in a wide forest. The water took on their hues, and glittered with stripes as though from a brush, as it calmed itself, the entire surface became a gilded mirror upon which we floated, silent and peaceful, watching the lake-gulls swarm overhead. There was no sound, the air was still, and the lake-breezes faltered; all was silent. There was only the light, and the dancing colours upon the water: gold, green, and blue.

The shimmer of the water was dazzling; it almost hurt to look upon it. One longed to capture the light, the colour, the reflection of it, to scoop it up into a fine glass, and to drink from it, that it might become part of one's skin and one's blood, a living, aqueous creature, moving and breathing.

The children on the boat are silent, they sense your contemplation of the water, and the skies slowly turn to soft, lavender blue; the sun has slipped beneath the waves, and the night is upon us.

Overture in E-Flat Major

I had been told by my friends in Charlevoix that the fireworks display, which marked the end of Venetian Week, was the most spectacular in northern Michigan; many of them had enjoyed the event, in past years, from the porch of my house. I did not think this possible; there were too many trees, I said, and the view of the water was lost. No, my friends answered, wait and see; the fireworks will be directly over your house; the sight will be dazzling.

It was a strange evening when it came; I had forgotten all about it. I was very tired, for I had had many client issues in Chicago, and had worked hard to resolve them. I had not noticed the sound of the festivities, moving and breathing around me. The air that night was heavy, weighted as if with lead, and I sat on the porch after dinner, with my Scotch and my cigar.

There was a hush, and a sense of anticipation, which I felt through the trees; it hovered above the grass, it trembled in the cedar hedges. The light was a cool grey colour, like a hawk's feather; it was evening, and not yet dark. I set down my book, I could not focus, and all had come to a halt. The world seemed to have stopped; I heard, far away, the sound of music across the water. If I had been able to see through the oak trees and the cottonwoods, I might have seen the boats, brilliant with electric lights, slowly passing before the docks, and moving into Round

Lake, like ladies at a ball, and I should have used the same words to describe them as the Baroness Rothschild: *Elle est charmante, distinguée, élégante.*

The skies clouded over, it was getting dark; I wondered if it might rain; the birds had stopped singing. There came a low, rumbling sound, like a far-off thunder; I looked to the southeast, where the long, narrow arm of Lake Charlevoix stretches down to Boyne City.

There was a quick, soaring movement upon the sky; the air ripped apart, and a white chrysanthemum of flame, reddening to crimson, burst against the clouds. I jumped from my chair and ran across the grass to catch the falling, burning sparks in my hand; I watched the lights exploding through my glass of whiskey, and the liquid glittered like fine champagne. The fireworks were dazzling, bursting, screaming flowers of light, in every colour, scarlet, sapphire, emerald, silver, amethyst, and gold; they shone through the curtains like many flashes of lightning. There was a recording playing, of the Overture in E-Flat Major; it called me back to Notre Dame, and the salute of the students to their coach; their arms flung out in unison as they chanted, *Lou, Lou, Lou.* It was a fitting souvenir, for the overture is a celebration in the midst of great adversity, the deliverance of the people from their enemies; they have prepared a net for my steps; my soul is bowed down. They

have digged a pit before me, into which they have fallen themselves. I
had never seen such a display; it continued with many wonderful explosions for a long time; they were so close that I did feel, during the length of it, I was standing beneath a shower of sparks, the hammer of Hephaestus sounding upon his great anvil. The mighty forge of the Olympian gods sang in the night, and the crashing fires cascaded all around me; the rain of sparks glittered over my head, and I caught them in my glass, laughing, as I danced upon the lawn, silver beneath their flames.

The East Jordan Road

I do not think I shall ever forget the day I moved, finally and formally, to northern Michigan. After many delays, I made the long, long drive north, coming around the lake, through Chicago and Indiana, with the sun setting in a golden, swelling light along the highway. I was bouncing and swaying in my rented movers' van with Jane shackled down behind, on her own flatbed.

The daylight faded long before I reached Cadillac; it was nearly dark as I turned for the Lake City detour, which I utterly despised: there had been roadwork on the north road for many months. It was still not finished, and the summer was upon us; there seemed no end to its duration, and the detour was not a picturesque alternative. It was a long, dreary road through bare country; in the day, it was severely beautiful in its remoteness, if one were travelling through a wild, strange land at one's leisure.

Arriving in Lake City, I pulled to the side of the road with some difficulty; it was necessary to check that Jane's tie-downs were secure and she was not jolted too badly. One of her chains had come loose, and with some effort, and some verbal encouragement, I re-attached it, this had been done for me in Wisconsin before my departure.

I wished I might not take this road; there were no towns or resorts, or any other life along it north of Lake Missaukee, it is mostly pine forest. As the road descends from the uplands to the wide, flat plains, the land spreads out and flattens, thickly planted with nurseries and potato and soybean fields. The nurseries are mostly pines and spruce trees; they are harvested in December, and painted a uniform deep blue-green colour; in that wild, rolling landscape, it is a chromatic anomaly. When I had first travelled there, I had exclaimed at the colours of the pine trees; in my ignorance, I had not realised that they had been spray-painted. It is a sight, I think, that might make an effective visual art; but I do not know who might find it credible.

The road ran straight for many long, long miles; as it crossed the Manistee River bottoms, there were wide pine forests and marshes; I saw signs for hunting and fishing grounds, but little else; the sky was dark overhead.

At last, at last, I saw the flashing amber lights upon the Grayling road, and felt a great relief; the longest part of my journey was over. The road dipped down from the hills; I was descending from the dark heights, and the skies no longer held me; I had returned, like Antaeus, to the Earth. I turned west briefly, before rejoining the highway into Kalkaska and then to Antrim and Mancelona. A drizzling rain came up, cold and damp in that late spring. It was not a warm spring rain, such as fell in the south, but a chill, shivering drizzle that chattered my teeth; I was very cold.

For the first time in my life, I turned onto the East Jordan Road, northwest out of Mancelona; the night was pitch-black, and I realised, with some alarm, that the brakes were not good; they squealed and ground badly on the wet, shining pavement. Nor did the windscreen wipers effectively sweep the rain from my vision; only one seemed to work.

The East Jordan Road does not provide the best path for a heavily laden, poorly maintained truck, towing another on a flatbed, late at night. I should have taken the north road, to Petoskey, which runs straight and clear, between wide, flat fields on either side; it was well-travelled, it was safe. The East Jordan Road slowly winds towards a high escarpment, and then falls suddenly down its slope in one long, curving sweep; I was unprepared for its steep surface, and crept blindly down towards the valley. I could not see the road ahead, all was black to me, and I kept my foot on the faulty brakes, hoping that I should not encounter a deer, or anything else. There were no other vehicles, either ahead or behind; I was alone, and moving forward through the darkness and the rain.

The road flattened out, and wound and curved through the Green River bottoms, heavily wooded on both sides. There are breaks in the trees where fields have been cleared, and there are houses and barns. There are solitary lights in the darkness; there is life here. Even in the night, I was not alone; I heard the frogs croaking in the swamps and realised, with a thrill, I was in the northern country at last, for one does not hear them anywhere else.

Their chorus accompanied me through the river-bottoms, all along the flat, wide forestlands, and up into the East Jordan hills. There, the land rose up again, in many gentle slopes, and the frogs' voices were muted behind me.

I had reached East Jordan at last, climbing up into the first wooded slopes of Charlevoix County and leaving the wide, wooded lands behind. There were a few street-lamps to mark the town, and I came to the only stoplight. The light was red; I waited alone for the police cruisers to pass, heading west, out towards Ellsworth. I wondered what they thought of my rig, with Jane hanging on for dear life, and laughed at the absurdity of it all; I was very, very tired, but almost to Charlevoix; I dared not stop now.

I headed north, out of East Jordan, where the road passes along the shore of the South Arm. One skirts the water's edge almost on top of the rocks; there are dinghies and rowboats drawn up, and floating dock platforms. It is a long, wide reach of flat water, which I have always loved. I have never seen it in daylight; each time I have passed by, it has been dark. It was dark that night, smooth and undisturbed, a vast, deep-blue glass reflecting the lights across the shore. The land rises in short, tumbling hillocks along its length, and the road follows it, sweeping up and down in swift, flowing curves; one is presented with views of vacation cottages and resort lodges. The pine forests press close to the road and often the view is obscured, with only passing glimpses of the water. Even now, as I have written this, I can smell the pine trees in the darkness, damp from the evening mists, and I am returned to that road, in the night, when I first drove upon it.

I came, suddenly, into Ironton, and was surprised; it appeared upon the road, behind the trees, and I saw signs for the Boyne City ferryboat; I was near Charlevoix. A few more miles, and I was in the town, hushed and still. As I drove past the post-office and the stores, it occurred to me that my life would now be passed in this place, a place that was now my home.

The road into Charlevoix drops sharply down a hill, and the trees are floodlit along Bridge Street; there was no traffic. I passed the bars and cafés on my left, and thought longingly of a drink, and of friends waiting at the bar, but I could not stop. Crossing the Pine River bridge, I did not think that in a few weeks, the summer season would be at its height, and that there might be delays when I went into town.

The road rose up from the bridge, past the Weathervane and the Edgewater, and past the summer resorts; the lake was near. It turned to the east in a great, sweeping curve that in winter would be treacherous, and headed out on Petoskey Avenue; I was nearly home. I passed the churches, and the butcher, and then saw the golf course, grey in the night, and the hotel beyond; the drive to my house was near. With a wide, swinging turn, I rolled in, and saw that my porch-lights were on, and I was grateful.

It is no small welcome to the traveller, after a long journey, to find the lights on and friends waiting. There was no one there at such a late hour, but the lights still shone, and in my tiredness and relief, I felt that they were there, somehow, for me. There was a bottle of champagne, on ice, waiting on the bar; I was very tired, but I opened it, and had a drink. It was perfectly cold and very dry; I wandered out onto the porch, black against the night, and looked up at the night sky. The stars glittered faintly behind the grey, silent clouds, and I raised my glass to them, and to my house; I spoke at last, yes, I am here. *Mes amis et mes frères, je suis arrivé, en fin, en fin.*

Should I be queried, and answer
Then I should say, yes, I have known this man.

Light, Dancing on Water

A red fox once occupied the porch of my house in Charlevoix, sitting quite calmly and washing himself; his presence was a greeting; an acknowledgement of Nature, interrupted by Man. He was beautifully coloured; the morning sun flamed his fur into a deep, glowing scarlet and orange, which I have not seen anywhere else. He looked at me, unperturbed but surprised, as though he were the master of the house, and I the intruder; my appearance on the porch was of no concern to him. When he had finished, he casually jumped down and trotted off, across the lawn and into the trees, returning east into the forests that border the shoreline; I saw his bushy tail disappearing into the brush. He came to my house several times after that, and I would hear his scrabbling feet beneath the porch, where he had made an opening in the gravel. I always felt better, when he was there, for then I knew I was not alone, and there was a unique comfort to know my hospitality was welcomed, and received; the gift was shared between us, and we both took pleasure from it.

There was another visitor to the house, of whom I have often thought; his presence was unseen, but felt. He first made himself known on a cool night in July; I was alone in my sitting room. I heard a faint tapping sound, like a hammer on metal, and I could not distinguish its source; it was puzzling to me.

I first thought someone had come into the house and was playing a trick; I looked behind all the chairs and even under the bed. The sound continued and I realised, slowly and suddenly, that it came from beneath my feet; perhaps an animal had become entangled in the ductwork. Strangely, the tapping was regular in its count and its rhythm, a cadence of three, and then the *caesura*. One, two, three, the pause, and then it began again.

The realisations of a moment do not always announce themselves; they come to us slowly, like the lift of the sun over the trees. The shadows move upon the grass, the light hovers upon the air; we are aware of new warmth upon our faces.

There was a sudden shift within the room, a soft creaking; a heavy weight had moved beneath me. The sounds stopped for a moment and then, while I waited, perched upon the sofa, they started again, moving closer beneath the floor.

It then occurred to me a response might be of some benefit; I tapped on the register, three times with a pencil. There was a silence, and the sound came once more, three soft taps beneath my feet. I heard a rushing noise of air, a great breath, and all was quiet; I was not disturbed again.

I have often wondered about my visitor: who he was, and why he had come there. Perhaps he had done so, only to introduce himself and to communicate in some fashion, distinctive to his purpose. I did not hear him again, but he came and went several times that summer; the air in the house would move when he walked beneath it. Perhaps he tapped upon the ductwork as a means of proving not his existence but my own, which might have been foreign to him, and was comforted by my response, late in the night, with my pencil.

The White Shadow

My visitor came again in August, very early one morning. I was seated on the porch with my coffee and my book; it was a peaceful, calm Sunday, and the day spread wide and uneventful before me. It was a fine day; the sun was just rising. Off to the east, I heard a crashing noise of footsteps, and suddenly caught a glimpse of a tall, heavy figure in a white fur coat, walking quickly across the street below the garden; he disappeared into the brush, and I heard his steps as he walked through the trees. The vision made no impact upon me; I did not think further of it, and returned to my book. Only later did I think, at an odd moment, of the futility of wearing a white fur coat, in August; even in northern Michigan, the weather is warm and fine.

It is often the chance word or phrase, in the midst of a conversation, which resonates with us; it is a sudden arrangement of syllables at random, borne out of the maelstrom, our thoughts are arrested by it. We cannot move, and the world has suddenly stood still; indeed, is it we who have become petrified, or the world itself? Various cinematic scenes have presented this form of eureka; an amusing presentation of Newton's laws, for it portrays the essence yet betrays the meaning.

I did not think of my visitor until many weeks later; the image of a large, white figure, one I had seen in South Dakota as a child, came again into my mind, and I remembered him. His presence was as vivid and clear as though he stood before me in the room, and the clock spun itself backwards as I recalled that August morning. I had not thought it possible; such things did not exist here. I had not heard of them in Charlevoix, but I had encountered them outside Grayling and Johannesburg, far to the southeast. Here, in Charlevoix, such things could not possibly walk across a street, in the centre of town; it was not real, it was a trick of the light; I thought I must be mistaken.

      I then recalled my encounter in Pellston, before I had come to Charlevoix. The mirror of that vision became a reality; it walked upright in the early morning, and strode across the sparkling glass; it was real, I had seen it with my own eyes, but I had not comprehended its presence. It took a very long time for me to acknowledge my visitor, and in the end, I still did not quite believe it; yet he had been there, and he had walked across the street, while I sat on my porch, past my garden.

The Possum

A large grey possum once waddled across my garden, very soon after my arrival, and I, still mired in my urban perspective, assumed her a very large rat. I was rather upset by her presence, for I hoped I had left that species behind me in Chicago; the rats are everywhere, even on the streets and pavements, scurrying beneath the bushes. My announcement prompted a series of humourous messages from my Michigan friends, who correctly identified it, and from my Illinois friends, who could not do so. It was very ungainly, yet moved very quickly across the lawn, following the deer-path down to the shore. I like to think she may have been thirsty, looking for a drink of cool water in the evening. I was advised by my friends to look for her babies, but I never found them, and I did not see her again.

The Birds

In the summer mornings, it was delightful to sit on the porch over my breakfast, watching the swift, whirring flocks of sparrows rush over the yellow pine-trees, or later, during luncheon, watching the blue jays, calling raucously and joyously as they flitted through the high cedar hedge.

In the early hours of dawn, I would be awakened by a chorus of songbirds with their clear, musical notes; the sun would have just begin to lift its head over the far horizon; all else was still in the soft, grey light. There were many different species outside my bedroom: robins, orioles, chickadees, sparrows, and woodpeckers, many different colours of finches, warblers, mourning doves, nuthatches, blackbirds, and hummingbirds. Their voices rang in the air, as the eastern sky grew pale and the trees changed from black to dark green. I had not heard the birds like this; I was unused to it; in northern Michigan, it was a sound of welcome.

In the city, one awakens, and is then kept awake, by all manner of noises: ambulances, fire engines, motorcycles, and stereos. Their clanging gongs would echo along Sheridan Road, reaching into the apartment towers. There are no trees or forests to absorb the sound; all was cast vertically, up, up into the night. Buses and automobiles add to the commotion, even the sound of a barking dog can penetrate your windows.

The trees and hedges in my garden would come alive with flashes of bright colour, like gay, animated confetti. I was singularly blessed to have them in my garden, forming a living row of trees, as though adorned for Christmas; I resolved to keep it if I could throughout the year, for it stood no equal. Many finches, in red, yellow, orange, and purple could be seen its foliage; they would alight on the branches, preening their feathers and sharpening their beaks. When it rained, they would find little pools of water in the hollows of the grass to bathe themselves; they were animated and social in all their habits. The blue jays were larger, with their bright, coloured plumage and sharp, defined crest; they were my favourite birds at the house.

The Red and the Blue

The blue jay maintains a special place in the spiritual traditions of the indigenous peoples of the American continent, and in the shamanic practises. His colouring is a reflection of the balance between heaven and earth, and the air in-between, no other creature possesses it. His feathers are a deep, vibrant blue, with markings of black and white; his call is loud and strident. I once found a brilliant blue feather beneath the trees; but when I picked it up the colour faded, and it became pale and transparent in my hand. When he speaks in the trees, his voice can be heard far across the lawns. His arrival is a signal for the other birds to depart, for he will inhabit their nests and steal their eggs; he is very greedy.

Once, in March, I saw three blue jays flying across the highway in a perfectly straight line, and I wondered at their message. I knew they were speaking to me, and telling me important things; they are messengers.

I also had many cardinals in my garden, foraging for seeds in the cedar hedges. Their colouring is a brilliant shade of red, with a slight orange cast, matching their beaks. They bear a patch of black over their eyes, as though they were wearing masks, like bandits or robbers; they are very clever. They are best seen in the late autumn and winter when the trees are bare; their plumage flashes brightly against the cold branches. Their wives have a plainer colouring; it is duller, and softer. I have often imagined them like eager young men at Carnival, with their gaily coloured waistcoats; *un bal masqué où tout cacher leur vrai caractère, mais tout est révélé en se cachant.* It would be a fine sight, I have often thought, to see a cardinal of the Church in his robes, striding purposefully across the Piazza San Marco, wearing a red-feathered headdress instead of his usual cap, and a black silk domino; the resemblance would be striking.

    These two crested birds, the cardinal and the blue jay, bear a resemblance, yet they are different; the jays are larger and louder; the cardinals are smaller and more refined. The cardinals are very polite; they will not speak to you without a formal introduction. The blue jays will call to you vociferously, and announce themselves in the mornings when they pay you a visit; they are gregarious creatures.

    I have often thought these two, the one blue and the one red, were the two halves of the same whole, to be compared to a sapphire and a ruby. Their classifications are the same; they bear the same degree of hardness; they are distinguished only by their colouring. In history, these combine in the badge of the Herberts, their flags of equal parts red and blue flutter in the pale, English skies over Wilton and Highclere. In my own work, I have often combined red and blue in my own home; they are two of my favourite colours. I once presented two samples of lustrous, silk mohair to a colleague, the one in deep cobalt blue and the other in glowing scarlet. When asked how I should best use them, I answered, truly and simply, "Together!"

Perhaps we humans, in all our varieties, are but a living embodiment of a single, precious substance distinguished only by our colouring, and by our personalities, while we wander upon the earth, and into which we shall be transformed, when we shall at last be with God. From a lump of clay, He has breathed life into us, and to the dust, we shall return, but that is only our physical body; our soul, which is eternal, is made of finer stuff, and it is this we must acknowledge, and for which we give thanks, to the Creator.

The Wild Ducks

There are many water birds in northern Michigan: Canada and barnacle geese, common loons, and the great blue herons. The wild ducks, however, are the most numerous, and their flocks inhabit the lakes and ponds throughout the countryside; there are many different species: widgeons, mallards, black ducks, and wood ducks. The mallards are the most common, but the black ducks resemble them; only by looking at their bills could I distinguish them. The male widgeons resemble the mallard drakes with their teal heads, but do not possess their brilliant blue-black spectrum feathers, which separate the species; they are very beautiful. I have often longed to capture them, in art.

The ducks often waddled across the lawns of my house, searching for a path to the water, or a place to lay their eggs. Their progress was slow and unhurried, the way of all life in the northern country; their ducklings would follow them like bits of bright yellow confetti, tied upon a string. It was an amusing sight, the parents seemed strangely unconcerned about the parade winding out behind them; the ducklings, however, followed closely. Often, the ducklings would investigate some spot where a worm had been taken, in hope of a quick meal, but they did not linger; the water called to them. They had bright yellow downy feathers; at times, I would find bits of fluff on the grass and realise the summer was passing. I did not approach them; we had not been introduced, their parents were very strict.

Often, the adults would scoop out a small nest beneath the pine trees, and take turns guarding it. For them to do so was a source of great pride, it was a reassurance that my house and my gardens were a safe haven. It is a great responsibility to have the wild animals come to you; they do not do so easily, and they will depart at the slightest provocation.

I have photographed them along the docks in Round Lake, where they float in the sparkling, clear green water, paddling here and there near the shore. The lake surface will seem quite empty, until someone drops a sandwich. There is suddenly much quacking and ruffling of feathers, the water becomes a churning froth. The effect is of a kettle on a furious boil, instead of water leaping and jumping, one sees different feathers in many colours: brown, teal, black, and gold. The noise is deafening, and the ducks, as they gather, squawk furiously, before lifting off the water in a rapid beating of wings.

The flight of a duck as it rises is of comic proportions, for the spectacle of it does not pretend to any artistic value. They do not lift themselves up like the swans, which sometimes dot the lakes and pools, nor do they wing effortlessly overhead like the herons. The ducks do everything with much noise and commotion, like a group of sincere, civic-minded women.

The Great Blue Herons

The great blue herons are often glimpsed in the freshwater lakes, or in the reed pools and marshes of the deep forests. They wade slowly and gracefully through the shallows, their steel-blue feathers glistening in the light. When they take flight, they do so gracefully and easily; their wings spread wide and flat, and they lift from the ground with no effort. The herons are distinguished by the carriage of their long, sinuous necks; they do not extend them like the cranes or the spoonbills, but maintain them in a single, curving line, like the letter 'S'.

When I would take my walks in the early mornings, they would often take wing from the trees as I approached; they would stand motionless, almost invisible, until I ventured too close to their nests. A great, spreading shadow would suddenly darken the grass at my feet, and as I looked up, they would be winging away, silently and splendidly. They did not speak to me; we had not been introduced, and I felt myself an intruder.

At Crooked Lake, they are numerous; as one drives through Conway, they can be seen along the sandbanks, looking for crayfish. I have often smiled at them, for they are very solemn in their appearance, like a group of Englishmen playing cricket; they are very proper. One longs to join their game, either as batsman or bowler, but such requests are always denied; the herons, like a famous actress, prefer to be alone.

The Red-Tailed Hawk

The red-tailed hawk is a predator of northern Michigan; his appearance is always a sign of great import. He paid me a visit one winter, flying straight towards me across a field. I thought he might collide with the truck, but he came to me as I drove, and provided an escort, a flying guard of honour. He was magnificent, with a wingspread greater than the bumper; he flew above the grille, pacing me for an endless, thrilling moment. His tail-feathers were a deep rust colour, and his gaze was proud; he did not look at me. By his glance, he said, I am here, because of you, but you are not here, because of me. I was greatly honoured by his presence; while he flew with me, my truck could boast an ornament unlike any other.

    The visit of the red-tail was a great blessing, and a rare sight; one does not see them often in the wild; when I told this to a shaman, he nodded many times, and said, *yes, yes*. The shaman then explained his meaning, for the red-tail is connected to the Kundalini, that force residing within all persons. It is a reflection of an intensity of the spirit; all forces will be strengthened: physical, emotional, mental, and spiritual. His appearance is a sign from God; He has seen us and heard our prayers, as we have spoken to Him in the night. Thus, as we have spoken to Him in our own fashion, so now has He spoken to us as He, and His ways are mighty to behold.

The Wild Turkeys

There are wild turkeys in abundance in northern Michigan; they are usually seen by the roadside or in the woods. They have every appearance of being attired in their Sunday best, like fine old ladies walking to church in their black, ruffled cloaks. Often they will gather in small flocks of seven or eight, and make their stately progress upon the road; it is so strong a likeness to a group of elderly, dignified matrons I have often burst out laughing. I did not do so in their presence, however; I had a feeling they would not approve; like all matrons of a certain age, they are very critical of youthful behaviour, and such things are frowned upon. As they walk slowly along, for they are in no hurry, they chatter loudly among themselves; they have many things to discuss.

The wild turkeys will avoid you; they maintain their own fraternity and they do not proselytise. Only once in the wild did the wild turkeys approach me, and I knew I was in danger; they were being pursued by another, more dangerous creature. He walked swiftly and silently through the dark forest; I saw his shape in the gloom, and I knew I must depart from that place. The wild turkeys gathered around my feet, as though I should be their protector, but I could not save them. Their plaintive cries echoed behind me, and as I turned to leave, the darkness rose up from the dead leaves.

The Trilliums

In the spring, the trilliums emerge throughout the north woods of Michigan, spreading their creamy white blossoms across the ground, beneath the trees. The trillium does not grow in the open, and it is illegal to cut them; I have seen banks of them in May, filling the slopes of the north hills like a snowdrift. I have often thought this the last gasp of winter before giving way to spring: a final covering of white to remind us of the snows that have gone, but will soon come again, in the approaching winter.

When I first came to Michigan, I did not recognise the strange, oddly shaped flowers; the car sped by the spreading white blossoms in an evening of green and gold colours; we did not have time to stop. Later, I returned, and I walked among them; they spread their white petals across the ground, and I thought I might be wading through a vast, rolling landscape of white, flecked with green, which existed for me only; I was alone, that day. I came back, with friends, that I might share the beauty of it with them, but the gesture was wasted; there was little novelty in it for them, and they did not inhale the pale, sweet scent as I had done.

The trillium is shaped unlike any other flower I have seen; it is composed of three petals, which spread wide to form a perfect triangle. Its colour is a luminous, creamy white, with a pale green cast. Sometimes the petals will have very pale, pinkish shading, which darkens, as the days grow warmer. In the centre is a small cluster of bright yellow pistils and stamens, like the boiled yolk of an egg, hard and full. When in bloom, it seems not of this world, but a strange creature that has landed only briefly in the great forests, pausing to refresh itself before it departs.

The Monarch Butterflies

The monarch butterfly is the most welcome sight of summer, for his arrival is a sure indication of warmth. His colouring, of deep copper and black, is unlike any other; it sets him apart, as befitting a sovereign. He does not speak; he has no voice, yet his presence is an arrest, a moment that focuses your gaze upon his wings; you have received a gift. They are very fond of milkweed, and it is common to see stands of it along the roads, and in the wild meadows. There one will find the monarchs feeding on the sweet nectar, and fluttering off gracefully. I had a friend in Petoskey whose gardens attracted them in great number; many monarchs hovered in the Japanese maple trees, and in the milkweed that bordered the drive.

I have often wondered if the monarch himself was aware of the colour and pattern of his wings; his flight does not betray such fancies. Like Hemingway's assessment of Fitzgerald, one hopes his awareness might slumber and not awaken; like the fatal drop of oil upon Eros' cheek, to be betrayed by its own recognition.

Once, while camped on Beaver Island, I lay out in the afternoon in a large, rolling pasture, bordered with juniper bushes and planted with tall grasses. There had been a settlement here a hundred years ago, the buildings had collapsed, leaving only deep, mossy trenches in the high weeds; it was easy to fall into them.

The afternoon was clear and warm; the skies were that perfect shade of blue only found here; it is a vivid, brilliant colour appearing at the end of the summer. It continues into the autumn; it is not found anywhere else. There was a small maple tree in the pasture; I lay in its shade, staring at the brilliant, pointed green leaves.

I saw a quick, sudden flash of colour in the air, and a very large monarch butterfly flew in his quick, darting fashion to the tree, as though it were a type of magnet; he did not detract from his course, but came directly to me. He hovered above me and it was strange to see something of such delicacy maintain our rough company; we were a boisterous group of men that afternoon, and our merriment continued long into the evening.

How long he remained there, dancing above our heads, I cannot recall; it is a moment we shall encounter in the presence of God, where we are motionless and yet moving; time is not measured in the throne-room of Heaven. In the early Church, the butterfly was a symbol of the Eternal Soul, a transmutation of the joy of the spirit, when it is released from its earthly body to become one with the presence of God.

The butterfly remained, and then fluttered off a short distance, as though to take his departure, then returned; he had further things to say to us; he flew over our heads in many wide, smooth circles.

We all commented on it, and discussed it many times; it has only happened once again, to me. When I have talked with my friends of that trip, they have asked me, "Do you remember, Sanjay, the monarch butterfly, which came and flew above our heads? Do you remember? Do you remember?"

I have remembered, and I have wondered what the butterfly must have thought of the strange male creatures he found, lying in the pasture that afternoon. Perhaps he thought we might be larger versions of his own kind, or other bizarrely shaped and coloured insects, come to rest beneath the maple tree. I often think, in a happier mood, that he had invited me to dance with him upon the afternoon breezes, where the air was warm above the tall, swaying grasses, and I wonder, at times, if he dances there still.

The Butterfly and His Wings

There is a legend I have heard of the monarch butterfly's wings and how they came to possess such vibrant colouring; I will tell what I recall of it:

    Once upon a time, the monarch was not acknowledged the king of the butterflies, but ranked the lowliest; his wings were a plain whitish-grey, like the cabbage butterflies, or indeed, like some of the moths, who are contemptible.

    His wings, nonetheless, were magnificent in their breadth and their shape; there was none other who possessed such beautiful proportion and dimension. However, they had no colour, no pattern; they were as unstained linen, and this the butterfly could not abide. When he looked upon the other butterflies, in their bright, flashing colours of blue, yellow, and green, he pondered the will of God that his own wings should not share in such vibrant shades, and questioned how he might resolve its absence.

    After much reflection, therefore, the butterfly went to the Devil, and asked for a drop of his tears, that he might colour his wings or at least tincture them to become more fashionable. The Devil received him and smiled; he does not shed his tears over God's creatures, but reserves them strictly for himself. In the night, when he is alone and contemplates his fate, the Devil weeps, and his pain is terrible.

"Nay," said the Devil, when the monarch had made his request. "I will not weep for you, butterfly, you are a creature of God, and what God has made, I cannot render anew."

"What about your daemons, Devil?" asked the butterfly, "Are they not borne upon black wings?"

"I did not fashion their wings," answered the Devil, "For the daemons are also God's creatures; they were angels once, pure beings of Light that dwelt in the Holy Presence. Yet when I fell, they chose to fall with me, and when they broke upon the stones of the earth, their wings were blackened forever."

"Then this I shall do," said the butterfly, "I shall fall upon the earth, and so I shall blacken my wings."

"Nay, butterfly," said the Devil, "Your wings are woven of gossamer silk, finer than a spider's thread; you cannot fall, but only flutter in the breeze. Were you to cast yourself down, you should simply float away."

"Then I shall find another colour," said the butterfly, "And affect my transformation. Thank you, Devil, and good day to you; I will take my leave."

The Devil bade the butterfly farewell, stretching out his black hand towards him. The butterfly, forgetting his manners, alighted on the tip of the Devil's finger, and screamed in agony.

"Devil, what has happened?" he cried, flapping and falling about the room, "I am burned to a cinder!"

"Nay, butterfly," laughed the Devil. "You have only touched the tip of my finger, and you have been burned by it. Be grateful therefore; many have tried to achieve what you have now done."

The butterfly was subdued by the gravity of this remark, and fluttered over to the looking-glass.

"Devil," he spoke, after some contemplation, "I have turned black; my wings are black as the soul of night."

"Yes, butterfly," said the Devil, "The touch of my finger turns all things black, black as night, and black as the heart of evil that rots my soul."

"But I am not evil," said the butterfly, and he then began to weep. "Yet thus I have sinned, and thus I have paid; my beautiful wings are black, they are blackened forever."

The butterfly's weeping moved the Devil to pity, who has never been moved, before or since. "Come, little one," he said, holding out his hand once more. "I will comfort you."

The butterfly touched gently down, and lowered his bruised, blackened wings; they fluttered softly in the palm of his hand. The Devil looked upon him and he also wept; his hot tears flowed down like water upon the rocks, when the snows begin to melt. They splashed upon the butterfly's wings, and dripped slowly off, washing away the blackness. Where the tears had streaked across the wings, however, a rich, beautiful red colour remained, like newly minted copper, which the Devil could not erase, try as he might.

"What is this colour, butterfly?" asked the Devil. "I have not seen it before, so beautiful, it is like a burning ember."

"It is My colour," said a Voice, and the Devil rose swiftly from his chair, and bowed. There stood the Lord God, in all His splendour and majesty, enthroned in the Light that shines over the world, and which even the Devil, seated in the depths of Hell, must acknowledge.

"Butterfly, come here," said the Lord, and the butterfly, rather embarrassed, fluttered over to Him.

"This colour I would have given you, had you only asked Me," the Lord said. "Why did you not do so?"

"Oh, Lord," said the butterfly, "I did not wish to disturb You with such trivia. After all, they are only wings."

"Butterfly," said the Lord, "Yes, they are only wings, but the Angels have wings, do they not? The Lord held the timid, quivering butterfly in His hand, and spoke again.

"Butterfly," He said, at last. "You have touched the Devil's finger, and blackened yourself with sin. I will leave these markings as a reminder, no matter how dark our appearance, the true colour of God, the colour I have given you, shall always be present, for it is the fire of the spirit, which lives and breathes within us, and so it is our true form."

So it is that the monarch butterfly, having once had wings he did not value, now has those touched by the Devil's finger, and blessed by the Hand of God, which makes, and preserves, all things.

The Deer Hunter

There is, each November, a great migration into the woods; it is deer-hunting season. Work schedules are put off, and the boys are released from school. Everything stopped; my projects in Petoskey all came to a halt; everyone was gone. They had told me in advance, but I had not imagined such vacation; the towns were deserted, and the woods and swamps echoed with the shots from their rifles. It is not like this throughout the year; turkey, duck, grouse, and even the small game all have their own schedules and licences. The November season, however, means food for many hunters and their families, and they are very skilled at the taking of deer.

  I once thought I might learn to shoot, and to master the art of the rifle; there were many deer near my house and in the woods and fields south of town, and I had friends with large acreages and forestlands where hunting was permitted. I liked venison very much, and found many old recipes for it; it is a fine meat for the table. From my old cookbooks that I had gathered in the Savoie, I had many receipts for stews and roasts with it.

  I had a friend in Harbour Springs, an avid hunter, who promised to take me out with him. He was a very big man, broad-shouldered and heavy, with the comfortably bronze skin of one who has spent much of his life outdoors. He possessed large, well-formed hands, which could build or repair any piece of carpentry or leather; he had a large shop behind his garage, and often invited me to watch him at work. It was good for him, he said, to have someone to talk to; I would sit quietly through the cold afternoons, watching his constructions take shape on the long, flat tables; we shared many whiskeys and cigars together. He often consulted me on the form and design of his cabinets, and I would give him the benefit of my own technique and application; he always listened, and often would utilise my suggestions.

As November approached, he began to collect his gear and his rifles together, bringing them out of the tall, glass-fronted cabinets and cleaning them; he had many different models. Some of them were very old, but still fired well; others he had purchased across the country, and used for specific types of game. When he cleaned them, he stripped their parts on the long, wooden tables, and allowed me to watch. He offered to teach me, but I did not handle his guns; they were not mine.

He took me out one fine October day to his parents' farm; in the woods behind the house, the trees were gold and red, brilliant against the blue sky; it is that colouring peculiar to the north. He showed me how to hold the rifle steady against my shoulder, and how to sight it through the lens.

"Now squeeze it gently," he said. "Try not to fall."

I took a shot at a target, and was successful; he said I needed to practise before I could go out.

"That is alright," I said, "I would only be in your way."

He laughed, "You would probably have beginner's luck, and bag a fourteen-point buck."

"That would be something," I agreed.

He suggested I try again; he praised my mark, but cautioned me to practise even more.

"What game have you shot?" I asked him.

"The usual," he said. "Deer, rabbits, pheasant, grouse."

"Have you ever shot larger animals?"

"Oh yes," he said. "A few bears and cougars."

"Have you," I paused, "Ever seen anything larger?"

He looked at me strangely, for a long moment; I wondered what he thought of my question.

"They're out there," he said.

I knew what he had seen, and what he had felt; he had known fear, while he had waited, motionless in the shadows beneath his hunting-blind. The fear had come out of the forest, it had walked upright before him, and passed into the woods; he had not hunted there, again.

What is real, or is imagined
Is but the shadow of the past
Where we dwell not, behind the curtains
Yet still our minds wander.

6101 North Sheridan Road

Northern Michigan, when I first visited there, did not present itself as a place where I might live; I knew, nonetheless, that I must reach beyond the realm of my present existence, into the drifting waters of a stream, the loaf now to be cast upon the current.

The high glass canyons of Chicago held my interest no longer; their artifice and glitter did not entice me with their brilliance. It was a pretty world, to be certain, of gleaming lacquer and polish, illuminating and reflecting only itself. Like a collection of brightly coloured fish in a tank, I looked upon it; I heard the voices and saw the lights; I witnessed the movement within the shadowed, green liquid, but I was not of their species; I did not swim with them; I had not been invited to their strange, floating feasts. I was not a welcomed guest; there was no place set for me at their tables.

One finds a strange aspect of a calamitous event that one has survived: it does not seem real, when you look back upon it. It is a sequence of moving images, coloured in sepia; it is a glimpse into a photograph, where one has put one's hand. One is passing in a train, through a foreign land, and a *mise en scène* is presented by a troupe; they are standing at the platform, or at a road crossing, but they do not move with you. They are familiar to you, they are friends; you know their faces and their postures, but the glass has misted over; they are strangers to you; the light and the music are gone.

I have been asked why I relocated to Michigan, and the answer has been a difficult element within the pattern of my life there, or before it; I have not yet stopped to examine it fully. Like Gilman's unnamed heroine, I knew only that I must ride very far, and very fast, so that sorrow might not touch me; he had already paid me a lengthy visit. I could not stop, but must keep moving, like the glimmering white sharks beneath the water; neither can they rest, for then they will die. *Istali mashi, kwar mashi, inshallah.*

The fate of Lot's wife fails to arouse sympathy of me; I have often wondered if I might turn back, just once, and if the action of it should paralyse my body; would the memory of it remain, if it were so? When I have thought of the places I have lived, I remember them fondly, for those chapters are now closed, and the pages have turned. I knew, always, that I should not remain there forever, and that I should be gone from that place but might return, if only once. Like a gaze across a faded looking-glass, I should see a different face staring back at mine, resembling mine, and yet different, and I should wonder who he was, or how he had come to be there.

Chariots of Fire

When I still lived in Chicago, I often gazed upon my wedding ring, and thought, when I looked at its gleaming bands, of Anne of Cleves. It was a very beautiful, handsome piece, of three different bands, intertwined colours of gold: red, white, and yellow. I had seen it only once before, long before my marriage, and vowed that I should wear it again, one day, for my own. I had never seen anything so beautiful; the man who carried it showed it to me, not without some pride; it was a distinctive item. He noticed me looking at it one winter morning, while we had breakfast.

"Are you looking at my ring?" he asked me.

"Forgive me," I said. "I should not be staring at your hands. But it is very beautiful."

"Would you like to see it?" he asked.

"Please."

The light from the window was pure and soft upon it; I held it up to the glass, to catch the different colours.

"Do you know what it means?" he asked me.

"It's your wedding ring," I said. "Is that not enough?"

"Tell me, how many different types of love are there?"

"I do not know," I said. "There are many, I suppose."

"There are three," he said. "Physical love, of course, which is represented by the colour red; romantic love, represented by yellow; and spiritual love, represented by white. Do you know which of these is the greatest?"

I did not know.

"They are all equal," he said. "And so the three bands are joined together, in one combination."

"That is very romantic," I said.

"It is also very true," he smiled. "But I see that you are very fond of this ring."

"Yes," I told him. "One day, when I am married, I will have a ring like this, for my very own. It is the most beautiful wedding ring, for a man, which I have ever seen."

"Would you like to wear it?"

"No," I answered. "It is not my ring; that is bad luck. And what would your wife say to you?"

He gave no answer, and I looked at him again. I could not see the colour in his eyes; they were grey in the morning, but they had been blue in the night.

"I can't wear another man's ring."

"I'm giving it to you."

"I could not take it."

"It doesn't fit me."

In that moment, of my own hesitation, he knelt and slipped it onto my finger, his large bare hand rested upon my knee.

"There, look, it fits perfectly."

I looked at the bands of coloured gold, gleaming in the cold winter light. I wondered if one of them might be made blue, to complement the gold and red bands, and so complete the spectrum of warmth and coolness.

"No."

"Yes."

Many years later, I thought of that morning, and the man in the hotel room, who gave me his wedding ring, if only for a few hours. I wondered if he still wore it upon his wide, shaped hand, or if there were others to whom it had been given. I wondered if they, like me, had returned it to him later, when the air was pale silver and the night was cold, on a winter morning.

When, at last, I tried on my own wedding ring, I stood in the pale, wood-panelled salon on Michigan Avenue, and the colours of it shimmered in the light, red, white, and yellow. I thought of that first man again, and the winter morning, when he set it upon my finger. I should not have done so; the thought was disloyal to my husband, and so I put the memory of him away. The box, of dark red leather impressed with gold, was lined with white satin; the reflection reminded me of that day, when I had worn it for the first time, and knew I should have it for my own.

The Land That Time Forgot

I have not yet willed myself to look at the pattern of my marriage; like Anne of Cleves' ring, it has become something of no force or value. Unlike her, I have neither destroyed it nor requested its destruction, for it is still beautiful. Although it has not embraced my hand for a long period, it has retained its meaning; it is a passage of time, frozen. Those memories are preserved in a golden light, which I should not wish to cast aside, for it is a part of me, my whole. If I were to cast it aside, then perhaps a portion of my life should be cast with it, that it might diminish me in some fashion, and I should be incomplete, void of some solidity, and thus my wounds be exposed.

Like an Impressionist painting, if one looks too closely, one sees only the individual strokes of the brush, the masked imperfections, and the blots of colour that are but minute fragments of the composition. From the correct perspective, however, one sees the painting in its full splendour. Mountains, trees, fields, and rivers come into view and their placement is as it should be, in perfect order. One says to oneself, *yes*. This is how it was intended, and so it was fashioned; *yes*, I understand.

I wonder what I shall see, in what colours and shapes, should this pattern present itself to me. Will it be in the deep cobalt-blues and vermillion reds of my sitting room, the glowing fuchsia and orange silks of my study, or the deep English greens, like antique leather, of my dining room? Will there be tigers, dragons, or other fanciful creatures?

I think the correct answer, at present, should be a length of finely embroidered silk, stiff with padding. Its colour will be a rich, deep golden yellow, found in the ancient court robes of Imperial China, with glowing reds and blues in fine, intricate patterns. There will be other colours, a vivid rose pink, and a delicate jade-green. It may be a garment too heavy for me to wear; it is to be put away, wrapped in silk paper, and laid in a trunk for many years.

When the cedar shavings have lost their scent and the attic stairs have squeaked a little louder, perhaps then it can be taken down and examined. It will not be in perfect condition; there will be stains and tears I have not seen before, whose origins I shall not remember. The striped silk cording will be worn away, and a puff of cotton wool exposed, where the threads have been pulled. The jade buttons will be loose, hanging on their pink silk tassels.

The sliding, falling collapse of my marriage did not happen overnight, or in a blinding flash of light; nor was I arrested on some road by its magnitude, like Saint Paul on his journey to Damascus. Yet, like all actors strutting and fretting their hour upon the stage, I remained in my rôle, speaking and moving, wearing my finest costumes. I continued to imagine, by some miraculous occurrence, the lights should not be dimmed, nor the curtain rung down and the bare, wooden boards of the empty stage should retain my presence, like the perfume from a scented glove.

Where those lilies are now, I wonder: who took them?

I have mentioned Anne of Cleves; she is my favourite of the six wives of Henry VIII. Perhaps she is so because of her loss; she was discarded, but survived, and I have held up her example as a pattern, perhaps to be copied. She left no diaries, and only a few letters, mostly to the King; we do not know the direction of her mind nor the counsels she took. She could not return to Germany, only death awaited her there; there was nowhere for her to go, no hidden avenue open to her. I have thought of her, alone in her silent, echoing rooms at Richmond or Bletchingley, waiting for the days to pass in their endless, weary procession.

Did she wonder if the King still loved her, or still thought of her, as he sported with Catherine Howard? Did she sit alone in her room, waiting for a message, any message, to come? Did she weep for him, or for herself?

I have often wondered how the news of the King's subsequent marriages affected her, if she walked through her day in a void of silence, not hearing those around her as she waited in line at the grocer's, or in an airport lounge, or sat in front of a blank television screen, seeing nothing, hearing nothing.

Did her mind retreat before the fact of it, that she was truly alone

The 400 Blows

In northern Michigan, I have seen a deer struck by a vehicle; she lay motionless on the ground, sprawling in all directions after the shock of the impact. The truck had been coming around a sharp curve in the road; the driver did not see her. His brakes had squealed loudly and shrilly in the dim, grey afternoon; I had come to a stop from the opposite way; he was standing on the road, looking down at her.

She was still alive and unhurt, staring blindly up at us. Her breathing was hard and laboured; I thought she might have been damaged internally. Her eyes were a dark, smoky black; they did not see me. The truck driver thought he might shoot it, but with some difficulty, I dissuaded him. He was a big man, a carpenter, a builder. His thick, raw fists were clenched tightly; his body, heavy with weight and muscle, was planted upright on the road like a tree. A whiff of smoke from a good cigar clung to his clothing and his skin; when he helped me to my feet, I smelled it on his hands. I wiped my face with my handkerchief, and remained seated, on the ground.

"I can't leave it here," he told me.

"It's in shock," I said. "She doesn't know what hit her."

"How do you know?" he asked. His voice was angry, and his eyes were a deep steel blue, the colour of cold, hardened metal at dawn. I thought of the wild ducks, winging over the marshes where he would be sitting, low in the water, with his dogs and his guns.

We waited at a distance, so that the doe might not be frightened. No other cars came; it was very cold, and there was no breeze. Along the road, the bare trees stretched forth their limbs over the ground, red and brown with the fallen leaves.

"It's not moving," he said.

"Please," I said.

"Look," he replied, and I saw his eyes flash. "I can't sit here all day. I have to be somewhere."

"So do I," I answered, and I knew he would not shoot her.

He did not say anything, but walked back to his truck and examined the grille.

"There's no damage," he called out.

Just then, the doe struggled to her feet, slowly, clumsily. I do not know if she heard us speaking, or if the sound of our voices had awakened her. Did she understand what had struck her so forcefully? Was she conscious of any pain, I wondered, and wished I might speak to her, in her own language.

The doe stood there for a long moment, looking at the driver. Then, with great care and precision, she stepped forward with one foot, then another. Walking past the truck, she glanced at it, as if to say, I do not know you, and trotted off. I lost sight of her in the trees, but thought I saw her stop, just for an instant. I saw a flicker of white, and she was gone.

The other driver drove off; he did not look at me. I sat in my own truck, for a moment. I thought of a *nécessaire* I had once owned, of gleaming, polished nickel, wrapped in aged, cognac-coloured leather; I needed a drink, badly.

There was a braking noise again; the white and red lights flashed, and he reversed the engine, backing it along the road until he was even with my window. I put down the glass.

"Hey," he said. "I didn't want to shoot her. Not like this. Are you alright?"

I nodded, but I did not speak.

"Listen," he said. "Deer get hit around here, all the time. There are too many of them. They killed off the wolves, and the bears, and now the deer have no natural predators."

"Yes," I said. "Yes, I know."

"First time, huh?" he asked me.

"Yes," I said. "No."

"You look like you could use a drink," he said. "You're as white as a sheet."

Despite the roughness in his voice, he himself was shaking; I felt the timbre of it. I did not know if saw my face as it was at that moment, or as it had been when I had first stopped on the narrow gravel. At the roadhouse, where I had followed behind him, I looked at my face in the mirror of the dark, grey bathroom. I felt very pale; it was difficult to stand.

He ordered a large brandy, for each of us. The bartender, seeing my face, must have had many thoughts, but said nothing, and spoke to the driver.

"What happened?" He asked. It was a long, deep bar of dark, polished wood; we were alone. There was a jukebox in the corner; Patsy Cline was singing *Crazy*.

"It's alright, Bob," he said. "Just hit a deer, that's all."

"Did you kill it?"

"Now why would you say that?"

The bartender chuckled. "Didn't you hit one out here a few weeks ago?"

I looked up at him. "Did you?"

He did not say anything, and looked down at his hands. "Yes."

"Did you...kill it?"

"Yes." His eyes were shiny in the dim light, but I could not see into them. I felt his hand, heavy with weight, upon my back, the room dimmed and I had to brace myself. My hands could not stop trembling; I did not know where to put them.

"It's okay," he said. "Drink this."

The Razor's Edge

In the preparations of my departure from Chicago, my life there began to slip, inexorably and inevitably, out of my fingers. The long, slow death of my urban existence was drawing to a final curtain on an increasingly empty stage, but there were still many performances. Even an audience of one must have its reward; there was no one watching, but the show, as they say, must go on. There were arrangements for my apartment, and tense, drawn-out meetings with my lawyers, which I could not ignore; many things had to be discussed, resolved, and implemented. A hundred details of packing and moving needed to be scheduled, and fixed; I also had the affairs of my business.

It was, perhaps, most painful to discuss my departure with my clients; they had all been enthusiasts of my work, and I was grateful for their patronage. I resolved to tell them all in person, so they might not hear it from others. I could not tell them the real, true reason; the reality of it still bled; I could not seem to beg for favours. Nor could I invent some wild, imaginative tale, despite my gifts as a storyteller, it was not within me to create a new fantasy; I had no voice for it.

What worlds I have created for my clients have come from a fantasy, nonetheless; it is the fantasy of creation; the empty, waiting space that needs but the touch of the sure hand and the careful eye to enliven it.

One's vision is conceived in colour and texture, form and pattern, in an arrangement both creative and disciplined; it is all there; one sees it within the depths of one's thought, and it is translated into a living, breathing reality; it is a room to be lived in, appreciated, and enjoyed.

One has created a space that lives and breathes; it does so around the life of its occupants; they lend it colour and the currents of their passage give it movement. It is not your room any longer; it belongs to them, yet it bears your signature. To some, it is an assemblage, a composition of disparate materials and pieces bound in harmony; to others, it is a witches' brew, a cauldron boiled and its contents rendered; it is a heady dish, a *cassoulet* of taste and dimension.

There was no fantasy appended to my departure, however; it was a bare, unadorned fact that rose up each day when I lay in bed and stared at the dull light from the windows. High above Sheridan Road, the empty streets resounded with the noise of traffic I did not hear.

I looked at the broken pavements of Glenlake Avenue, littered with filth, excrement and dung, and saw only the smooth, flat ribbons of the highways in northern Michigan, curving through the hills and across the meadows. I thought of the wide, empty roads at night under the stars, while I sat in the choking, greasy vomit of Lake Shore Drive.

The boys who parked Jane in my building were polite and friendly, but my truck was invariably returned with more miles and less fuel the next morning. The price of gasoline was very high; I could not subsidise their illicit joyrides. After some commotion, I moved her to a private lot where I could be assured she was not being commandeered for a midnight jaunt to the local hamburger stand, or across town to the hardware store, the grocer's, or the coffee shops on Clark Street. They would pick up their girlfriends in my truck, and I would find their empty lipstick cases on the floor; the truck would reek of their cheap, dime-store perfumes and be dusty with their white face powders.

The last day of my life in Chicago, I collected my bags and walked through the empty rooms of my apartment one last time; it was mine no longer, it belonged to someone else. I could not say whether it had been mine for a very long time; much had passed out of my door. I looked at the bare walls, once hung with many framed photographs, and their colours, in dark shades of moss, rosemary, and sage, were the colours I had first selected, when I had made it my home. Light, in different shades of pure, clear green poured through the wide windows, and the lake was a perfect blue; there was a regatta upon the horizon, a handful of confetti cast upon the water. The bare mahoghany floors gleamed in the light, and I did not see them, I only saw that my remaining

possessions had been removed; there was nothing left; everything had gone, and my life in
Chicago had gone with it.

    I shut the door behind me, softly and gently; I did not wish to hear it shutting, for it is a terrible, final sound. I was leaving it all behind me, when that door closed for the last time, and the light, the music, and the colours all remained; I did not take them with me; they were a part of my life no longer. I walked slowly, for the last time, down the curving hallway to the lift, and pressed the button, and as I did so, my heart gave a great jump; I felt very strange. Inside the lift, I was alone, and as it slowly descended, I gripped the rails tightly, so I might not fall.

Vivit Post Funera Virtus

My last week in Chicago was filled to the brim; all the patterns and courses of my life there ran together and poured themselves out from it, a gushing froth of champagne from a sword-lifted bottle. In that last, strange week, I received a gift, a strange treasure, which I did not expect.

A man came into my life, and then went back out from it; I have not seen him again. He took me in his arms with his whole, open heart and soul; he welcomed me into his house, that I might share it. He was not perfect, yet he was whole; he was himself; he was a man.

I was not in good form the evening of our introduction; I was in a favourite bar with friends, knowing I must leave them soon. Our friendships had changed, I had told them the story of my departure, and why I was leaving; it had changed them. A string had snapped upon the bridge, the soundboard was mute, and there was no one to repair the instrument; I have not seen them again. I had taken a risk, in telling them of my reasons for leaving, and the circumstances that made it necessary; they had only watched me through receding eyes. I had begged no favours from them; I did not expect any. Their embrace of me had dissolved; they had stepped back across the room, and we did not speak further of it.

He came to me across the room, he had been watching me at the table, and introduced himself; we began to speak, and he sat next to me. I told him my name and we spoke of many things; I do not now remember them. I told him of my work and my research; he told me of his career and his travels. We drank and laughed, we talked, and drank again; it was a merry evening. He put his hand on my leg during the course of it, and I did not object; he had very nice hands.

I jested with him, that he should make me lame, and that he should not let me go, except that he blessed me. He comprehended my speech, and laughed.

"I will not let you go," he said, "It will be you who will leave, and I will still bless you with all my heart."

I did not answer him; he had spoken the truth of the matter, and I did not think to see him again, after that night.

I do not know if his path upon this earth has continued or has ended; he was a visitor, a thief in the night, who came into my life, and blessed it. If I were to look back, as I see him now, and wonder if his hand touched me, that I should be lame, or that he should let me go, except he blessed me?

The wheels of God turn of their own accord; they are not accountable to Man; he has no voice in their mechanism. Their paths are fixed upon the stars, immutable and irrevocable, for what God has joined together, Man may not put asunder. Yet we are also given the choice, to go or to return, to rise up or to lie down, to speak or to be silent; all these are given that we might plot out the course of our lives; they are the fruits of Love, borne for us alone. How must we choose when such a gift is presented, to accept or to refuse; in the night, how does one turn it away?

He was very kind, and sheltered me in his house; I made his home my own for the time we shared. My own apartment was a hollow shell, with blank walls and wide, bare floors; all the furniture was gone, and my pictures taken down. There were only echoes there; they still resounded in the night; the spaces did not like the thought of my departure.

There came an evening when we were both in my apartment, strangely, there was no longer any place to receive guests. I should not be there much longer; the weeks had shortened into days; I could count them upon my fingers, and soon, I would count them upon one hand only.

"Why did I meet you?" He asked me. "Why?"

"I do not know," I said. "I did not expect to meet anyone like you, and now I am leaving."

"You can stay," he said. "I do not want you to leave, ever. Please say that you will."

"I have to leave, I cannot stay."

"Stay with me."

"No, I cannot do that."

The radio burst into life, and a song I had not heard, for a very long time, came over the air. I had always enjoyed it; its lyrics spoke of a hope beyond the hope of men, a spiritual perspective, a desire that comfort might be found. I looked at the man standing before me, and then I looked at him again; I realised who he was, for the first, and the last, time.

"Who is that singing?" he asked me. "I do not know them, do you?"

"Yes," I said.

In the Jewish faith, it is said, the Angels must take on human form when they appear to us, lest we be terrified by their true presence, for they are Beings of Light. The Book of Genesis presents them as Visitors, who are sent to us with messages, in the shape of men. This concept is removed from the plane of the earth; Light, a pure element, consists neither of Fire nor Air, nor of anything solid or liquid, save by its own reflection within us. If we are to walk in the Light, then we must accept its presence both upon us and within us; that is all. We can neither grasp its essence, nor can we horde it in a box, yet it fills all our days and our thoughts turn to it, in the darkness.

The Gift of the Magi

There is another moment I still remember, in the last, long weeks before my departure. It was a precious gift, and I both realised and understood it at the presentation, it came to me unexpectedly, and its meaning was clear. Thus, does the voice of God speak to us in those instances, ambushed by other forces; we are made to listen, the Word is everything, and nothing we expect to hear. It speaks to us, it moves us; we are held captive by it, as Elijah the Prophet heard it; the still, small voice in the storm, holding the world in its grasp.

I had clients in Chicago, a charming, handsome couple; they owned a charming, handsome pied-à-terre in Streeterville, which I had designed for them. In the middle of March, they invited me to luncheon; it was the Saturday of the annual St Patrick's Day festival; the wife's birthday was the same date. They invited me to walk along the river with them, to see it dyed emerald green. This enhancement is unique to Chicago; no other city, not even Dublin, performs this office and it is very popular.

I was not eager to go, the crowds and the noise would depress me, I thought, and I had no taste for it. Nevertheless, they insisted, saying, "We have always wanted to see this, and we'd like you to join us. And we will go to luncheon afterwards."

I could not refuse; they were, and are, good, kind people, with generous hearts. We walked down State Street to the river, the crowds swelled and surged around us; there was an air of festivity, of shiny, happy people dressed in varying shades and textures of emerald green. They offered us drinks from their flasks and their bottles, they wore silly hats and costumes, like leprechauns or barmaids, wenches and pirates; all were gathered together in the celebration.

The river was green, a bright, fluorescent colour not found in nature; it was a glowing, shimmering shade that did not resemble any I had seen before. The dye-boats moved down its length, pouring out the dye; it was blue from their pails, but turned green in the water.

I stood with my clients, laughing and pointing, and taking photographs; the towers along the river reared up into the sky, and about them moved swarms of people; the green of the water was reflected in the glass windows. Everyone was happy, and smiling, enjoying the moment, the river, and the crowds.

My thoughts moved within my head, and it seemed to me, as I stood here, that I heard a still, small voice speaking; *I will remember this day*.

We walked back along Michigan Avenue to the restaurant; I had made our reservation in advance. The bar was very crowded, but there were drinks waiting; we were shown to our table with its white linen cover and the gleaming white plates, set with the owner's marque. Every seat was full, the air buzzed and hummed, like a swarm of bees; we had to raise our voices to be heard.

There was a commotion at the door; the maître d' went outside and I saw a crowd of people through the tall windows, with buskins and pipes. He returned, leading them; they were a troop of Irish bagpipers, fully attired in kilt, scarves, and hose, with their sporrans and flashes; there were some women in the band. They gathered in the centre of the restaurant, lifted their pipes, and began to play.

The music gathered itself and spread outwards, it swept me along with it; the room dissolved into a fine, grey light, the colour of a silver rifle. I saw lines of men marching in the mists, from the high hills, the lavender-grey heather in the morning, and the battles, and the sorrows. The lamentations that are the heart of the Irish ballads surrounded me and took me into their soul, where the peat-fires burn at daybreak.

I was not there, my spirit had flown away with the music, and I could not return easily to my chair, I had been to the hill of Tara, and the castles of the River Shannon. In the stir of the slow, rising music, and the calling of the pipes, I seemed to hear again the still, small voice, speaking the words that I had heard before. I was aware of nothing else, not the elegant dining room, nor the people within it; I was not even aware of the musicians. Only the music kept me; I was lost in the sound of mourning, and the pipes wailed upon the cold air. The song ended suddenly, and I found myself applauding, and thinking: *Yes, I shall remember this day.*

We finished our luncheon; my clients asked to see the dessert menu. I was surprised; I usually took my coffee alone. The waiter, beaming, discussed the menu with the husband, who asked him, "Do you have cheesecake?"

"Yes," said the waiter, "We have an excellent New York style cheesecake today; it is very good."

"But, what are you serving with it?" asked the husband.

I thought the answer might be themed to reflect the day, an Irish whiskey sauce, perhaps, or something with mint leaves, fashioned from white chocolate.

"We have a very special topping today," answered the waiter, "Michigan cherries."

I had drawn in my breath sharply; the waiter turned his head, politely, for my response. My clients looked at me; I had something to say. The moment had come, as the French would have said, *entre la poire et le fromage*, but I said nothing.

It was all flowing away, dropping, falling, like the jetting of a rock from a great height; I could not stop it. A great hole had opened, and many aspects of my life had passed through it, which could not be recovered. Like a series of sharp, shining knives piercing my body, the skin, the bones, and the muscle, I could not react, I could not speak; the pain of it was too great, and the words to describe it would not come. They looked at me again, my clients and the waiter, and still, I could not speak; I could not hurt them, but only remember the moment, that I might, in a far-off place, look back to that silver afternoon, and the music that drew me from that place.

When we had said our goodbyes, and I rode home later, the Outer Drive Express rocketed over the hill at Fullerton; the towers of Michigan Avenue behind me were grey in the mist. I sat alone in the swaying coach, looking upon the flat waters of Lake Michigan, and my life there. The music rose up again around me, and I was again carried away by it, to a distant land; I was going north, and as the bus came down the hill at Diversey, they disappeared behind me altogether.

Come, my love, my lover, dance
Upon the spangled green
Where lilies bloom and roses climb
In summer's golden sheen.

The Beaver Island Boat Ferry

Journeying to northern Michigan in that long-ago, golden summer, I began, finally, to realise that my life in Chicago, as with my marriage, was now to be set behind me. It had taken much time and effort to move beyond both of them; I did not know what I should find, but only that I should look for it; it was out there, it waited for me. I myself did not know what hand directed my steps to the north; it was unknown to me.

Beaver Island was my first destination that summer; I had never visited it, but my sister's husband had family there, and I had planned to call on them. Our meeting did not occur, for my steps were directed elsewhere that summer; there were other visitors there, whose paths crossed my own. Like the pawn that takes its first, hesitant step upon the board, I set forth, and looked across the checkered field to the other players, shining and terrible, that stood before me in their long, unbroken ranks.

The trip to Beaver Island is a pleasant one when one has not done it very often. After a time, however, it becomes tedious, and one cannot wait for the journey to end; it is as if one were being ferried on multiple passages by Charon, across the River Styx, yet never so long a voyage as the trip to the island. One arrives at the dock in Charlevoix; there do not appear to be very many people about, and one wonders at the bare pavement, stretching out to the water; it is deserted. Then, as one descends from the main street, the view widens, and Round Lake spreads out before you; there are people everywhere, bringing up their cars, unloading their bags, and gathering at the dock. The boat offices are tucked under a deep brick portico; they are cool and pleasant. One realises, in the early morning, the heat of the sun.

The ferryboat to Beaver Island is large and white, with green awnings and deck furniture. People crowd about happily; there are large sun decks in front and shelters amidships. It is pleasant to sit on the decks, feeling the breeze upon your skin as the boat moves upon the water.

There is a gay, holiday spirit as the ship prepares to leave the dock; the gates are lowered and a deep horn sounds. Gently, the boat pulls away and turns to enter the Pine River. The bridge lifts slowly, gracefully, into the air, the gulls flutter overhead. The sky is a clear blue, and the trees are green.

As the boat heads into the channel, people along the shore wave from the restaurants and the parks upon its steep banks. There is a feeling of abandonment as the land is left behind, and the wide, blue waters of Lake Michigan spread out before you; now is the time, you think, when you are truly embarking upon an adventure. Anything may happen; you are perfectly prepared.

The ride out is smooth and uneventful; it takes a little too long, for the boat travels at a leisurely pace. Other boats ride past swiftly; they are the focus of many envious glances. Yet the slow, measured turn of the engines is reassuring, there is no hurry. The island will be there, and one will arrive, one is on holiday; there is no schedule, no timetable to which one must adhere.

The first sight of the island, as one is approaching from the east, is unobtrusive; it is a long, green shadow upon the water. As the boat pushes forward, the shadow begins to widen, and to hover strangely; the trees along the shoreline lift their heads above the horizon. Far, far out in the distance, one sees the deep blue-green outlines of other islands, the Fox Islands to the south and to the north; there is Hog Island, with the Hat and the Shoe beyond. Turning back to the east, there is only a dim, faint line of dark blue-green across the horizon, where the Charlevoix shoreline is still visible.

The sun is high overhead, and the heat warms the body; the lakebed is shallower. In the depths, the colours change from deep, sapphire blue to the gleam of an opal, now blue-green, now green-blue. The white, rushing foam streams past one's gaze and the water is still, smooth, like a vast, unruffled sheet.

The water is now a full, clear green, like that of a bottle of Champagne held to the sun; the sand is white and clean beneath it. A flash of silver marks the passage of a trout; a lake-gull comes winging low across the surface. The sand is perfectly smooth beneath the water; there are no plants in these depths.

The island is nearer and the trees are magnificent, lining the shore from one end to the other. Houses are visible along its length, in colours of white, yellow, and pale blue; there is a cluster of them at the harbour, among the shops and cafés.

There is a flicker of white that remains steady, coming into view, widening to form the perfect triangular sail of a boat, cruising out for the day. The people aboard look happy and carefree; they are waving; one realises there are other, white curving sails upon the water, like a vast pond adorned with many children's toys; one is reminded of the wading-pools in London, or Paris, in the Tuileries or the Luxembourg.

The arrival of the boat is a festive affair; one is not aware of the journey's end, for another is beginning as the dock comes nearer, and the lines are fastened. The ramp is brought down, and the queue forms. There is an air of celebration; it is palpable beneath the blazing sun, it is very hot.

The town of St James is a dry, dusty place, with a main road running past the dock-houses and the wharf; there is a space where the cars are brought off for the passengers. I have taken Jane there, on a camping trip; it was strange to see her in such a foreign setting; she did not belong on the island.

When one returns to the mainland, one is aware only of the departure; the memory of it has not yet developed. It is a photograph held beneath the water; the image has not yet materialised; there is only a blank square of paper. One does not have a sense that one is departing, only returning, it has been a *caesura* in the motion of one's life.

The boat departure from Beaver Island is in the early morning, when the sun has barely risen. There is a high, white mist over the waters, it is not possible to see into the distance; there is only the prow pointing outward. The water is perfectly still, like a mirror, even the ducks do not disturb it. Slowly, slowly the sun begins to lift its head over the horizon, in a blaze of red and gold, the day has come. In a molten blaze, it turns the waters to flame, and one is set forth upon a lake of fire. The reflection is blinding; it dazzles the eye.

The cold air of the night hovers about the boat; one is still warmly dressed in long, heavy trousers, boots, and even a sweater and coat. On the boat deck, one waits patiently, for the cars are still being loaded. There are friends on the dock waving and drinking coffee, waiting for your departure, when they will return to their own lives.

There is a deep, booming sound, the horns have blown, and with a great push, the boat moves off. Standing at the prow, one is carried forward smoothly and easily, as though a great jinni were holding you in the palm of his hand, propelling you through space.

The sun is a ball of white now, and the water a shimmering steel blue, the colour of fish beneath the surface. Out on the lake, the heat has returned, and the weather is clear, but one is heading back to all that one has known, and taking up one's life once more. The telephones begin ringing; there are messages waiting, appointments to keep, and friends are calling.

The Campfire

On the island, I always preferred to set up my tent beneath the trees, where it would be shaded during the day. It was some distance from the others, and I would set my lanterns inside, during the evenings. When I would be walking back from dinner, the tent would glow with a soft, golden light, a beacon in the darkness to guide me to my bed.

As night falls, the shadows lengthen across the fields and the air becomes cold; one needs heavy layers of clothing even in summer. There is a freedom to the night, which is embarrassed by the sun; the shadows envelop our bodies, concealing dimension and depth. Here, in the darkness, one is only aware of the shape, the outline of things; the intricacies are removed. The light draws one into the circle of fire; it is a sacred trust, and all that is spoken there is in confidence.

Many secrets are shared around the fire, and many things are seen which are not otherwise visible; the voice of a man who speaks to you in the night is not the same after the sun has arisen; he is a different creature altogether, he is unknown. You do not recognise him, for he has been changed by the sunrise; the light has modelled his features. In the night, when only his voice has marked his passage, you have seen him more clearly.

The fire reaches up into the trees, and their shapes change, they become friendlier, and evolve into figures, and animals.

One's imagination takes command; there are fantastic creatures among us. When the fires are banked late in the evening, they recover themselves with the night-blanket, and root themselves in the shadows once more.

The great dome of the heavens revolves slowly overhead and we are amazed, we ourselves are standing still, mute witnesses to their splendour. Yet as we wander upon the silver-grey pastures, the world has continued its dancing orbit, and the night is passing. We do not judge its movement by its own design, all things must relate to ourselves; in our conceit, were we not made for this purpose? We centre our bodies upon the grass, and the stars and heavens look down upon us, but they see nothing.

We cry out; here is someone greater than you, yet the stars and the heavens remain silent; they do not answer.

We have been made by God; this belief is a tenet of our faith. We serve His purpose and His will, and are the first amongst all His creations. Who is mightier than we are, for we have been set before the Angels, who themselves only serve God?

Do the heavens know this, and acknowledge it, in their eternal dance? What must they be thinking as they look down upon us, those puny creatures, which are the human race? How could God possibly love something so small? Look at me, God, they declare, for I am the Milky Way, I am vast, ever widening and spreading myself into the universe, blessed with innumerable stars, and yet this is not enough, for I have no soul.

It is the soul of Man, which has lifted him into a superior footing, above the heavens and the earth, and all creation bows before him, for he has been set there by God.

The Kindness of Strangers

There was a woman I first met in northern Michigan when I arrived on Beaver Island; the paths of our lives had crossed, and had combined to run together for many miles. When I met her, on the docks of Paradise Bay, she greeted me as an old friend, with her warm, smiling face and her sparkling, blue eyes; her cheeks dimpled when she laughed, loud and long. She welcomed me into her life, and made me a fixture; I knew I should not be alone, while she was there.

Our sojourn on the island was cemented by our love of good, single-malt Scotch; together, we shared our stories of good liquors and the conversations that accompanied them. In one of the local restaurants, we found, against all expectations, a well-stocked bar with an excellent range of Scotch; it was a hidden treasure. I ordered a Glenmorangie for both of us; she had not drunk it before.

"I think you will really love this," I said. "It is one of my favourites." When the glasses arrived, I asked the bartender for some clear, tepid water and a silver spoon.

"Taste it first," I said. "Then I will add the water."

Carefully, as I had been taught, I added three drops to each glass.

"Now, tilt it around," I said. "The water will release the bouquet. Can you taste the difference?"

She could, and did, exclaiming at its enhancement of her drink. It was amazing Scotch, soft and warm, and the colour of it, deep gold in the light, and honeyed amber in the shadows, was the colour of the afternoon. Had I looked through the memory of that time, I should have viewed it in the same colours, as though I had held the glass to my eye and peered within its swimming depths. I have often looked back upon that golden, perfect afternoon, and wondered at the course of my life, because of it. Whenever I have drunk a Glenmorangie, I have thought of my friend, and remembered that day, with fondness.

The Sacred Grove

Together, we found a pond deep in the woods, not far from our camp, spreading wide and flat under the sun, bordered by thick groves of oak and hickory trees. The trees were very old, knotted, and twisted by the storms of their existence; it was not possible to guess their age.

The trees on Beaver Island are old, older than anyone who has seen them; they themselves have seen many people pass beneath their branches. When the great logging camps first came into the northern country, their forebears were the first to be felled. Their size now can only be guessed, for they were the giants of the forest. Their children have now succeeded them, and have grown strong, but their blood has thinned; it has become watered with the tears of the forest, Rachel, weeping for her children.

When I stood beneath their branches, I felt the life of the trees pulsating through their veins, still strong, fresh, and green. It filled my hands as I caressed their gnarled trunks, coming straight up from the ground; my hands were numb from the shock of it. I had not experienced such strength in a living thing; it was a mystery to me. I asked my friends about this, but they could not answer; it was outside their perspective.

There was, in the centre of the grove, a peculiar sight: a large, forked limb hanging in the air, suspended in the branches of another tree. It had fallen long ago and remained there, a rustic

Damocles' sword, high above a green throne. When I stood beneath it and reached up to touch the bare end of the limb, I felt a great current sweep through me; a vibrant, living wind swirled up, and I felt my hair blowing about; my clothes flung out into the air, I felt I might rise from the ground.

Thus do the wild things dance in the woods, when the leaves are green, and their raiment is blue. Did Lúthien, in her dress of evening stars, dance on this lawn when the stars glimmered in the eastern sky, and did Beren, spying through the wooded banks of Esgalduin, see her there? Was some enchanted place here, where all should dance beneath the trees, when the beech leaves first unfurled themselves in the soft mornings?

It was strange to feel such things, I had not felt them before; I was not aware of them, yet they rose within me, as though they had merely slumbered through the long history of my life. They seemed to be awakening, and I was not aware of their strength, only that they filled me with amazement and delight.

One may not always realise one's gifts. I was given a glimpse, there in the grove, into the power of other living things, possessed of a force and a life of their own, which took no notice of me. They allowed me to touch them, the sap running through their branches was like hot, swiftly coursing blood. I could hear its rhythm, like a soft, muffled drum, beneath the smooth grey boles of the trees, when I stood very still, and held my ear to their trunks.

The Field of the Cloth of Gold

There is, in the slow, graceful mornings, a golden cast to the light as the sun comes up over the trees on the island, green-black in the darkness. The light, as it swells up into the sky, winking out the last stars, is a soft, blushing pink, suffused with pearl, which warms itself into a rising, golden colour.

In the wide, grey pastures, the mists linger as the daylight warms the air, and hover gently along the edge of the trees; one has entered into another world, a separate dimension bounded by the fogged walls. Beyond the mist there is nothing, even the tents are invisible; you are truly alone, at last. For a long, perfectly silent moment you do not speak, for your voice will break the spell; were you to do so, the mist would tremble like a shattering glass and your reflection should fall to pieces within it. There is no other noise, not even your breath is heard, but the hushed sounds of trees dripping on the grass-beds and the pine-branches glisten with sparkling drops.

Now the sun comes, gracefully, almost shyly, the light rising from its faint, rose-coloured stain to a rich gold, and the mist takes its colour from the sun, rising above the ground. For a long, exquisite moment, the world is poised on the brink of night, and then it is gone. A doe and her fawn step gracefully through the grass, as if to announce the new day, and then they too are gone, silently in the woods.

The Secret Garden

The pinewoods on Beaver Island are silent, majestic groves of dark green, carpeted with rust-coloured needles. There is no undergrowth; the pine resins quickly blight any seedlings. The forest is hushed and still, and the light, filtered through the fine branches, is softer than the oak and beech woods. I have often walked there, and felt the cool air upon my face as I moved through the shadows.

There is a strange *mouvement* in the clearings, as you step out from the trees; there is a presence there, which is not felt in the towns. I once asked aloud, "Is someone there?" when I walked through the forest, and there came no answer; I was alone. Yet through the shadows, other shapes moved and other shadows; they followed me and watched from a distance, as though unsure of my intent, they did not announce themselves. I heard their music, like the sound of soft, trembling violins, upon the summer evenings, but they would dismount their instruments in the twilight, and I would not see them again. The people of the island shrugged their shoulders, and said, "They are only shadows," but I wanted to see them for myself, to speak with them, and to dance within their magic rings, where the circles are laid out in the green grass of the forest clearings.

Freude, Schöner Götterfunken

The stars, on Beaver Island, are at once brighter and more numerous than any other place I have travelled. The sun, setting late, disappears behind the hickory trees, and slowly, slowly the first stars wink into the deepening blue. As one lies on the grass, it is possible to feel complete with the heavens; the sky is a blaze of blue-white diamonds slowly revolving above. I have never seen majestic beauty as the spectacle of the stars in such multitude.

The perspective of the night sky, when lying on the grass, is so full and so splendid that the depths of the star-fields seem to be not placed upon the dome of heaven, but affixed to the bottom of a great pool, filled with perfectly clear water. One is not looking up, but downwards, seeing an underwater civilisation, glittering far beneath the surface. It is a glimpse into another world, which one cannot enter, but only admire, for as Man cannot breathe in the depths of space, neither can he survive beneath the waves. Were one to reach towards it, however, the water would shimmer and ripple; the mirage should be dissolved and the lights would wink out quickly and not return. The strange, myriad creatures inhabiting that world would scatter in swift, silent flashes of copper and gold, and disappear; one would be left swimming alone, staring into the void. This world we have glimpsed, what is it? Is it something we have known, have seen before, or is it new to us, an alien creation now become visible?

If I should go back there, it would be to that warm, sweet pasture on the island, to that place and that night full of stars. Somewhere in the woods behind me, there would be a campfire, and the sound of men's voices, low in the air.

Once, I managed to align my body upon the wet grass, magnetically to the North Pole, and gazed for hours at the spectacle overhead. The stars, gracefully dancing in their prescribed orbits, resembled a great ballroom, splendid with bright, flashing jewels, revolving to a silent orchestra. Did I hear, somewhere, the faint echo of a waltz and the rustle of swirling silk dresses, blushing white with petticoats? I once stood on the balcony of the Aragon Ballroom, when the lights were dimmed, and in the dusty, misted light a hundred dancers slowly revolved in graceful silence, the echoes were still there.

One feels one might be lost in such a display, and indeed, it is difficult to tear one's sight away. At times, high, distant flashes of green and red announced an aircraft, winging its way to some unknown destination. I did not feel jealousy at those who travelled at such hours; I had my own journey to follow, and for the moment, it was here on this island, on this grass where the trees pressed back against the deep blue night, and the stars were my only light.

The Heel-Stone

I have felt and seen many strange things on Beaver Island; upon my first visit there, I asked my host, "Are there any snakes on this island?"

My host was rather startled; this was not a usual question to be asked by a guest, but he answered me truthfully.

"Yes, there are snakes here," he said, "But they are not poisonous; you don't have to worry about them," He was glancing at me while he drove.

"Thank you," I said.

"Why did you ask about snakes?" he asked me.

"I felt them, when I came here," I told him. "And I do not know why; I am terrified of them."

I had *felt* them, as we left the boat-dock in Paradise Bay, driving down the white, dusty road in the blazing sunshine. There were many different kinds of them; they called to me, they spoke to me. Later, I chanced upon one, a long, wriggling black specimen moving quickly through the grass. It frightened me, but not so much as what I encountered later, on my last day there.

There is, on Beaver Island, an ancient ring of stones, like a medicine-wheel; it is a remnant of the indigenous Odawa peoples. Much of it is now hidden in the dense forest, but there are components still visible along the roadside, and in the meadows, including the heel-stone.

On the eve of the summer solstice, the Odawa gather here as they have done for centuries; the sounds of their drums and flutes rise gently upon the night. It is a sad, plaintive music of longing and remembrance; it speaks of blue smoke curling through dark-green forests, and white-birch canoes upon still waters. Hiawatha came here, and his mother Nokomis, Daughter of the Moon. Then, as she rises over the water, the music falls slowly and sadly, to a whisper; Grandmother Moon she is named by her people, and they revere her silver light.

The heel-stone of the medicine wheel is a large, square-shaped piece of white granite; it sits alone by the roadside west of town, in a wide, circular meadow. It is not a gigantic stone, like some of the others in the arrangement, but its importance is paramount, and one often finds gifts at its base. Feathers, small decorative stones, pottery, and figurines have all been placed here, at one time or another. They do not remain; someone takes them away after a few days, and then they return.

We came to the heel-stone to see if we might find other pieces of its arrangements in the woods, there is a map of the wheel, but it is incomplete. I had found other stones in other fields, and they had called to me; I felt their presence, and their living, breathing energies were strong.

As I walked towards the heel-stone I realised, strangely, there was a snake beneath it, and I could not comprehend my perception. It was thick and black, with many coloured stripes; it lay curled about the base, invisible. The grass grows thick around the stone, yet I saw nothing. We gathered around it, and laid our hands on the scarred, white surface and began to pray in unison; I do not know remember what we said, for it was not a prayer I had heard before. I felt a force rising from the stone, of ancient strength, and of a spirit waiting to be summoned. Did it wait, like Caliban, for some long-forgotten master, that it might be released from its bondage?

    I stepped back suddenly, and there was a soft rustle, a breeze moved in the grass; my friends spoke, "Look at the big snake!" and I backed away quickly; I could not look at it. It was enormous; it circled the stone with the length of its body, once, twice, then it flowed like a black stream around its base once more, and disappeared from view. I ran down the road, and I could not confront my fear; I was shaking. The propulsion of its spirit collided within me, and I did not understand why this fear, of such things, could rise so quickly, and with such strength.

La Belle Au Bois Dormant

Before I had first come to Beaver Island, I had seen a vision in the pasture: a woman of surpassing elegance and beauty, attired in a wide, full-skirted gown of palest lavender silk, with gold embroidery. Her hair, rich and auburn-coloured, was fashioned into a heavy chignon, set off by sparkling gold and diamonds.

I did not know who she was, and asked my host. He did not know, either.

"Many people have seen things here, on the island," he said, "It's quite possible you are seeing something, too."

"Yes, but *what* am I seeing?"

"There are ghosts on this island, you know, and there are many haunted places here; I have been told."

"I do not think this is a ghost."

All this was forgotten in the excitement of my holiday, the ferryboat passage, and the landing in the bay. As my host was driving me, we passed the wide, open pasture, and I suddenly sat up; I saw the woman, *my* woman, standing there; she beckoned to me.

"Stop, please," I asked my host, "There's someone under that tree."

"Which tree?" he asked me.

"That bell-shaped tree, in the centre," I told him.

There she stood, the beautiful Frenchwoman in her lavender ball-gown, looking at me. I did not know her, but she smiled at me, and beckoned.

"*Mais qui est-elle?*"

"I don't know what you're seeing," my host said.

"But she's right there," I said. "I'm looking at her."

"No, I don't see anything."

His expression was puzzled; he did not see her.

"You don't see her?" I asked him.

"No, I don't."

"But she's standing there, she's waving to us."

"Perhaps she's only waving to you, Sanjay."

She remained there, throughout the long weekend of my first visit to the island, and I approached her later that afternoon, not without some hesitation, for I was very shy about it. She smiled graciously, but she did not speak, nor did she leave the shelter of her tree, which shaded her from the hot sun. She stood there, always, watching me, whenever I would come to the pasture, and would gesture to me; if I could not join her, I would wave, but she watched me, always. She was kind and gracious, but aloof, as a lady should be; her manners were always proper and she was formal in her habits and her deportment. I apologised to her, very often, for my own attire, for I had come there for camping, swimming, and hiking; I carried neither a dinner jacket nor a tailcoat, but she did not question the selection of my costumes.

In the evenings, her skirts would catch the last, fading gleam of the setting sun; the sparkling jewels would flash beneath her tree, I would go to her, and we would dance, very slowly together, in the twilight. It was appropriate, I think, that we maintained the rhythms of the dances she had known in Paris; they were very formal, and slow.

I do not know who she was, and whether she was a wood nymph or some other sort of dryad, I cannot say, or guess. I did not understand my vision of her, for only I saw her, and knew her, as a woman both beautiful and mysterious, whose wide lavender skirts, once upon a time, had rustled along the streets of Paris, in a long-forgotten spring.

Brighid

She was not the only strange, beautiful creature who danced with me in the trees that summer. The lovely Brighid, ancient and wise, bare-footed and red-haired, came and stepped nimbly among the branches of trees of our campground, and greeted me; warmly, as a friend. In joy, I called out to her, for who would not greet such a noble personage? She was eager and cruel, demanding of strange, bloody sacrifices, but she honoured me with her presence; her golden bracelets would jingle when she lifted her arms to dance with me. When she leaped through the trees, I called out to her; her appearance was there in front of me. My friends looked strangely at me, and did not accept the revelations of my perception; it was outside their experience. I offered Brighid my bottle, but she would not accept it; I had to procure some Irish whiskey instead. For her meals, I presented her with raw meat, and she was satisfied with it; the blood ran down her chin as she ate.

    I did not understand the ways of the old religions; they were foreign to me. The Brighid who came to me in the forest was a different creature, wholly feminine, and resplendent within her existence; she was like a wild animal of the forest, a doe upon the mountain of spices. I made haste unto her, together we journeyed beneath the green roof of the forest, and our paths strayed through the woods, where the others could not follow.

The Cairn

At the end of my stay, I came, as was the custom there, to a high cairn in the woods bordering the pasture; it was piled high with stones, placed by other visitors to the camp. It stretched out beneath the trees like a sacred altar that one might find in a barren, windswept cove across the sea. Many had come here; it was a tradition of the island, honoured by all who travelled there. I placed upon it a small rock, a lump of deep forest-green granite, which I had brought with me.

As I set down the stone, I knew, suddenly, that I should not return; I knew not why, but only that I should depart. The walls of the forest and the embrace of the pasture would no longer hold me to that place; my journey would not find its way there again, and I knew not why. In the grey light of the last morning, we drove to the ferryboat, and I looked upon my beautiful woman in the pasture, beneath her bell-shaped tree, and waved farewell to her, farewell, farewell, my lovely.

The Blue Grotto

There was another strange episode on the island, which, I must disclose, was not counter to the peculiarities of my experience. All things were new to me, I was eager to explore every route presented. To what destination they might lead, I did not know, nor did I care; it was enough that the tracks were laid, in all directions. I had only to choose among them, and great things would be revealed at each of their endings. I felt myself to be a mighty, many-limbed tree, emerging into the sun, feeling the air moving about me as I reached forth, up, up into the clear, warm light; the green shoots came forth and branched themselves out from the stalk, the bees gathered to feast on the rich nectar.

We had gone out one afternoon on the island, and were having a picnic, when a strange car arrived, I recognised its make, and a very pretty woman emerged. We greeted each other warmly as old friends, and then realised, with some amusement, that we had never met before.

Yet I knew her, she was familiar to me. She said the same thing; I was someone she had known for a very long time; we had met, and smiled, before.

"Have you been to Chicago?" I asked her.

"No, never," she said. "Only once, on a plane, for a few hours, that is not the same thing."

"South Dakota, perhaps," I suggested.

"No," she said.

"Paris?"

"No, not Paris," She smiled.

Our association was puzzling; we could not find a place where our paths, somehow, might have met. Yet we were completely comfortable in the presence of the other, a warm, soft sweater that one puts on, while the storms rage outside, as one draws near to the wood-stove. Neither our school nor our careers had brought us together, nor had we lived in the same town or place. We knew no one in common, nor did we have any friends or relations through whom we might have met, somehow, in our long journeys together.

"I want to tell you something," she said to me later, as we were wrapping up our picnic. "I hope you will not be offended."

"What is it?" I asked her.

"This feeling," she said. "Do you think we might have known one another…somewhere else?"

"Yes," I answered. "And no."

"What do you mean?" She asked me. "You cannot answer both yes, and no."

"Yes," I said to her. "Yes, we have known each other, somewhere."

"And what did you mean, when you said 'no'?"

"No," I hesitated. "Not like this."

She looked at me again, and then I touched her gently, on the soft skin of her arm, beneath her white cotton dress.

"Yes," she said, and she did not look at me. "Yes."

We turned into her drive, golden in the fading afternoon light, and I stopped suddenly. I stepped from the car, and looked about me; I had been here before, I did not know how, or when. Everything was the same, in the same places, with the same colours. It was all familiar, the house, the gardens, the greenhouse with its rows of seedlings; I had been there before.

Her dog came bounding towards me; I picked up a faded, yellow-green tennis-ball and tossed it into the woods. The dog went running away and brought it back; I threw it out, again, and again. Always, the dog would retrieve the ball and return it to me; we played together all evening. There were other guests at the house, who tossed out the ball, but the dog would return it, only to me; they all noticed, and commented upon his behaviour.

Since then, I have noticed, I have witnessed an attraction for strange dogs, and they have retrieved items for me, or come to me, unexpectedly, ignoring all others who might be present. Once, walking along the beach, I saw a man training his Labradors, one golden, one black; he was tossing brightly coloured footballs into the water. I stopped some distance away, so that I might not interfere; the dogs, however, swam out for the balls, brought them to me, and then laid them at my feet. I had not beckoned or called to them; still, they came to me and remained, wagging their tails and panting with pride as I patted them. I was rather embarrassed; I had interrupted their training, but I had done nothing. The man was very nice about it, but I could see behind his eyes a question he did not ask. "They have never done that before," he told me later.

It happened again at an orchard; I had gone there with friends to pick fruit; they had fine trees and the apples were ripe; they were heaped up in baskets, red, gold, and green. The farm was very crowded; it was a perfect autumn day. The owners had a beautiful golden spaniel that ignored all the children running about, and all the adults who tried to play with him. I was standing in the yard taking a photograph; I saw the dog away across the lawns, and smiled at his disregard. I noticed him walking towards me and thought, this cannot be happening; but it was happening, he came to me without hesitation, wagging his large, furry tail and laying at my feet a well-chewed plastic toy; I thanked him for it. He sat there for some time and did not speak, but allowed me to pat him and to praise him, and then he gathered up his toy and trotted off. He did not play with any of the children and disappeared into the white barn. Some of the adults noticed, and spoke to me about it; I could not answer them; I had no explanation.

The night came upon me as I slept, and in her garden, the moon rose full and glowing; a light filled the room, which I have seen before but once. On the island of Capri, there is a famous grotto, accessible only by rowboat, filled with a deep, shimmering blue light. One finds oneself floating upon a sea of light, there is no longer water supporting you; along the edge of the cliff, a pair of crumbling stone columns flanks an empty, stone chair. I looked at it, wondering if I might see the Emperor Tiberius himself looking down upon us. The light is all around you, it is a real, moving substance, and you have entered a dimension existing nowhere else; the boatmen who sing to you are creatures from another realm.

The light was that same colour of blue, richer and fuller, more mysterious, passing through the open window. It filled the room and all it contained; all were coloured by its touch. The lace curtains, the walls, even the furniture, were transformed, and mixed it into their own hues. The mahoghany furniture became the colour of a deep purple, where the red grains of the wood were blended; it was the view through a perfect, hard sapphire, held close to the eye.

I felt something brush my skin; she had laid her hand on my arm, blue in the moonlight; I opened my eyes.

"What is it?" I asked her.

"Nothing," she said. Her eyes were deep violet-black, like a shadowed pool in the forest. "I was just listening to the sound of your breathing."

"I'm sorry, did I wake you?"

"You have a good rhythm," she said. "It is not fast, or slow. You sleep as though you had not a care in the world."

"It has been a very long day," I said.

She paused.

"Yes?" I asked her.

"Will you stay...for a few days?"

"I have to see about my ticket."

"Go down to the boat-dock in the morning. They can change it for you."

"Sunday?"

"Sunday."

In the early morning, I walked along the pale, narrow gravelled road to the town; under the trees, the light was dim, and the shadows were deep green-black. There was a quiet to the world; all was at peace here. The sound of my boots crunching over the stones was muffled by the stillness of the trees, breathing heavily. Across the wide, flat fields to the south, the mist hovered silently and I saw a doe feeding in the corn.

"Sister Deer," I said, "Have you come to greet me?"

She turned her head; her wide, brown eyes looked at me without fear, and turned back to the corn. Away in the east, the sky was a soft grey colour, a pearl tinged with the faintest blue. Slowly, it blushed pink, a paeony unfolding, the light grew stronger, a white radiance which turned to gold. The trees began to take on their summer hues of many different colours of green, yet still shadowed; the darkness hovered behind their branches, and I could not see into their depths. I heard footsteps in the woods, parallel to mine, and stopped for a moment. The sound was not repeated, but I waited.

"Hello," I called. "Who is that?"

No answer came; the early morning was silent, listening, as if holding its breath. All was hushed and still. There was a single, loud footstep on the dry leaves and it was gone; I did not hear it again.

The Way of All Flesh

There was a camper with us on the island one summer, a young man of some relation to the others; he approached me on the path and beckoned to me. I did not know him very well; we had only just met for the first time, he was a stranger.

He was not unattractive but possessed of an odd, nervous energy, which permitted him to remain apart from us; he did not drink our whiskey nor did he share our cigars. His comings and goings were unknown to us, and his tent was a strange affair; it resembled a bright, yellow cocoon, when he wrapped it around himself, and like the dead skin of an insect when he took it off in the morning. It lay on the grass like a flaccid carapace; it was ugly, the rotting skin of a corpse. When he spoke of those things that held his gaze, they failed to interest me; I cannot now remember a single word he uttered.

He stood there in front of me, on the path, looking at me directly, and then removed his shirt; his thin, smooth chest did not entice me. There was no definition, no contour, no shape; all was one smooth length of pale flesh. If I tried hard enough, I thought, I might have easily snapped his torso in two with my bare hands. He said nothing, but continued to look at me, and then, finally, I said, "Is that for me?"

"Yes," he said. "Do you want it?"

I looked at him.

"No," I said. "I do not."

It has been my singular fortune in romance that I have been approached, usually years later, by someone with whom I might have made an interesting life; some might label this a misfortune. Remarkably, it has happened more than once and has always been a surprise; I have never anticipated such confidences.

These approaches, invariably, have taken the form of a strange confession, delivered in the midst of an awkward reunion, heart-felt and sincere, ineffective and intrusive. It is insulting, I have often thought, to be considered an accessory to someone else's story, still in the white-hot blaze of my own fire, that my own life was incomplete without their presence in it. The culpability must lie with the other; our stories together are over, they are finished, and new stories have begun and ended. There are more stories to come, with new characters and new settings; there is never a dearth of romance if one goes about it properly. I have lived better and laughed louder, and this has served me as the finest rejoinder, *negotium est factum.*

The currents of our life, like the black, swiftly flowing streams of winter beneath icy banks, rush on to find warmth. It is found where the white and yellow flags nod gently among the rushes; there are green leaves floating on the surface of the water, and a dragonfly hovers. The stream may eddy for a moment, and the cold, clear waters stir slowly in a forest pool, where can be found the swarming, silver flashes of a fish's mail. The pool widens, rising, until a new outlet is formed, and it spills over a new bank, creating a new stream and a new channel, it finds its way to the sea below. Thus, do all stories end, and thus begin again, determining their way out of one stream, and leaping over the rocks to find another.

In that realm, between earth and heaven,
I have known him
He has come to me, in the night
When the moon has departed
And the stars, now silent
Pass over the trees.

Ghosts of Boyne City

A portion of my professional work took me to Boyne City for one of my clients; it was always a pleasure for Jane and I to drive there. The Boyne City Road branched off Petoskey Avenue, out of Charlevoix; it was usually deserted, with only a few cars one might pass easily. The road, as in most of the county passages, was in poor condition, filled with inadequate patches of asphalt laid over other, inadequate patches; it was not maintained, and rarely ploughed. When a portion was resurfaced, it was considered a victory of appropriation by the populace; the county government did not spend its monies on the roads.

In northern Michigan, it was a popular joke to claim one drove in the *opposite* lane out of Boyne City, heading northwest, back to Charlevoix. This was neither an exaggeration nor an idle boast; I myself have done so many times, and I have seen other motorists doing the same. I did not see any patrol cars doing so, but that region was only barely monitored, and, at times, a long procession of cars would drive, in the English style, on the left as they headed out of town. The northbound lane, if one had driven on the right, was impassable, a series of ruts, patched asphalt, potholes, and buckled pavement. The road shook my truck violently; I would not subject Jane to such abuse, she did not deserve rough treatment.

Despite these failings, the drive down was always a pleasant one, and I made many trips; the road swoops and curves gracefully across a rolling landscape. It is not the same drive from the east, through Boyne Falls; there the land is very flat, and wide, with spreading views to the Boyne Hills. Farmlands and woods pass in succession, and one must take care that deer do not leap across the road, or that one does not strike a deer; I have seen their carcasses along the roads, through all the seasons, and the crows hovered over them.

On my drives, I have often seen a herd of whitetails stepping gracefully across the road; it happened one winter morning. The air was frozen, almost white, and the steam from their nostrils, snorting as they walked, was like puffs of smoke from an old-fashioned engine, in miniature. They came out of the woods in a single, ordered procession, and crossed the road in front of me, paying no attention to Jane or the other cars that had stopped, suddenly, to let them pass. They looked neither left nor right; they cantered across gracefully, as though the passage of the road was reserved exclusively for them; they took their time about it, and did not hurry. I counted twelve of them, before they finished crossing, and disappeared into the trees.

There is a section of the Boyne City Road, climbing a steep hill, which affords one a view of Lake Charlevoix. Beyond the shoreline, one can see the west shoulder of the Boyne Hills, rising up on the end of town, and there are many summer homes built on the water's edge. To the east, one can see the faint patch of blue that is Walloon Lake; to the south, there is another smear of steel-blue paint, which is the South Arm, extending to East Jordan.

When I worked in Boyne City, I would often slow the car at the crest of the hill, to view the calm, placid waters, faintly rouched in the morning light. Then, I would slowly put the truck back in gear, descend into the town, and begin my day's work. I was never approached while I remained there, stopped upon the hill; perhaps the townspeople were used to having their domain admired, and reflected upon, in the summer mornings.

The town of Boyne City is not large; its centre is only a few blocks extending north and south, at the very tip of Lake Charlevoix; the Boyne River debouches into it from the east. There are many historic buildings, but not so many as when it was a thriving port; some of them are very handsome. In the great days when the timber companies spread across the northern country, the logs, floating down the Boyne River, were processed through numerous mills and warehouses, before being loaded onto boats. From there, they were shipped up Lake Charlevoix, out across Lake Michigan, and south to Chicago. It is no small conceit that the forests of Michigan supplied much of the lumber in the Windy City, before and after the Great Fire.

It is not noisy here; the streets are quiet at all hours; I heard no echoes when I walked there. The old, brick buildings with their blank, staring windows hold no secrets; it is not possible to conceive of ghosts. It was strange to walk through the town, from one end to the other, and hear no stories, no remembrances of things as they once were; there is a history here, but it is forgotten. There are a few scattered photographs, dim with age, filling paperbound volumes at the old station house, but nothing else.

Footsteps on the Ceiling

It puzzled me that I did not see any ghosts, when I worked in Boyne City, for others had told me of them. There was an old, abandoned café, where I carried out some work for a client; the roof needed repair and I assisted the workmen. Once, when I waited inside for the men to arrive, I heard footsteps above me, walking purposely across the floor; they were heavy and solid in the still morning. It was a strange thing, to hear those sounds in the quiet space, and I should not have remembered it, save for what happened at the end of the day.

Later that afternoon, the workmen called me, I met them at a bar, and they spoke to me. They were big men, they had served in the army; they hunted, trapped, and fished; they did not frighten easily. The men would not set foot in the café again; not alone, they said, not without someone else to remain on duty. I did not understand, I said, what had happened?

"It is haunted," the men said in unison, staring at me over their drinks, foaming upon the counter. "It is haunted; we are not working in that building, not alone."

I watched their faces; they were not lying.

"Are you certain?" I asked them. "It is an old building; there are many things that can creak, or make a noise, from time to time. I myself have heard the floors settling, or the windows rattling, when I have been there."

"It is haunted," they said. "Something watches us; it follows us from room to room."

I took a sip of my whiskey, and wished I had a cigar.

"Might this have been a bird, or a squirrel?" I asked them. "Could an animal have entered the building?"

"No," they said, "It was not an animal; it walked on two feet, it followed us across the floor."

"Could someone have come inside, after I left?"

"Sanjay," they said, "You opened the door for us, and you locked it again. We did not open it, how could we? We do not have the key."

I rang up the owner, and asked if he had been there, or any of his staff. No, he answered, no one had been there, and why was I calling him about such things?

I apologised and rang off. "Where did you hear the noise?" I asked them. "Was this on the roof?"

"No," they answered, "It was on the second floor, directly over the vestibule."

"Are you quite certain?" I asked, and then I was silent, for I had remembered the sound I heard.

"What did it sound like?"

"It was the sound," they said, "Of someone walking, in very heavy boots, across the floor."

The Night Watch

There is an old, abandoned theatre in Boyne City, where I once exorcised a spirit; it was the night watchman. When I had visited the building for the first time, I had felt his presence; he was watching me; he saw me, and acknowledged my invasion of the projection room where he stood guard. There were other spirits on the balcony and in the glass booths; I could not address them, they were angry, their hatred trembled in the dusty air.

The night watchman held my attention, I returned to the theatre alone, to speak with him. He had remained in the theatre after the lights had dimmed, and the power cut off, after the last reels had been wound, and the ushers had escorted the last guests from their seats.

Did he hear, as he stood in the corner, the easy laughter of the flappers in their tissue-pleated, gold dresses and their pearls? Their bobbed hair was dark under their glittering headpieces adorned with marabou feathers, as they made their way through the audience, calling and laughing to each other. Somewhere, glasses clinked and white cuffs gleamed under black dinner jackets. Were there black, polished opera pumps that danced in the saloons, on the road to Walloon Lake?

The lights were softer and dimmer then, a misty, golden-coloured hue, it caressed the figures of the young ladies. Were there really men in full evening dress, their dark hair slicked back, smoking their cigarettes in the plush velvet seats? Were there college boys, still driving old jalopies and looking enviously at the newer Packards, were they still wearing their raccoon coats over their varsity sweaters? Their evenings would end differently, not at some speakeasy but a roadside diner. There, in the fog of cigarette smoke and great cups of coffee, they would chat earnestly with their girlfriends about football, and the great rivalries between South Bend and Ann Arbour.

I sent him into the Light, which awaits us all, whether we accept it or not, at the time of our passing; such is the way of things. I helped him to leave; he did not wish to go. His duty was there, he said, to watch the theatre; he had been there for many years. No, I said, you may go now, there are others who will watch the theatre, it will be guarded, it will be safe.

This is my life, he said, standing there, gripping the projectors, I have been here my whole life; it is everything to me. I know that, I said, and I thank you, you have done well, and now it is time for your rest, go now, go with our gratitude.

I still see him, at times, when I think of that theatre, and the dark, cramped little projection room at the back, dirty with grease; the red paint was flaking from the walls, and the film equipment was mounted in the centre of the room. There were film canisters stacked in the corner; I could not read the labels.

He had been born and raised there, he told me, on a farm somewhere to the south of town. He had come to the theatre as a young man; he had an eye for machines and motors, and had worked the projectors on more than one occasion. There had been a girl there, whom he had once loved, but she was gone now, and he had never seen her again; he had remained behind, the last sentry of a forgotten post. He looked at me one last time in his dark, faded overalls, his greasy white shirt with its rolled-up sleeves, and his workman's hat pushed back, high upon his forehead. He was chewing on a blade of grass, and his face was dirty from the oil and the grease. Then, without a sound, he went quickly and easily, through the Doorway and into the Light, and the room became warmer and brighter. I closed the Door, and stepped back into the room, and I said goodbye, my friend, goodbye, goodbye.

La Règle du Jeu

There was a monthly gathering of gay men in Boyne City, which I sometimes attended; we met in the loft of an abandoned, shuttered café, dusty and forgotten, on Sunday afternoons. As with all groups gathered for a purpose, there were common features of the stereotype, despite the distance from Chicago, or even Grand Rapids. The same pieces, in their shape and in their function, were set upon the same board and moved across it; only the faces had changed.

The newly established couples maintained their own segregation, behaving in similar fashion as the Lowells to the Cabots; they spoke only to God, and to each other. They were arrogant and cruel in the gleaming varnish of their coupling, yet they would pursue others, if no one were looking. The dancers changed partners, and formed new pairs, which then changed again before your eyes.

The older couples stayed together, secure in the longevity and stability of their partnership; they made friends with the other, older couples, and sometimes with the adult, single men. Most of the single men, as is universally recognised, were there for a good time, whether at the bar or elsewhere; they held no prejudice against the janitor's closet or the back seat of a car. There was a single, desperate older man who propositioned everyone; he accosted me on my first visit, promising various favours, which I could only decline. There was, as always, the flamboyant young man, possessed of no physical attraction, wildly dumb and incredibly stupid. He was popular with the older men, and was exploited for the vague freshness of his body and the quivering down on his cheeks; he had no personal attributes of intelligence, grace, or charm; I myself had very little to say to him.

Whenever I attended these affairs, I invariably found myself pressed into service by the host; he advertised my presence for his guests, so that I became, for the afternoon, a type of performing seal, barking for treats across the bar. Once, he made a tantalising statement: I had once dated a serial killer, and lived to tell of it. It was not a fabrication; it was true; it had happened many years ago, in Chicago.

There were two men there, of my own age, who asked me to do a reading for them, as a couple. I had not done this before, but I was willing to try; I told them, however, that my efforts might not be successful, or that I might say things, which they should rather not hear. I took their hands in mine, closed my eyes, and told them what I saw.

"You are at a crossroads," I said, "As a couple, and your relationship is in doubt; one of you is thinking of leaving, and the other does not wish it. And, there is something else."

I opened my eyes; one of the men was staring into my face, his eyes were red, and wet. The other man glared at me angrily; his eyes were flashing, and I knew that he wished to leave, it was over; he had found someone else.

"I need a drink," he said, and walked away, the other man trembled; he was shivering.

"I'm so sorry," I said, "I didn't know, I just saw it as we joined hands."

"No, that's alright," he said, still shaking, "We've been trying to work it out for a long time, but I think he's found someone else; I don't know what to do."

Later, they asked me to call on them, to visit their house in Boyne Falls; they tempted with me with the offer of work. It was a very old game, and I knew the rules. I had played it before, but did not wish to play it again.

We played another game one afternoon; it was a version of 'Murder'; there were various rôles assigned to the guests, including a detective, a murder victim, various clues of a rather adult nature, and several suspects. I was enjoined to participate as a mysterious French person 'of some interest to the case'. The particulars of my costume I shall not relate, for they were of dubious origin and distinctly uncomfortable; my belt, however, was Versace.

There were lulls in the afternoon as the game continued, and I became rather bored. Convincing someone to play the jukebox, I danced on the dark, empty stage by myself, unheeding of any audience. When the song had finished, I heard the sound of applause, and turned around.

A friend of mine stood there smiling, he was holding a small movie camera up to his eye.

"I tried to film you," he said, "You were dancing."

"The music was too much for me."

"I wish I could show you," he said, "The look on your face just now."

"Phillip, whatever do you mean?"

"You looked so happy just dancing there, all by yourself; there was no other thought in your head."

"I was rather carried away, I think."

He looked at his camera, and swore. "This camera is not working, there is no recording."

"I'm sorry about that; I should have liked to see my audition. Did you like my dancing?"

"I'm sorry, too."

"Phillip, it was nothing; I was just dancing."

"I've never seen you like that before."

"Phillip, I'm not certain I understand you."

"You looked so happy, dancing there, as though nothing in the world could touch you."

He looked very sad, as he said it.

"Then I will dance again for you, if you like," I said.

"It will not be the same," he said, "Because then you will be dancing for me, not for yourself."

He paused, and drew a deep breath.

"I don't think I will ever see that again."

Many times later, when we would be talking or together in his house, he would say to me, "Do you remember that afternoon, at the Murder game, when you were dancing? Do you remember it, and how I tried to film you?"

"Yes, Phillip, I remember."

"I have a wish," he would say, after a moment.

"What is it, Phillip?"

"I wish I might see you dancing like that again, just once, when you were so happy, and thought no one was looking."

He rested his head on my shoulder, and was very quiet for a time. I did not say anything; I knew that the moment had come and gone, my dancing had come, and had gone, and what paths our lives together might now take could not be foreseen.

Where the summer sun rises, and the moon is setting
Here, in the golden meadow
My brother, run with me
We shall live forever
My brother, I have spoken these words.

Barton Briley and the New Moon

You have not lived a full life, it has been said, unless you have shared that life with friends, for no man is an island, and no man is truly alone, should he have friends. Of those friends who came into my life, and blessed it, there is one I have missed the most. His name is Barton Briley; he was there at the beginning and at the end of my journeys in northern Michigan, and in the ever twining, branching paths of our lives, he has been a true friend to me. In that long-ago summer, when I had first travelled to the northern country, I met him at the farm, at the end of a long, golden afternoon; the light was new, and all about me were things I had not seen before. He had just come in from the fields, and he greeted me warmly, but as an old friend, not a stranger to his house. I had not expected such a greeting, but it was a sincere gesture, and a welcome one.

It is an unusual fashion to be greeted in such a manner. Someone, whom we have never met, has welcomed us; we have been received; we are a friend, a companion at the table. When I saw Barton several weeks later, he again greeted me and welcomed me warmly; it was the weekend of the festival, and many people were about. Still, he took time to show me over the farm, and the projects he had planned for it. He performed a great kindness to me on that visit; he had mapped out a special, secluded place in the woods for my camping site, and terraced it out with many rocks, that I might have a clear view of the stage.

The Hundred-Acre Wood

Barton invited me to his house in Gaylord, on the long stretch of road heading west out of the town; I often stayed there. It was a fine, log-built house, of cedar planking and deep green shingles, with a wide porch in front, raised high off the ground. It sat almost hidden from the road, deep in a grove of tall pine trees with a wide lawn before it; it was always shady and cool there. The driveway curved through the woods from the road, it came slowly into view, revealing itself gradually, and the strange, serene beauty of it emerged before you; it called to you, it spoke; here am I, come and find rest. There were no other houses nearby, it stood alone. This was the usual fashion in the country, where land is plentiful, but for Barton's house, the peculiarity of its setting became it well. It was a precious enclave within the living forest, a jewel box of living trees, housing a rustic, wooden gem.

  Inside, the house was bare of furniture; Barton had been living at the farm for many years. Yet its structure was sound, and the rooms large and well proportioned. The interior décor was not to my taste; it featured heavily of flowering vines and twigs, but that was a personal consideration, not a professional assessment. Had I lived there, as I once thought I might, I should have made many changes to the interior; the exterior, however, was perfect in every way, well suited to its climate and its surroundings.

When I first entered the house, I felt the hand and the weight of Barton's skill in its construction; he had done all the work himself. He had planned its layout, studied building techniques, and raised the house with his own hands; I felt it was loved, as a fine automobile is loved by its mechanic. The beauty of a fine piece of construction is not a feature of the craft, but of the craftsman, for they transmit the perfection and symmetry of their minds into a concrete reality; the finished product may be enjoyed by many persons, but it belongs to them alone; it is their own creation.

Barton and I spent many weekends there, when the farm women were celebrating the new moon, and it was a time of great value to us; we spoke of many things there. He was neither pleased nor displeased by the pattern of his life; he realised its importance and its value, and struck his own course through its waters. Nor did he withstand the effect and the meaning of the presence of the Spirit in his life; he was very holy. We had many talks about God and spirituality; he took his own view, firmly and clearly, and shared it with me when I would ask him.

The Elder Children

To Barton I must give credit for first expressing in words what I could not comprehend in thought: the physical and spiritual essence of the Elder Children, which some men call our brothers, and which I, in that time of my ignorance, considered only apes. I had shared my views on the topic with Barton, he had expressed an interest, and we discussed it often. The Elder Children were real, they had been seen; I had felt their presence often, at the farm, and elsewhere in the northern country.

"I would believe in such things," he told me, "But they are not flesh and blood, and if they are not so, then how can they exist here, on this earth?"

"What do you mean, Barton?" I would ask him, for his response had taken the form of a concept unknown to me; I was still learning much about the Elder Children, and understood only a portion of the whole.

"I do not think they are physical beings," he said, firmly. "They are of the spirit world, and they return to it when they are pursued or hunted by us. This is why they cannot be found."

This was an entirely new thought for me, as the true reality of the Elder Children had not yet impressed itself; I had not looked upon them through Barton's eye. I had encountered them many times in a spiritual arena, but the truth of their substance had eluded me. Nor had I considered the import of Barton's words, for he was correct in his view.

I had not considered such things possible, but it took Barton, with his clear, unimpeded beliefs, to clarify them. After my conversations with him, I began to view the Elder Children in a different shape, that of light and colour, bending through the air to masque their appearance.

Therefore, our talks would continue, running along new, uncharted trails in the forest where neither of us had walked before; the entire world was laid out to us. It was never difficult for Barton and I to engage in conversation; his mind turned easily to many topics, and it was pleasant to share new thoughts with him.

The Farm Pavillions

Barton often shared with me his ideas for the farm and the buildings there; I was able to lay out many diagrams and details for him. He would analyse my drawings for their practicality; he looked at them, not as the scribbling of an architect, but as lengths of lumber, sacks of concrete, and quantities of nails. It would emerge before our eyes in three dimensions; the reality of it would unfold itself as we gathered around the layers of tracing paper. I would wield the pencil, Barton wielded the ruler; thus were our tasks divided, to a common purpose.

The festival was growing; every year larger crowds attended and the old buildings could not accommodate them. The festival kitchen and the bar needed a new, roofed area for tables and chairs, where guests might take their meals; Barton had conceived of it with translucent, glazed walls, which could be lifted in the summer and lowered in the winter, and thus utilised for bedding out plants and seedlings. He showed me his ideas, and I was very excited to see them; the walls hinged up from the top plate, like the wings of a butterfly, and hovered over the ground.

I sketched out a diagram, showing how the walls could be folded, as a bird's wing is tucked beneath its body, to be suspended over the ground, creating a shelter with wide, overhanging eaves.

"Use triangular forms for the framing," I told him, "And this will brace the panels for you. The shape of the wall panels, when they are folded, will also form a triangle, and this will give you even more strength."

"But that is extra lumber," said Barton. "Are you sure that we will need to do this?"

"Yes," I said, "The prevailing wind comes from the northwest. Look at bridges, derricks, and cranes; they are always braced with diagonal framing. The triangle is the simplest structure you can create; it is inherently stable."

Barton listened to me and followed my advice; he did me a great honour by doing so, for he was very practical. I did not know it then, but he respected my training; I had once described the balloon-type framing of an old general store accurately and completely; he had been very surprised I should have noticed it, for no other architect had done so.

It was a great pleasure for me, when I was next at the farm, to see the shelter completed, and the great, folding wings lifted up, high above the ground. Barton had built them from pine lumber and sheathed them with clear, transparent plastic; they hovered above our heads like the breathless wings of a dragonfly, and their diagonal bracing was sound. The winds, coming from the northwest, rattled at them, but they did not flutter; they stood firmly upon their posts.

The Artist in His Studio

If I should name one great excitement of Barton's career, it would be tractors, and machines, and all types of farm implements. Many times, when we were out driving, we would pass an old, rusted tractor abandoned in a field, and Barton would signal me to stop. I would pull to the side of the road; Jane's engine would idly softly while I waited for him. He would get out, walk over to the battered hulk, and describe its manufacture, its engine, and its capacities. I have never seen him unable to analyse any motor he encountered; they were all familiar; he was enamoured of them, as a woman might be enamoured of the flowers in her garden, or a child enamoured of his blanket or his bears.

Whenever I had difficulties with Jane, he would have me bring her outside, so that he could watch her manoeuvre on the wide, flat drive. He would open her hood, poke around inside, and diagnose her ailments immediately. He knew how to listen to her, as I did not, but tried to do so; Jane could be very naughty at times, when she was feeling her oats. He showed me how to check her oil and her radiator fluid, and to keep extra supplies on hand for emergencies. He fixed her bonnet, inserting new springs for it, and showed me where to buy accessories for her. He was very patient with both my queries and my ignorance, and I was grateful; it was a balance, a levelling guide, a plumb in our friendship.

I do not think there is an implement made which Barton did not own; his large, wooden shed at the farm was crowded with them, as were his trucks and his farm vehicles. He had several of these, electric golf-carts, pick-up trucks, and the like; they all carried tools and equipment, many of them had special, sliding racks he had designed and fitted himself. The walls of his sheds were lined with hooks and shelves, filled with various items; the floor was mapped out, foot by foot, with mowers, lawn machines, and such. Much of it I could not identify, but all of them had been used, and often. Barton could dissemble any motor or machine, and reassemble it quickly; he worked hard hours, and long, at the farm.

The Northern Country

Barton and I would often go for drives through the countryside; it was a distinct pleasure for both of us. The weather, even during the winter months, can be extraordinarily fine; we were out nearly every day.

Once, we drove around Little Traverse Bay and then north, into Cross Village, which lies along the uppermost shore of Lake Michigan, northwest of Petoskey. There is a very good restaurant there, with wide, flat roofs decorated with the legs of old cast-iron stoves; we enjoyed a fine luncheon in the dining room. From our table, we could see through the tall, blue-green windows over the gardens; they ended, suddenly and briefly, where the ground slopes sharply to the lake. The land here is raised up high above the water; there are many summer cottages down at the shore. They are not visible from the road, which skirts the escarpment high above them; one is only aware of iron gates and narrow, sandy drives that descend into the trees. The deep blue water was flat and wrinkled, like rain across a windscreen; clouds were scudding low overhead. Outside, there is a historical plaque written in English and Polish, dedicated to the builder.

We drove home through the Tunnel of Trees, which is that stretch of road from Cross Village to Harbour Springs; it is rumoured to be haunted, but I have never driven there at night. It is a uniquely pleasant drive, much of it wild country, with steep cliffs to the west and wide, green forest to the east. In the clear autumn light, the trees were a long, winding canopy of golden leaves, spreading their branches high overhead; one felt that one was gliding slowly, slowly, beneath the petals of some enormous flower. I felt, at times, that we had somehow stepped through a looking glass, and were travelling, as did the Odawa peoples; their long canoes traversed the broad, flat rivers beneath the golden trees, and the sky was still that same, perfect blue colour that is found only here.

We once stopped at a farm near Harbour Springs; it was a large concern with many wide, spreading gardens, bordered with long, caterpillar-like hoop-houses and a series of barns with livestock, and a small café, with a farm store. They sold many different preserves, all bottled on the farm, and vegetables and fruits in their season. Behind the farm, tucked into the trees, was a trout pond that was well stocked; there was a miniature train which ran about its shore. The grounds and the buildings were spotlessly clean; everything was organised and efficient, despite the bustle of visitors and children. There were pumpkins, squash, and other autumn vegetables for sale on the long tables; we saw children everywhere, scampering across the grass. In the barns and in the sheds were many different animals; I petted a small, black sheep in a pen, and fed some grunting, eager hogs in another. In one stall, we found tiny, pink and brown piglets, fast asleep on the straw; we did not wake them. There were horses in one of the paddocks, saddled and carrying children, and several small, grey donkeys, patiently waiting for their feed.

There were hills rising up behind the farm, terraced to make a vineyard, and we thought this an interesting feature to install in Johannesburg. The hoop-houses were also of great interest; Barton had built one at the farm, and it had been a great success; he grew bedding plants and seedlings all through the winter. Over time, it was extended and a second hoop-house constructed; I toured it many times, and Barton delighted to show me its workings; like many other things at the farm, he had designed and built it himself, with his own hands.

When the Moon Was High

Each month when the new moon rose, the women would gather at the farm, it was a weekend reserved exclusively for Diana. Then Barton would absent himself, and come to my house; my kitchen would be bursting with food: meats, cheeses, breads, vegetables, and many little tidbits: pickles, relishes, and other savoury treats. He would bring me food as well, venison for stews and chili, and fresh, whole milk from his family's dairy. Sometimes he would bring vegetables he had raised in his gardens; they were a delight to use and always fresh. They tasted of the earth in which they had grown, the water that had caressed them, and the sun that had given them life.

Barton liked to eat, he had a good appetite, and it was a pleasure to have him in my kitchen; he was a fine helper and a patient one. We experimented with old recipes and new ones, adapting them to our tastes and palates; we were always hungry.

It was a great thing for me to have a guest appreciative of my culinary art; Barton enjoyed my cooking very much. Our weekends were spent in the planning and preparation of our meals; there is a unique fellowship with a good friend at the stove. It is a truth universally acknowledged that every guest makes his way to the kitchen and stays there, if one is to paraphrase Jane Austen.

With Barton's help, I began to draw out my old recipes from Paris, which I had put away long ago; I had not used them while I was married. The flavours and the textures returned in new, different forms; the old triumphs resounded on the palate.

When I opened the dusty, worn pages, cramped with tiny, almost invisible writing, I felt that I stood on the edge of a deep ravine, whose bottom I could not see; staring across the void, there stood a man. He was like unto me, but also unlike; I recognised him, he bore my appearance. No bridge spanned the chasm between us, but with ease, he handed the gift to me again, through a dust of time and distance; it was still whole, and fresh; it had not changed in the passage.

Who was the giver, and the receiver, I could not distinguish. Was I the young, excited student of architecture, of art, of all things French, beaming with happiness? *À l'autre face*, was I the older man, the experienced architect, still learning but looking backwards, to a past of fond memory? The passing of many years had weathered me; I was not the same person who had first hesitantly stirred the giant soup pots on the ancient black stove in Versailles, nor was I the same person who stirred the gleaming stainless-steel pots on my modern stove in Charlevoix. The circle had drawn itself together, a strange *ouroboros*, united in the pleasure of the feast and in the company of a dear, cherished friend.

Potage Crème des Champignons

Mushrooms are the pride of northern Michigan cuisine, and of which I could never find enough; they are very popular. They are offered for sale in booths along the road, but in the early spring, when the snows recede from the wooded hillsides, the morel makes its appearance. It has a rather obscene shape, with its swollen, phallic head and its dull gold colouring; it is not a suitable topic for polite conversation. Once plucked, however, it is richly fragrant and fills the room with its scent. It is second only to the truffles of the Périgord in the fullness of its aroma, and is as highly prized.

In the spring, it was delightful to join my friends in the morel hunts, searching on hands and knees deep in the wet, mossy woods north of Little Traverse Bay. Here, in the rolling hills, can be found the choicest selections; plucked and carried safely home in a damp cloth, they are at their best sautéed in a white wine sauce, with roast chicken fresh from the market. It is best to pick the morels in the morning, before the sun has become too hot, and they wilt under the advancing heat.

One weekend, faced with a rather large amount of mushrooms, I put them into a soup, which I had first learned to make in the Loire Valley. As the stovetop reddened, and the scent of the simmering mushrooms filled the air, I was whirled back through the snow, over many years, to Fontevraud, and the three hundred-year-old farmhouse of pale stone. The flames roared in the hearth; I can still feel the heat of it, even as I write.

As with most successful inventions, its creation was accidental: I had left the mushrooms to simmer in white wine, over very low heat, for much longer than necessary, to cook them with the roast chicken. Out of this came the soup and I prepared it as I had been taught, it was delicious; Barton and I stood over the stove with long wooden spoons tasting it; I will not exaggerate, it was *amazing*.

I remembered, as I prepared the soup again, the station café in the Haute-Saône, where the blue-stubbled men sat over their coffee and newspapers in the smoke-filled air, and the big shepherd dog bit my leg. He did not draw blood, but he clasped his jaws firmly about my calf, as I walked past him; I did not shout, but waited for the owner to pull him back. I had ordered soup there; I was very tired from a long, restless night on the train; I had not slept. When I disembarked in Ronchamps, a fog engulfed me; I could not see my way ahead, and then the golden, warm light from the café came shining through the grey mist; it had drawn me into its embrace. The soup came steaming hot, scalding my tongue, as I lifted the large, silver spoon to my lips, sipping its delicious creaminess, and ordering more to take in my thermos. When I drank it later, for my luncheon in Belfort, it was waiting for me, and like Max's dinner, it was still hot.

Scotch and the Single Man

Barton liked a very good Scotch, as did I, and we enjoyed many glasses of it; he was not a wine drinker, but appreciated the bouquets and the vintages that we enjoyed with our meals. He would drink them happily, and remark in delight at their complement; I was learning, again, to pair food with wine and the pleasure of it was a blissful enjoyment. Each enhanced the other; we often sat at the table long into the night, exclaiming at the flavours.

After dinner, with our coffee, we would serve ourselves from the drinks table, and take our glasses outside. We tried many different kinds of whiskey, both the Irish and the Scottish, and always returned, after many detours, to the single-malts of Islay. The domestic bourbons we rejected as too sweet; we both preferred the strong flavour of peat in our drink. The blended whiskeys did not hold our interest; they were used for cocktails, when other liquids might be added. I showed Barton my father's technique of adding three drops of clear, tepid water, and he enjoyed the bouquet that rose from the glass.

There, on the porch, surrounded by the night, we would raise our glasses to the meal we had just enjoyed, to the stars, and to ourselves. I like to wonder, in those moments when I am looking up at the stars, if their reflection might still sparkle within my glass, were I to hold it up to them.

I should like a very dry martini, please.
With a very good gin, and vermouth
Do you have Noilly Prat?
I like an olive in my martini, sir, thank you.
A good Spanish olive, if you have one?

A Bloody Good Time at the Bar

Riding into Petoskey, I always drove with anticipation and excitement, the drive was exhilarating to me. Jane would roar breathlessly, effortlessly down the Petoskey Road, taking delight in its smooth, grey surface; she mastered each curve and each bend with great skill. I always had the windows down, to catch the flying breezes; my hair was always tousled when I arrived, and my scarf invariably askew.

I enjoyed working with my clients there, and met with them several times a week; one of them had offices situated in a house converted to this purpose. It was nestled deep in the woods on the east side of town; the pine and cedar trees towered up on all sides, sheltering the house from the street, and casting their shadows on the grass late in the afternoon.

The house itself was sited oddly; it was aligned perpendicular to the road, with the garage at the far end; one had to navigate a long stretch of drive before reaching the front door. This, however, was far from unpleasant; there were many shade trees and flowers along its edges. The drive dipped into a hollow, and then rose up out of them, emerging into the yard and the sunlight. A small stream flowed across its crumbling surface in the summer, falling down over rocks into the ravine before it splashed away deep in the woods.

  I was set up there in a quiet room on the ground floor; the secretaries worked upstairs in the converted sitting room. The deep eaves of the sloping roof kept the house in continuous shade; it was cool in all weathers and very comfortable. From my room, a large, plate-glass window looked over a sloping patch of ground, heavily overgrown with wildflowers and creeping vines, shaded by a Japanese maple. The effect of this created a light of aqueous, dream-like ripples, as though I were looking through a green, glass bottle; I often felt, at times, I inhabited a large tank, an exotic marine creature that looked out upon the world.

  Such a view afforded me a glimpse into the variety of fauna that abounded in such a place. Their proximity to man was similar to the alleys of Chicago, where the coyotes patronised the delicatessens at luncheon. From time to time, a turkey hen with her poults would parade past the window, plucking fat, delicious worms from the earth; their appearance was always welcome. They made their progress slowly across the lawns and disappeared into the trees; they took no notice of us; we did not matter to them. There were white-tailed deer who camped out on the lawns in the summer afternoons; they liked the cool shade of the cedar trees, and used to nibble at my client's flowerbeds. Once, a bleating fawn staggered strangely across the grass, and in our mounting despair we realised it had been injured. We set off to find it, that we might help it, but it vanished into the woods away to the south, where the land drops down into steep ravines; we could not find him, nor could we track him there. My client sent one of his friends to track it, a hunter of some experience, but he could not do so; the woods there were impassable, he said.

When I first began working in Petoskey, a large, red fox trotted across the deck, behind the house, and stopped for a moment to wash his paws. I was delighted at his appearance, for he bore a great resemblance to the red foxes that played in my own garden. My client did not think it the same creature, but I felt that it was my friend from Charlevoix, coming to my new place of work to greet me, and to offer his blessings. Despite the encroachment of man into the hills, the wild animals still made their homes in the forest, and there carried out their lives.

Petoskey

Petoskey Avenue, running east from Charlevoix, skirts the southern edge of Little Traverse Bay, extending like a finger into the green hills. It is edged by forested slopes rising gently to the south that soften, almost imperceptibly, into wide, rolling farmlands. One can see across the bay, to Harbour Springs and beyond, where the hills mount up to Boyne Highlands and Nubs Nob, and the forests of Cross Village; Pellston is due north, and the road leads, as do all roads in northern Michigan, to the Mackinac Bridge.

The road slopes down to the shoreline, and the old rail line parallels it for many miles. Then it turns again, and the land is wide and flat, where the bay comes up close, and there are many parks and hiking paths. There are thick pinewoods here, and hidden swamps where the deer and the elk can be found; the hunters populate the woods in November, and you can see their orange caps in the grey trees. The land rises again to the steep, rocky cliffs of Bay Shore, where there are houses, a gas station and a liquor store, and then runs straight into Bay Harbour. Here are the large summer homes, the riding club, and the big hotels; they are thronged with people during the season.

The road winds through the sloping hillsides, heavily forested, which are very steep; I have tried to take Jane up there in the winter. As you come into town, the land stretches out, wide and flat like a sloping shelf, and there are many shops and restaurants on both sides.

There is another approach to Petoskey from the south, as one comes up from Gaylord. The road rises to the top of a steep hill, and the view, at first glance, is breathtaking; you see the whole spread of the bay, wide and glittering, before you. As one descends into town, the view is becomes marred by the local hospital. It is badly sited; it masques the view and does not command it. It is an ugly box of brown brick, with many additions and growths, resembling a square, cancerous stump.

Along this road, as one turns to the east, there is the pleasant sight of Mitchell Street, rising towards a fine church with a high steeple. The view is marred, once again, by a gaping void in the earth, a large, square emptiness where the theatre and shops once stood.

Mitchell Street is the main thoroughfare in Petoskey; it runs in a perfectly straight line to the east, rising up from the Bear River and over the hills, where it leads out to Vanderbilt.

The downtown area is filled with many old buildings and shops, catering mostly to the summer trade. There are several boutiques, and a well-stocked bookstore, with a fireplace, where it is pleasant to read in the winter. It is rumoured to be haunted, and I have felt the presence of spirits there, in the basement and on the staircase.

Only Wise Men Know....

I once lunched with a client at a small café in Petoskey, where the patrons were familiar to the waitresses; there were no tourists. There was nothing in its décor or its location to tempt the unwary traveller; it was not on the main streets, but tucked into a grey, wooden rectangle the exact size and shape of a two-car garage. The food was memorable in its blandness; it was of no distinction. Were it in Chicago, I should not have set foot in it; it was not of a quality to compare with M Henry or even Ann Sather's, whether in Lakeview or Andersonville.

One of my clients often ate there, however, and he asked me to join him; he did not like to eat alone. We took a late breakfast there; it was a brilliant summer day and quiet on that side of town. As we waited for our meal, seated in the corner booth, an old woman shuffled slowly into the café. She was greeted kindly by the hostess, and was seated next to us, which irritated my client; he valued his privacy. Like all persons of his disposition, he supposed it to be of some value.

He whispered furiously, "Why does she have to sit next to us? I don't want her here, do you?"

The old woman said nothing, but sat quietly. I hoped she had not heard my client's mutterings; I should have been embarrassed for her. The waitress emerged from the kitchen and set down a small bowl of cottage cheese, garnished with some orange slices. I cannot recall what she drank; perhaps it was only water, or iced tea.

My client whispered, "That's all she's going to eat for the day, Sanjay, that's all she can afford."

"Stop it, Peter," I said.

"Maybe that will be you, someday," he said.

"*Stop it.*"

"Do you think, one day, all you'll have to eat is a bowl of cottage cheese? Sanjay, just think; this is probably the highlight of her day. When she's done here, she'll shuffle back to the nursing home and stare at the television, waiting for someone to call."

"Stop it, Peter," I said. "Don't."

"Waiting for someone to call, who never will? Her family has completely forgotten about her. They've shut her up in a nursing home to die; they are just waiting."

"Stop it."

He did not speak again, but looked at me over his scrambled eggs and his toast, his bacon and his cinnamon rolls, that he would not finish, and would not take with him; it would be thrown away, after he left the café.

"Stop it," I said. "I don't want to hear anymore."

"Maybe your life will be like that."

I could not look at him.

"No," I said, finally, and with much effort. "It will not be like this. It will not end this way; it will not happen like this."

"How do you know?"

I finally looked at him.

"I know it will not end like this."

"How will it end, Sanjay?"

"It will happen quickly, and I will be laughing; I will not be sitting down, but standing…and it will happen in the woods."

"In the woods?"

"Yes, in the woods."

"How do you know these things?"

"I don't know, Peter. They just come to me, and they show me things; that is all."

"Do you know how I will die?"

"Yes."

"Can you tell me?"

"No."

"Why?"

"I can't."

"I think I have a right to know how I die."

I looked at him.

"Peter, I cannot tell you, how you will die."

"You already know, don't you?"

"Yes, Peter, I do."

"So, tell me."

"No…I will not."

"I don't understand why you can't tell me something, if you already know what it is."

I looked at him again.

"Peter…the day I tell you…it will be on the day that it happens."

"What do you mean?"

"That's exactly what I mean…the day I tell you, is the day that it happens. It will be the day that you die."

"And how, exactly, do I die?"

"I can't tell you, Peter."

The old woman did not look up; I do not think she heard us. She was eating her cottage cheese, taking her time and enjoying her food. She did not speak, nor did she seem aware of our presence. I looked at her, but she did not see me, and I hoped that she had not overheard our conversation.

Did she think of, or remember, other meals when she had not been alone? Had there been a time when she said to herself, my life should not end like this, I shall be happy and be surrounded by those I have loved, cherished, and fed with meals prepared with my own hands. They will always love me; they will remain with me. Did she wonder where everyone had gone, her husband, parents, children?

The promises we were told, on those days when our lives lay spread before us; where are they now, the bright burning fires of our youth? What has happened, that they should have been extinguished, before our eyes, yet without our knowledge? Which star will next fall to earth, to grant our heart's desire?

In the darkness, where is the lover?

We finished our breakfast, and paid the check. I went to the waitress, and pressed a five-dollar bill into her hand. "For the lady, seated next to us," I said.

She thanked me profusely and asked, "Do you want me to tell her? She will be so grateful, you are very kind."

"No," I said. "Please wait, until we have left."

We stood for a moment on the sidewalk, while Peter smoked a cigarette; we did not speak. When he had finished, he asked me, "Why did you do that?"

"I wanted to," I said.

"Why?"

I sometimes think of her, the old woman in the café. I wonder if she is still sitting there on her bare, wooden seat, and I hope she is enjoying her cottage cheese and her slices of orange, and I hope, somewhere, in some small portion of her life, she is happy.

The Potteries

The decorative arts in northern Michigan are exemplified in its pottery, which one finds at the fairs and markets and at some of the shops; they can be, and often are, very good. They are not, perhaps, worthy of the imprimatur of Stoke-on-Trent, but they can be very beautiful. I often sent photographs and descriptions to my clients; they were very popular in Chicago, and in much demand.

The signature of each artisan is distinctive; there are many different styles, which sometimes display the influence of the Ojibwe culture. You will find the pieces adorned with feathers or dried flowers; I have seen larger vases incorporate shells, butterflies, and pinecones in their fashion; they can be very striking compositions. The pottery comes in many sizes and shapes, and many different colours: mossy greens, rich tobacco browns, soft blues, and golden-earth hues are prevalent. I have not seen red pottery, or white; I suppose this is due to the composition of the clay and the minerals of the earth; the northern country once boasted large copper mines, but they are empty now, and forgotten. The colours of each piece are also a hallmark of the artisan; many of them have adopted unique clays for their works, and they are a signature of their skill. There was one craftsman I found, who used a deep, mossy green biscuit-ware for his pieces; they were very distinctive, and very beautiful. I offered him a special composition, to create special pieces for my clients in Illinois, but he refused.

When the detailling of a piece is executed carefully and precisely, it becomes possessed of that quality which lifts it from the realm of the ordinary to that of the unusual, the different, and the unique; they have become beautiful, they are of value. It is an uncommon factor, for it is highly subjective, and not everyone will agree on its application. Nevertheless, as I used to tell my students, in the words of my old professor, when an object has become truly beautiful, when it has transcended mere physicality, it has become a living, breathing entity; it has a voice, a soul, and a spirit; it has begun to *sing*.

They did not understand, of course; they were only students. Their minds could not accept such appreciations or fantasies. It does not happen in every piece, or in every shop selling them; much is worthy only of the dustbin.

I had clients in Illinois who collected pottery; they were keen judges of form and shape; the quality of the colours and glazes were critically reviewed and assessed by them. Often, they would commission me to find pieces for them; it afforded me the chance to visit the fairs and to speak with the artisans. I made many trips, for one finds potteries and craftsmen across the breadth of northern Michigan; it is a ubiquitous feature of the region. The artisans did not attend the fairs; they were busy creating; they were devotés of their art, focussed on the concept, the design, and the execution; they had spent much time and effort to master their craft.

    Their studios were to be found in the most extraordinary of places, in garages and basements, pole-barns and sheds, and once, in Pellston, in an abandoned caravan, propped up on masonry blocks in the forest, heated with a kerosene lantern. They were crowded with slips and greenware; the kilns roared day and night; the glazing-pots littered the tables. The air was thick with the scent of the glazes and the firing chemicals; it was difficult, at times, to breathe.

    The artisans were very friendly; they were proud of their work, and often stopped their wheels to show me their particular signatures; one man, who had created a number of very beautiful vases, offered me a position, that I might learn his craft and thus create my own pieces for sale at the fairs. He told me his work was too traditional; he felt my designs might reflect a contemporary attitude, which might be sold in New York, or San Francisco. I declined his offer, to his regret; I was not skilled at such assembly; it was not my gift. My own tastes, moreover, followed that of Maria Martinez, but there was no one in northern Michigan who made black-on-black wares.

Portrait of the Artist as a Young Man

Ernest Hemingway's presence in northern Michigan is celebrated in Walloon Lake and Petoskey. His family's cottage 'Windermere' still stands, and there are many who have seen it, but it is privately owned; you cannot trespass upon the grounds. I had friends in Walloon Lake, who had been to the house; his ghost was seen in the hallway, they said; he still returned there, from time to time, but they would say nothing further.

In Petoskey, Hemingway's presence is celebrated at the Carnegie Library, where he spoke of his experiences in the war; I have often wondered if he described the impact of his accident, and the sensations he felt; they are vividly described in his work. I have seen the depth of his injuries manifested in his writing, but not directly, for he was a master of submersion. His writing of it, in *A Farewell To Arms*, was so similar to my own account that I felt a kinship in our experiences. The circumstances of Jane's death, and the accident which took her life, are still so unreal to me that I cannot describe them accurately, for the story would be an extremely intimate one, and the construction of it as fragile as the snowflakes that whirled about me on that road on that terrible, tragic day. I have not yet faced its reality, but in poetic format; even then, my attempts, I think, while clumsy, have struck very near the mark.

Hemingway is revered for his presence, but not for his writing, nor for the development of his form. I met no one there, in all my time in Charlevoix, who had read *The Old Man and the Sea*; if they had, they could not discuss it; it was a foreign literature to them. I had not come to it until later in my career, and it was fortunate that I did so; it was a fine way to complete my understanding of his oeuvre. My father had once told me that *The Old Man and the Sea* was Hemingway's finest writing, and I had not believed him; I had not thought that anything could surpass *For Whom the Bell Tolls*. When I read it, at last, I could not speak of it, or even of anything else; it was a work both incredible and powerful in its simplicity. Slim Keith, in her memoir, described a similar reaction; I knew what she felt, and how she perceived its brilliance. It was, and remains, one of the few great pieces of writing I have seen; a standard against which I might judge my own work.

Cava

I had been advised before leaving Chicago that I should not find good pizza in northern Michigan; many of my friends had felt it necessary to say something to me. I did not take heed of their warnings; I felt I might create my own version, if necessary. I had learned to knead and to throw the thin pizza dough with my bare hands, and to spread the rich, fragrant sauce upon its round, pallid surface; I had experimented with many different toppings. My favourite, which I have never successfully reproduced, was a combination of chunk tuna and artichokes, teased with anchovies and spices, set upon a very thin layer of tomato; there was no cheese. I was served this once, outside the Villa d'Este in Tivoli; I have never forgotten the sharpness of its flavours and its textures; it appealed to me.

    The pizza labelled Chicago-style or deep-dish is unique to the Midwest, it is not found anywhere else. It is the one, true American creation, of which all Chicagoans may be proud; it can be very good, and is in much demand. It has been claimed, and with some reason, to have been made first in Chicago; there are two chefs, at least, who have assumed this credit. A pizza-chef is appreciated and admired; he is sought-after; he is patronised. New York-style pizza, with its paper-thin crust, is altogether different and sometimes, I have felt, more preferable; it is a lighter, more delicate affair, and perhaps more authentic, deep-dish pizza is not an Italian invention.

Nonetheless, it was a true statement; there was no good pizza in northern Michigan, and I did not realise this until after my arrival. I had been warned, but I had not listened; what I found, in the various pizzerias in Petoskey, was nothing that I should have considered fit for consumption. Where delicacy of crust was needed, there was only a thick layer of heavy dough; where spices and flavouring were desired, one found only dull, tasteless meats. In a region that produced some very fine cheeses, only flat, limp slices of American-style Cheddar were to be found. It was an embarrassing reality; I could not comprehend it, nor find any reason for it.

It was not possible to find a true deep-dish pizza; I longed for the rich, flavourful concoctions I had once ordered in Mundelein; by my own reckoning, they were the best I have tasted. After much experimentation, I succeeded in producing my own version at home, but it was not something I should have served my guests; it was only an amateur effort.

I met clients one afternoon for luncheon at a quiet café in Bay Harbour. It was furnished, unusually, in a modern blend of shiny metals and smooth, polished woods; northern Michigan is not known for such things. The menu listed several different types of pizza, which intrigued me; I had not seen such offerings elsewhere. I asked my clients if they had ordered here, and they said they had done so.

"You may not enjoy the pizzas here," they said. "They are different from what we like."

"What do you mean?" I asked. "Is it deep-dish pizza?"

"No," they told me. "They are very thin."

"Do you mean New York-style pizza?" I asked.

"Sanjay, you know about these things," They said. "We have not heard of it here."

I ordered several small, thin slices with different toppings, to sample the flavours; the chef indulged my request, and sent several small plates out for me. It came to the table piping hot, with thin, thin strips of perfect crust, almost Neapolitan in fashion, and spread with only the thinnest layer of tomato or oil. The herbs were robust and vibrant on the palate; they enhanced the meats and vegetables, the mushrooms and the good, good cheese. The cheese, the cheese.

I burned my tongue, and then burned it again; I could not help it; it was very, very good, and reminded me of home. I laughed aloud, at the direction of my life, that I should have left Chicago, that I should have longed for the flavour of a New York-style pizza, and that I should have found it, in a café in Bay Harbour, in northern Michigan.

Chandler's

There is a restaurant in downtown Petoskey that serves very good food; I have lunched there many times. It may be the best cuisine in northern Michigan, and this is no small compliment; it is seconded only by the café in Bay Harbour.

I first ate there on a cold, drizzling morning when the light was grey and dull; the streets were damp and the stones chilled your feet. Inside, it was pleasantly warm and cheerful; there was a wood fire in the open kitchen and hot, fresh bread from the ovens. I sat at a long table with people I did not know; we had just been introduced; some of them later became my friends, but I do not know remember their names. Nor do I remember what I ordered, an omelet, perhaps, but it was very good, and the coffee was strong and hot.

When I next dined there, for a luncheon party, my hostess insisted I order a Bloody Mary, *le plus grand spécialité de la maison*. The drink came and was sent back; it was too bland, too boring; I could not abide it.

This scene repeated itself on subsequent visits, and the bartenders began to chaff me in a friendly manner when I would order my cocktails. They sent over tall, sweating glasses for me to sample; they were adorned with tiny, pickled vegetables: carrots, artichokes, and white asparagus, which I had never considered as a garnish, but enjoyed. The pretty, young waitresses would apologise profusely and return with another; it would be better and more heavily spiced, but still insufficient. I was used to the robust concoctions of the Twisted Spoke, and I needed, no, I demanded more flavour, more vigour, more bite.

The bartender, after some consultation, allowed me to mix my own cocktail at the bar, and was astonished at the spices and sauces I added. He took a sip, and then another, eyed me suspiciously, and then drank the entire contents.

"That was incredible," he told me, "But I'm not sure our customers will like this; it is very spicy."

"Perhaps you can set the spices out, on a tray," I suggested, "And people can add their own, when they order."

"Sanjay," he said, "You are the only customer who does that here. *No one* can drink this; it is *very* spicy."

"Oh dear," I stammered, "I am so sorry. I did not mean to be so difficult. Please forgive me."

He laughed, and said, "There is nothing to forgive; we want to make our customers happy. Sanjay, anytime you come here, we will have a very special Bloody just for you."

He was as good as his word; they kept the mixture to hand, and when I would take luncheon there, alone or with friends, I was always served a 'Bloody Sanjay' from the bar.

The Lives of Others

It is an idiosyncratic feature of northern Michigan that certain of my friends would only dine at certain establishments; they would not patronise another. The Side Door, Chandler's, and even Roast & Toast all maintained their own guest lists; there was no intermingling. I had no such reservations; I was not affixed to one place; still, my friends would segregate themselves, and so I would venture out, taking each café, pub, and restaurant in its turn, with each group of friends.

There was a small, dark pub on Mitchell Street, near the old rail lines; it may no longer be there. It was of no special appearance; it is a pub; it served burgers and beer, and other fried foods. I did not care for the cooking; it made me very ill, but I had friends who enjoyed dining there, and so I would join them at the bar.

The bar was in its own room; it was appropriately long and dark, built of heavily varnished oak, its walls were covered with photographs, clippings, memorabilia real and faked, and a variety of antique musical instruments. They served good, cheap drinks; I used to see my students there after classes, and sometimes before. They would then ask me, at our next class, whom was the pretty lady dining at my table? I would answer, only a pretty lady and they would then fall silent; I gave no other answer.

I usually ate at the pub with my friends Margaret and Rachel; they often invited to join them. Our conversations were loud and boisterous, full of double-entendre; we were all the same age; we were all divorced, and we all enjoyed the same type of men. It was all in fun, it was part of our lives; I took none of it seriously. Still, I was careful with my speech, I did not know what might be repeated; I did not know them well. *Qui vous parle des autres, les pourparlers à d'autres de vous.*

There was a chilling winter day when only my friend Rachel lunched with me; the rest of our friends had other engagements, and so we were alone. We enjoyed our luncheon, and then suddenly, Rachel began to speak of our mutual friends, the ones who were not there, and other people we knew.

"You know she's cheating on her husband," she said, her dark eyes flashing. "In fact, she has cheated on both of them."

"Please do not tell me these things," I said. "I don't want to know; it is not my business."

"You are living here now, Sanjay; these people are your friends. Everyone knows; it is all over town."

"That may be so," I said, "But their private lives are their own; they are nothing for me to concern myself."

"You need to know," she said. "Why these people have the reputation that they do, why people think a certain way about them. Did you think that they were perfect?"

"How can you say these things?" I asked her. "These people are my friends, and they are also my clients; it is not my business. They are your friends, too, or had you forgotten that?"

"You think they're so wonderful, don't you, Sanjay?" She leaned closer to me. "They are not. They sit in their fine houses, drinking their fine champagne, and you sit there with them, you think they are your friends."

"They are my friends, Rachel; they have been very kind, and very helpful to me."

"That is because you are useful to them."

"Stop it."

"And when you are done being useful to them, they will cast you aside. Did you ever wonder why some people refuse to speak to them, people who knew them, who worked for them, all these years?"

"Rachel, *no one* that I have talked to has ever said anything untoward about my friends. *No one.*"

"They are using you, Sanjay."

"Stop it."

"You think they are so perfect, so wonderful."

"No one is perfect, Rachel, least of all me. Or you."

"Did you not ever wonder, why they did not tell you about these things? Did you never ask?"

"It is none of my business, Rachel!"

"You need to *make* it your business, Sanjay."

"No, I do not."

Her speech continued after we had our coffee and paid our bill; I have forgotten it now.

No, I have not forgotten it; but I cannot write these things; they were hurtful, stabbing, wounding the people I loved, people I cared for and who, I thought, cared for me. She kept speaking after we left the pub, as we walked down Mitchell Street, and I could not look at her. I could not listen to her, as she revealed secret after secret, spoke lie upon lie, like tiny grains of some bitter, dark ore, and the cold wind whipped my face, and my skin, numb.

The Last Supper

Once, a friend invited me to dinner at the local casino, to join him in their private dining room; I was suitably astonished. I had lunched at the buffet, a hot, steamy room redolent with heat lamps and hard, wooden chairs; it did not appeal to my tastes or to my palate.

"But we are dining in the Grill Room," he said, "I think you will enjoy it."

I arrived early, and waited for my friend with no great anticipation. From where I sat in the lobby, looking into the vestibule, there was no hint or promise of a good dinner, and I resigned myself to an evening of extended boredom. I did not mind my friend's company, only that it should be wasted in such an environment. The casino décor, in its harsh, clanging shades of red, purple, and chocolate brown, failed to excite me.

"You know I don't like casinos," I told my friend. "I am not a gambler, I don't like gambling."

"Bring twenty dollars," he replied, "And if you lose that, it won't matter." I had brought twenty dollars, and promptly lost it; it was, and remains, a great deal of money to me.

I was not prepared for the interior of the Grill Room: it was a remarkable space, and I still see it clearly in my mind, both the vision and the reality of it. It was a product of care and precision, of a strong, firm eye and the means to fulfill it; no detail had been overlooked; nothing was left to chance. All aspects of its design were harmoniously realised; there was nothing to jar the senses, nor too much elaboration, where severity should have paid. The interior formed a wide, oval room, panelled in broad, vertical strips of black walnut, and highlighted by immensely tall, graceful blown-glass sculptures of deep flaming orange, like the pistils of a gigantic flower. They were arranged about the room like the pillars of a temple; their surfaces composed of many small, irregular pieces of glass, fused together by the heat of the kiln.

The room was hushed and quiet, with only the sound of glasses softly clinking at the oval bar in the centre; overhead, an oval, wooden trellis focussed the swirling dimensions of the room, and stabilised its curves. It was a skillful design, and a surprise that it should be there; it was worthy of Chicago, or New York, even San Francisco; no alteration was needed. I wondered who the designer had been, and if he had created other restaurants like this; I should have liked to thank him.

I exclaimed to my friend, at the design of the room, and he was surprised at my response. "I did not think that you would like this décor," he said, "I thought your tastes were more traditional, and more formal."

"This is a very formal space," I told him, "And it is also a very traditional arrangement."

"What do you mean?" he asked me.

"It is the materials, and the colours," I said, "Which make this room a contemporary design. The forms are quite lovely, too; these glass sculptures are superb."

He did not comprehend my words; my analyses were spoken to empty air; it was outside his knowledge.

I do not remember our meal, save only the wine: a young, triumphant Chateau Greysac Médoc, warm in our glasses and refreshing, clear and invigorating. The waiter smiled at my appreciation of it, and thanked me; it was rare, he said, for someone to enjoy such a wine. I told the waiter how much I enjoyed Bordeaux, and was always searching for good, young wines to be served at my own table. It is a memorable wine I have drunk since; I have drunk it often, and sometimes alone, it is not, I think, a wine to be shared in haste.

I have not shared it with my friend, however, for our paths took different directions from that evening; it was the last time we dined together. I neither knew nor realised that the storm would soon break upon us; it was only a dinner with my friend, and I enjoyed myself, but the forces of our lives, and the people within them, were sharpening their blades for the slaughter, to then feast upon the carcass, and to divide the spoils.

If You Could Read My Mind, Love

The old Carnegie library in Petoskey is a fine building of dove-grey stone, resembling the Villa Rotonda in its design. It is lacking in its isolation, however; it is crowded on all sides and commands no view. The books are no longer there; they have been moved to the new library across Mitchell Street. The interior spaces are lofty and well proportioned, with fine detailling and pleasing woodwork; there is a fireplace in one room, with a handsome, well-proportioned mantelpiece.

I was invited to provide readings as part of a fair, by some people who had heard of my skills, by other people who had benefitted from them. I did not know what to expect; my experiences in the trade fairs in Chicago had been subjected to a gross, extended tedium, and I planned accordingly, so I that might not be bored. I brought some books with me, and the boys, and planned to write in my journal, recording various thoughts on my life; I felt these might be of some value one day. Even if no one were to see them, they would still be there, my own notes and commentaries on various topics.

There were several readers there; the building was full of them; I was only one of several. I did not expect to meet many people, and settled myself in comfortably. A few friends had promised to stop in, and I looked forward to their visit, it appeared to be a long afternoon.

I was set up in the children's library; there are freshly painted murals of various storybook characters upon its walls. From its appearance, they were of a modern design, and not original to the building. I wondered if there had been murals before, products of the WPA, if they had been examples of the Art Moderne, which we now label Art Deco. There are murals like this at the Merchandise Mart, in Chicago, and they are very beautiful; I have always enjoyed looking at them.

The other readers set up their tables and I noticed their accoutrements; cards, stones, crystals, herbs, and other implements, which I did not possess and for which I had no use. I did not need them; I used only my hands and my gift; there was no need for ornament. The others were experienced; they had done this many times. I knew no one there; everyone was a stranger to me. I was a novice; this was all new; I had not so publicly paraded myself.

I expected an afternoon of boredom; I could not leave until three o'clock. The day was sunny and clear, I longed to be at the park or at the shore, watching the sailboats.

When the bell rang for the first round of appointments, one of the managers came to me and explained the structure of the fair; each reader could expect to see an individual for ten minutes, so that all might have their turn. I was surprised when she informed me I had someone waiting, at the start of the day.

My first sitter was a woman; she had attended these fairs; she was experienced in these matters. I was nervous but I did my best, taking her hands in mine and telling her what I saw, answering her questions. My diagnoses were accurate, she began to weep, and I realised I had not provided any tissues; I had not thought such revelations could arouse such emotion. I read for her until I felt I could go no further, and she departed, thanking me politely.

The day continued and I experienced a steady, continued roster of visitors. I began to grow very tired; the strain was very sharp; I was not feeling very well. With some difficulty, I pulled myself from the table, and spoke with the managers.

"I cannot go on much longer," I said. "Is there any way to close out my session early?"

"Sanjay, we cannot do that," they told me. "There is a long line of people; they are waiting to see you."

"What on earth do you mean?"

"You have a waiting-list, people have signed up; they are waiting below stairs, in the café."

"How many are there?"

"Sanjay, there are at least ten people waiting. Some of them have been here all morning."

"Please tell me you're joking; I've never done this before. This is all new to me."

"No," they smiled, "We are not joking; you are a very popular reader here."

"But I have never done this before," I said.

"Word has spread," they answered, "People are talking about your skills, and what you have done for them."

It was a surprise to me that my skills should be noticed and appreciated; I had not expected it. I did not know any of these people, waiting hour upon hour for my readings; they were strangers to me, although some of them later become close friends, and we shared many things together. I have often wondered how they came to choose my services, from a schedule full of readers; there were many who sat through the long afternoon with no one at their tables, and some gave me hard looks. Some of them even came to me for readings, and were very grateful for my insight.

I continued the readings and saw each person in turn, although I was very tired. The managers were right; some people had been waiting all day. I set a record for the fair, no one else was in such demand; my roster had been filled within the first hour of the fair's opening.

The Lightning Storm

I had a friend whose house was built upon a steep, bare hillside, where it commanded a fine view over the town and the bay, far to the west; I liked to watch the summer storms from his terrace. The skies over the bay are wide and high; the clouds mount up from Lake Superior as they drift slowly down from Canada, and assume many different shapes and colours.

The sky darkened, and the air changed while we watched the lightning flash high above us, silent and terrible; we did not see where it came from, only the quick, flashing bolt across the sky. There were strange, gleaming lights that sparkled in rhythm as the heat and the electricity collided; the lights moved up through the clouds, and their rays pierced them. The clouds mounted up, their layers were edged with gold; the last rays of the sun tinged them with light. All was tense before the approaching darkness; the cattle moved in the fields below us, but we remained. My friend took my hand; he was frightened, but I did not reject him.

The air sizzled, a sudden, stabbing blaze struck the earth, and the night echoed with thunder: where did it land? The winds rushed down from the cold lakes; there was nothing to stop them until they struck the slopes of the central massifs. The rain blew horizontally in our faces as we stood on the terrace laughing, our hands stretched out to the light and the heat and the cold and the darkness, in a display put on, as we imagined, for our sole benefit.

I thought, then, of the *feux d'artifice* of 1770 at Versailles, and wondered at their splendour and their colour; I have stood on the balcony of the Galerie des Glaces. As I looked out over the Water Parterres towards the Basin of Apollo, the setting sun ignited their surfaces, turning them to burning, flaming gold; the reflection of it, in the tall, wide mirrors, dazzled the eye, and I thought of them, again, as I stood on the terrace of the house in Petoskey. We had been permitted to witness a facsimile of that performance, an imitation of art, via Nature, that might have surpassed the original, and, if so, like the courtier's remark, they were truly priceless, indeed.

What fumbling hand has turned the light,
Of daylight's burning ember
Sleep well, my child, and do not dream
'Tis well not best remembered.

Under the Milky Way Tonight

Sleeping beneath the wide expanse of the star-filled night is an encounter not to be missed; the darkness rises up over your bed, and the depths of your vision seem vast and unending as you gaze into the night. The air is soft and cool, a caressing breeze that gently hovers above the grass; in the distance, there are the familiar sounds of men's voices around the campfires. The night is late, you are very tired, but the spectacle of the stars above you holds your interest; you stare up at it for a long time, until at last, the sky begins to gleam faintly, and the stars fade from view, one by one.

My first experience with camping occurred in northern Michigan, and it was a true *volte-face* for me; I had never done anything like it. It was not, as some of my friends in Chicago had imagined, an affair worthy of a designer's trade journal, complete with an antique mahoghany four-poster in a wide, green field, draped with delicate floral chintzes and netting, generously swathed with pillows in many different colours; pinks, blues, greens and yellows. Nor did I gracefully recline, attired in a midnight blue dressing gown with crest and piping, awakening to bluebirds alighting on my tray, gently caressing fawns, rabbits, and other silly creatures. It is a pretty picture, and I have painted it for my clients, but it is not to my taste. I might have done it for the camera, it would have made an amusing perspective. Nancy Lancaster might have done it after the war, and she probably did so; it was suitable to her temperament.

There is, in all first experiences, a blessing of good fortune; the proverbial beginner's luck held out its staff over my excursion, and all went well. A camping-trip requires careful methods of organisation and planning; there is much to be considered, for there is, invariably, a singular lack of appropriate facility. I relied on my camping friends; they could tell me what to pack, and how much; like Dominique Francon, I had never done these things, yet I did them, expertly.

It is a feature of my life that I have attempted, and often succeeded, in ensuring my comfort in the meanest circumstance, whether on a trip abroad, working in the city, or waiting at an air terminal. This is not a physical attribute but a spiritual one; the ideals of comfort are attained internally; one wraps the surroundings around oneself, like a heavy, secure garment, and by various turnings accommodates oneself. Thus attired, one is able to inhabit oneself as though in the mouth of a cave, cozy and warm, looking out upon the world. The great caravan of life passes before you and yet, you remain seated, watching its progression; *sic transit gloria mundi.*

Nowhere is this accomplishment more useful than a camping weekend; one must have one's small luxuries, for they are the essence of life, the perfume, the cosmetic glitter that sparkles in the sun. These luxuries are simple, a subtraction of those one might require at home. Whenever I have camped alone or with friends, it has always been accompanied by good coffee and better Scotch; the former upon rising and the latter upon retiring, but this has not always held to form.

Much of the activity of camping, I have since realised, is centred about one's meals, everything must be prepared on your small, propane camp-stove or over an open fire. I had never cooked such meals; it was a bold experiment for me, and one that might determine the outcome of future excursions. Fortunately, my meals were well received, and the plates and bowls wiped clean; there was never a waste of food.

My first trip was afforded a miracle of fine weather, a harbinger of great things to come. The days were long and warm, and the nights cool; the full moon cast her silver glow upon the woods for many hours. That first night, once the tent had been erected, my bed set up, and my gear arranged, we all gathered around the table for dinner.

Although I have cooked, and often, for a group of hungry men, I had never done so over a camp-stove in the dark, without my usual *batterie de cuisine*; what I held in my hands was all. That night, the dinner was a success; the steaks grilled perfectly, the salad was crisp and the dessert sweet, the hot, buttered rolls were light and airy, and the cheese ready to run off the plate. One of my friends later told me it was the best camp-meal he had ever been served. Its preparation was similar to a steak *au poivre*: the meat was sautéed in red wine with some olive oil, rubbed all over with sweet butter, and seasoned with sea salt and black pepper. The pan-juices were swirled with a spoonful of Dijon-style mustard, and then presented with the roasted potatoes and the vegetables.

I do not recall the wine I served, a Côtes du Rhone, I think; I do not remember if it was Côtes du Rhone Villages or something else. I was still learning about wines and their transport, and which would work best for my meals *al fresco*. It was superb for the evening, rustic and pleasant, without any pretense; my guests were not used to such things.

The dessert was also very simple, a selection of fruits purchased that morning from a roadside stand, peeled and sliced very thin, then marinated in fresh mint leaves and kirsch over ice, at the base of the cooler; the mint leaves were added to our lemonade, later in the evening.

It is a fine thing to enjoy a meal under the stars; the chairs are gathered around the long, wooden table and the fire casts long shadows across it. The lanterns are set on the checkered cloth, and they flicker softly; there is no music but the soft chirping of crickets in the grass. The voices of the men are low, and pleasant; they are enjoying their meal, and it is with some relief that you take your seat among them; you have earned your place there.

When I recall the various dishes that I have enjoyed, whether served as a guest, or prepared with my own hands, that first meal under the stars is remembered, with joy. Perhaps it was an accidental triumph, or the luck of the beginner; I do not think I have achieved such perfection, or such simplicity, since then. It was a night of many happy firsts, and many happy memories; I have thought of it often. I must agree with my friend: those steaks were the best I have had, anywhere, and the company of those who shared it, the best, also.

The Seed

It has not always been clear to me, how to best define and to proclaim my spiritual beliefs, especially when confronted with remarkably different perspectives; I encountered many of these at the farm, and throughout northern Michigan. I am a Christian, I believe that Christ died for my sins and rose on the third day; this is my faith, and I adhere to it. Yet this faith was not embraced by others, and there are moments when my declaration of it has been granted a silent, strange reception, like the arrival of a bastard at a family reunion; everyone suspects that he belongs, yet no one knows where, or how.

In the myriad versions and practises of faith found in northern Michigan, outside the establishments of Bay View or the Holy Church, the concept of Christianity is almost unknown. It is not considered, by the fringes of the populace, to be a part of their own religious learning; they make a practise of recognising and adhering to those customs pre-dating the Church, although they certainly do not comprehend them.

The hippies of northern Michigan especially refused all aspects of Christianity; they embraced other faiths, rooted in native lore, or borrowed from other sources. Nothing was omitted; all were welcomed, but Christ and His teachings were forbidden. They did not venerate Mary, but praised Isis and Ishtar. They did not say grace at the table, but ended each declaration of brotherhood with *Blessed Be*. Their feast days were derived from pre-Christian holidays, renamed, and restructured, but they celebrated Christmas and Easter with enthusiasm. Krishna and Diana walked among them, Hecate rose up from the depths to inflict her wounds, yet they turned not to the faith that eclipsed them all, and in which I remained; it was anathema to them. They blamed the Church, or the priests, or the deacons, for their own misgivings, they would not look past the follies of the human experience to the Light that outshone the world, and embraced all within it.

I once had a conversation of Jesus with a woman at the farm; I thought it might be an engagement of our minds, for she had discussed many topics with me. When I told her of my faith, and my own conversion, however, she refused to listen; to her, Jesus was only a man, and in her mind, not the Son of God.

This revelation astounded me, and I recalled CS Lewis's commentaries on this same subject; Jesus was not merely a man, for He was, and is, the Son of God. No man could have done as Jesus had; it was a testament of the Christian faith. I offered to send her my copy of *Mere Christianity*, so that she might read it; there was much that Lewis had stated which had been very helpful to me. She refused my suggestion outright; she had closed her mind to such possibilities, and rejected them completely.

The Labyrinth

I once told an audience that the outlines of the ancient labyrinths were akin to the paths of our daily lives, we cannot see its turnings or its outcome. The destination, I said, was the journey. I did not realise I was paraphrasing another man's words; I did not know it at the time. Many have laid claim to the statement, and I was neither the first, nor the last, to do so.

The path of a labyrinth is a strange ambulation; one's steps are traced repeatedly, circling further and further in. Your feet turn many times and in all directions, seemingly without purpose or destination, other than to reach the centre. What one finds is an empty space, awaiting the gift of your presence, and your contemplation. Sometimes there is a clever, fanciful little structure hidden within the greenery; it is not without reason named a folly, for to what purpose have we come there, if not to make a mischief? What one leaves behind, however, is part of the journey, a gift; it is a souvenir of the miles one has crossed.

I was once invited to walk in such a maze, at the farm; it was a meditation, a celebration of the spiritual life; I have since walked its path many times. The labyrinth itself was sheltered in the hollow of the land, as though held in a pair of cupped palms; it was depressed into the earth, almost hidden from view. The edges were formed by large, granite boulders, as one descended the steps; one had the impression of disappearing from the world. I have often wondered if the effect might have been more resonant to have the entire track sunken into the earth; it might have achieved a greater spiritual dimension. One then might be divorced from the physical reality of the fields in which it lay, and thus able to direct one's steps with greater purpose. It was not a maze like those found in English gardens, which are defined by tall, green hedges of yew and cedar; here the route was clearly laid, and the centre visible. The paths inside defined, many times, a large, single square outline with a continuous route, carefully bordered with many small, colourful stones.

Before entering the labyrinth, each guest was asked to carry a small rock or stone, to be placed inside as a gift, or a memento. I located a stone in the field nearby, a small, heart-shaped lump of green, mossy granite, and I took it with me. The rock seemed strangely heavy in my hand as I walked; it hurt me, as I carried it. I turned it over; the other side was a jagged, open cut, slicing into my skin; beneath the green surface of the rock there, lay exposed a dark, grey interior, almost black. A line of small, red drops was drawn across the palm of my hand, as though I bore a string of fine, glittering rubies. The pain was intense; I had not noticed it; I had not felt the sharp edges.

I have been fortunate, in my life, to receive a remarkable spiritual guidance when it was least expected: a clear, distinct message has come to me. It has not always been a foretelling, but it has always been correct, and the thought has remained; I have remembered many episodes where such guidance came, and was useful.

I held the rock as I walked, and the lights faded around me; there were other people on the path, but I did not see them.

I will carry this burden, said a Voice, and I looked around me; I thought a man had spoken.

I will carry this burden, said the Voice again, and I stopped on the path; there was no one near me; I was alone.

I will carry this burden, said the Voice, and again I saw no one near; I held out the rock and looked at it, and then I understood.

I set the rock upon a large boulder, its surface bleeding and visible in the damp mist of the evening. It has not moved from there, I have found it many times since then. Each time I have done so, I have remained before it, in silent contemplation; I have remembered that rock, and the weight of it in my hands. When I left the farm, for the last time, the rock was still mounted upon its boulder, and its scars had begun to fade, slowly and steadily.

The Music

Folk music is a popular form of celebration in northern Michigan; there are festivals dedicated to it nearly every weekend in the summers. Blessed by the warmth, one is able to enjoy the outdoors amidst a swirl of people, musicians, vendors, and partygoers; it is a happy, festive atmosphere. The sky is a perfect blue with a faint green cast; the light reflects the water, which reaches up into the air and colours it. The days can be very hot, but the nights quite cold; I have often dressed myself, as the afternoon waned and the evening advanced, in succeeding layers of shirt, sweater, jacket, and a heavy coat. In the early autumns, when it can be very cold beneath the stars, I have required a long, heavy scarf and gloves.

Folk music is borne of the land and its people; it is kin with country music and bluegrass; their roots are the same. When the country people came to the green valleys of the Appalachia, they carried their music with them; the forms and the rhythms have not changed, but endured, like a flint; there is still a strong, vivid spark to be drawn from it. There is freshness in the melody; it stimulates you, and you carry the vivid memory of it in your head. They are songs about the wide, spreading land, and the grasses bowing beneath the winds; the trees, and the water; when I have listened to the musicians late, late at night, I have seen clouds rising up in the sky, reflected in the wide, still ponds, and a blackbird has alighted in the reeds. It is the sound of the abandoned bus stop, on a wide, empty road under grey skies; it is the sound of a walk in the rain, through a country meadow. It is the sound of a bottle that you whistle into; the sound returns, full, rich, and mysterious, yet you have produced it yourself; it is a sound to be carried in your hands, as you walk along the path through the tall grasses. It can be very haunting, a reminder of those passages of our lives which are lost to us; the past is but an echo of the sound of our voices upon our journeys.

Folk music is played on guitars, banjoes, mandolins, and violins; there are very few drums, but sometimes one will see a djembe or a bongo, handled to great effect. One will often see a cello or a double bass; there are also many different reed pipes and wooden flutes, which have a haunting, sad fall as they are played around the campfires. I have seen some performers utilise the edge of a wood saw, across which they manoeuvred their bows; their music was strange and beautiful beneath the August moon.

The Musicians

At the festivals, one meets the musicians in their tie-dyed clothing and long, unwashed hair, walking barefoot in the dirt as the sun sets in the west; they are very friendly, and always eager to talk of their performances and to share their music. They carry their recordings with them; they are offered for sale, or for barter, and some of it is very good. Many times, we would engage in long discussions about particular songs or recordings; the musicians were always grateful to hear my thoughts, although I did not pretend to any great knowledge of music, other than my own likes. A client of mine, who ran a music publishing business, often asked me to accompany him to the festivals; the musicians were always glad to meet with him, and I saw many performances.

The musicians are great travellers; it is common for them to cross the width, or the length, of the state to make an appearance. Some will travel to Chicago on the weekends to perform at clubs and bars; I have attended their shows in Lincoln Park and Wrigleyville. To see them in an urban setting, removed from the forests and meadows, is like a shock of cold water; it is not expected. It is not the musician who has become lost, but the setting, which has become plastic and artificial by their presence; it is not worthy of their music. Folk music has been nurtured on the wide, dusty streets of the towns and villages dotting the landscape of Michigan;   it rises from the wide, spreading potato-fields and from the dark forests that punctuate the landscape. To see it under the amber lights of Chicago was to separate it from its reality; one's thoughts turned to the story of the nightingale, imprisoned in her golden cage.

Many of the musicians have been trained at Interlochen or Oberlin; they have spent long hours in the perfection of their talent; some have been performing since childhood. It is a delight to observe their performance; they possess great skill and demonstrate their techniques; many of them play several different instruments. It is not surprising to see them turn from the banjo to the ukulele to the violin, the guitar, or the mandolin, all within a set. The quality of the instruments is superb; rarely have I seen such fine pieces of artisanship except at the symphony or the opera. The musicians are proud of their instruments, and take great care in their transport; they are objects of great beauty.

The Festivals

The setting of each festival is different, but all are equipped with stages, widely roofed, with large, wooden platforms looking over a green expanse of lawn. On the farm, the stage was set at the bottom of a long, sloping hill, emerald-green with thick, lush grass, forming a perfect amphitheatre; its natural acoustics were superb, and required only a slight enhancement. By the end of the festival, the grass would be worn down and trodden into the earth, but after a few days, it would spring up again, as though the passing of hundreds of people was but a trifling ailment.

In the daytime, there is no boundary to the festival; it is only bordered by the trees, the caravans, and the vendors' tents; all movement passes before you. The wide, green lawns stretch to infinity, and are a swarm of people; they ebb and flow like a brightly coloured stream. The people in their festival attire are not entirely human-looking, but resemble fanciful creatures, butterflies, and exotic birds with bright plumage. Their tie-dyed clothing, often loose and unbelted, comprises no discernible shape; they resemble wings, hoods, and feathers, not sleeves and trousers. In the pavilions, at mealtimes, they resemble nothing so much as a flock of colourful birds collected on a branch, chattering happily together.

At night, the festival takes on a different air; there is no lighting save for the brilliant blue and red spots over the stage.

The world shrinks from its vastness; all else is eliminated. I have often thought the nighttime performances the most intimate spectacle; one cannot see into the darkness; the stage-lights blind one's vision of the outer world. The musicians must rely on their skill and talent to draw the audience from the night, and to share their music with them; you cannot see into the fields, but you know there are people there, and they are watching you. In the darkness, one can imagine that one is alone in a vast, boundless setting, yet all attention is focussed upon the brightly lit stage; you are the centre and the total of your world.

One is only aware of the music; all other features are submerged beneath the night. The music lifts its swift, running notes upon the air, and you are swept away on a river of song. It flows like a clear mountain stream, lively and chattering, and then slows, suddenly, to a still, dark pool within a forest glade. It hurries on again, falling and splashing over rocks, and then, in a plume of mist, it falls, gently and gracefully, from the edge of a cliff high above the world; you are carried with it, a leaf tossed upon the water, and the spray blinds you. The water tastes sweet upon your tongue, you are lifted over the edge; for a quick, breathless instant, you feel that you might fly into the air.

Late in the night, when the musicians have finished, but the drummers are warming up at the fire-pits, the crowds drift in pairs and groups to the tents; the bar is open. The sky has darkened, and clouds have come down from the north; the moon is in the west. She is going to bed, bidding farewell for the night as she sinks behind the trees.

At the bar, the lights are warm and bright; the night air is chilly. Jackets and coats are put on as the people gather at the long, white counter and the drinks are poured. It was delightful to share a good glass of scotch, gleaming honey-dark in the light, with my friends; we all brought our own bottles; there were single-malts and blended whiskies; we enjoyed them all.

At times, the lack of some liquor or the other will lead to some rather inventive combinations; these are not served in most bars, and have very strange names. The release of the day opened the gates of the bartender's imagination; they created strange and wonderful concoctions. I have, at the festivals, drunk a Peach-Blossom Nectar, a Running Horse Sampler, and a Dog's Curly Whisker, none of which I can now remember. It is probable I should not drink these again, for the next day my head was splitting; I could not tell you the ingredients, how they were mixed, or even blended, but only that I enjoyed them, and they were delicious.

The Word

In the mornings, the festival grounds are empty and silent; everyone has finally gone to bed. There are only a few people about, farm workers and vendors, preparing their booths for the day. In the kitchen, brightly lighted and warm, there is piping hot coffee, and the warm, delicious smell of eggs and bacon. Laughter floats softly from the pavilions; the crews are gossiping about the night's activities.

The air in the morning is heavy and damp; a soft grey fog shrouds the trees and lawns. Everything is dripping wet, and the birds are silent. Out of the mist come strange figures, random folk with a purpose, while everyone else is asleep.

At the fire-pits, still glowing, faint wisps of white smoke rise slowly into the air, dissolving into the pale light. The fires are still warm, and there are to be found, inevitably, one or two people reclining around its edges, having lost their way. I have had many intriguing and sometimes nonsensical conversations there in the cold mornings; I was an early riser and needed my coffee. With steaming pot in hand, I would make my way to the log benches, and take in the quiet around me. The world was asleep; it would not awaken for many hours, but there was a breathless hush; now, I thought, was the moment for something to happen.

The mist hovers, and drifts slowly over the grass; it dissolves into a sparkling, effervescent light as the sun rises, but that is far away; she is still asleep, rousing herself reluctantly; it has been a wild night.

At the fire-pits one morning, a child came up to me, and asked me for some of my coffee; she was very strangely attired, and I did not know if she had dressed herself. I did not give her any; she was very small, and I said, "I'm not sure you're old enough...what was your name?"

"My name is Cora," she said, reaching for the mug. "And I drink coffee all the time."

"Does your mother let you have coffee?" I asked her.

"Sure," she said. "She lets me have whatever is left in the coffeepot; I drink it all the time."

"Cora," I said, "that is a beautiful name. Do you know what it means?"

"Yes," she answered, in an odd way, "It means 'little heart'."

"Yes," I said, "It means 'little heart'."

"Do you want to know," she asked me, "How I know what my name means?"

"Please."

"I have a bad heart," she said.

"What do you mean, Cora?"

"I have a bad heart," she said. "When I was born they had to get a machine, to breathe for me."

"Cora," I said, "I am very sorry to hear that. Do you have to take heart medicine?"

"Yes, all the time," she said. "But I didn't take any today, so my fingers are turning blue."

"Let me see your hand." She held it out to me; her fingers were a soft, violet-blue colour, in the grey mist.

"Cora," I said, "*Where is your mother?*"

"She's sleeping," she said.

"Is she here, at the festival?"

"Yes, she came back last night, and she went to sleep."

"Cora, where is your heart medicine?"

"It's in the tent."

"Will you wait here, for a minute?"

I ran to the vendor booths, where I found someone who knew her mother; he sent a boy to fetch her. Another friend, a woman I did not know, took Cora for her heart medicine; she thanked me for my attention.

"It was nothing," I said, "I saw her hand, and realised she needed help."

"Thank you, again," the friend said, "She slipped out this morning, and I couldn't find her; I was frantic."

"I'm just glad you found her," I said.

I later found my coffee mug nearly empty; she had drunk most of it, and written me a charming note in crayon on yellow, lined paper. I still have it, in my hamper. I looked at the colourful, careful printing, the letters spread across the page, thanking me for the coffee and for being her friend; it was signed, at the bottom, 'C♥RA'. I stared at it for a long time, while the coffeepot whistled and the smell of it rose on the morning air, and then I folded it carefully, and put it away.

The Flower Children

Around the music stages, the young people hover like fluttering, jumping insects engaged in loose, freely interpreted dancing. Children, women, and men all take part, in groups or in couples. There is a solitary, lithe female with a stolen hula-hoop, who performs alone and ignores all attempts to speak to, or dance with her. Later, I realised, her fluid movements were not entirely natural. Often, these girls will pass onto the stage with the musicians, and dance freely among them as they play, like an errant petal drifting on a breeze.

The women at the festival are very comfortably attired; their dresses in bright cotton are loose and flowing, their headscarves are dyed to match. The men dress in odd assortments of patched-together clothing, comprising old army pants, blue jeans, madras, and many combinations thereof. A number of festival shirts are to be seen, offered for sale by the organisers; some are beautifully designed, with superb, colourful graphics and images; I have several that I still wear.

The old men are thinner, but possessed of strong, protruding stomachs, which give them the appearance of strangely pregnant storks, stepping resolutely among the tents and pavilions of the festival grounds. Cigarettes, and the occasional cigar or pipe, protrude from their mouths, adding to the illusion of a freshly caught, white minnow in the bill of a large, wading bird. They are accompanied by their grandchildren, for this is a family affair, and the children run and scamper over the grass. It was always a surprise for me, to see men of my own age, with offspring spanning multiple generations; it was not the pattern of my own life.

The younger men, however, are thinner, and usually more athletic; they are often very handsome. They have come from the surrounding farms, where they have been working their fathers' or their grandfathers' lands. Their necks and faces are sunburned bright red; their smiles are wide and genuine. They wear large, floppy hats to shield their burnt, red skin, and sport unusual necklaces of shell or teeth, strung with beads of carved wood and stone. Tattoos are everywhere, on arms, chests, backs, and legs; one man, with whom I later became good friends, showed me an unusually shaped design on his leg. He hinted rather broadly he might have other decorations to show me, but I declined; I did not wish to see any more. Another man, a wrestler with a broad, muscular build, pulled off his shirt to show me his back one afternoon; across his wide shoulders, there pranced a team of draught horses pulling a barrel wagon, proudly labelled with the name of his favourite beer.

There are one or two fragile young flower girls, in their early twenties; one hopes they are of the age of consent; they do not say very much about themselves. Their names are Amber,

Tiffany, or Heather; they have no surnames. They are possessed of extremely slender bodies, such as may be demanded in London or Paris, to serve as mannequins for the couture houses. Their hair is either dirty blonde or pale brown; they wear little or no makeup. Their clothes appear from nowhere, a handful of patched-up garments cast-off from some other girl, from some other festival. Who these girls are, and where they have come from, is unknown; they are from a town no one has heard of, but everyone knows. They appear and disappear at regular intervals, usually with an older man. During the musical performances, they become highly visible, and dance strangely in front of the stages. Many of them are possessed of brightly coloured hula-hoops, with which they are greatly skilled; they perform with them throughout the day, like a collection of strange, circular insects fluttering on the breeze. There are younger men, who try to dance with them, but they are not together; they are only dancing. The young men will ask the girls to meet them later; they are always refused.

It is amusing to witness the extraordinary lengths some men will go to impress a desirable female; they are very pretty. A lone, unattached woman is watched carefully, more than once I have been pressed into escort service to keep her safe from roaming predators. A handsome man, however, is subject to much flirtation and welcomes it, a distraction after the labours of the day. I have seen this during the night, when the bar opens and the women gather around its long, shiny surface, clamouring for attention. The men will welcome their advances, and respond in kind. Their girlfriends will be watching carefully, however, and will interrupt the conversation before it has become too friendly.

The Lilies of the Field

There is a welcome air at the festivals and in the camping-grounds; no one is turned away. As at all festivals, there is a wide, open field lined with long rows of caravans, tents and other shelters for the weekend. There are friends camping close together, sharing a love of music; they are often musicians themselves, or will have instruments to play, for an impromptu performance after dark. It is a habit for the same friends to stay together year after year in the choicest spots; these spaces are highly prized and much desired; they are guarded fiercely and reserved months in advance. Their clusters of caravans, tents, and trucks form an enclosed, open space, a village in miniature, with areas for cooking and cleaning, lounging and playing music. These are decorated with wildly coloured banners and flags, serving as markers or signposts in the long rows; the designs are somewhat eastern in their fashion.

There are also larger caravans at the festivals, enormous, wheeled mastodons of *café au lait* ridged sheet metal. I have never seen one arrive or depart; they simply materialise, like the ghosts of foundered ships on a rocky beach. Parked amidst the tall grasses of the pastures, they give every appearance of floating above the ground; they do not belong here. Their drivers and passengers are not a type common to the festival crowds; they do not mingle with the others. They remain sequestered within their metallic holds, and keep their doors locked. One sees them at night through the windows, playing at cards, and wonders what they are doing there, and why.

I have often wondered how these behemoths managed to negotiate the rutted fields; they are not easily navigated. Only once have I driven one; it was, I felt, a labour worthy of Hercules. I myself have been grateful for four-wheel drive in Jane; I could not have taken her over such rough, muddy paths. Yet there they are, and at the end of the festival, they disappear.

There are refurbished school buses, short or long, painted dark blue or army green, splattered carefully with sprayed-on graffiti. Usually, this takes the form of political messages, calling for the legalisation of hemp, or universal peace and brotherhood, free love, and ending the nuclear arms race, amongst other slogans; one is not certain if the owners are advertising their own politics, or have been hired by someone else. Inside, one has the impression of a large, mobile dormitory, its owners have collected several passengers en route, and the names of these persons are not known, or even correct.

Rose-Lipped Maidens; Lightfoot Lads

I had many friends at the festivals; it was a true joy for me, to spend time with them. After setting up my camp, it was a welcome prospect to walk down the long rows of tents and vans, exchanging greetings, and small talk with everyone; I met many people there, year after year. An atmosphere of merriment prevailed; we were all happy to be there, to enjoy the music and the company.

I have had good fortune in the friendships that I made at the festivals; many of my friends there are still part of my life, and we remain in contact with each other, throughout the year; it is always pleasant to speak with them. They are kind, thoughtful persons, who welcomed me and made me a part of their lives; for several weekends every summer, I became part of an extended family, a gathering of cherished souls.

A festival friendship is not like any other; one may not see one's friend again, for a full year, and in that time, other people may enter and may leave your domain; they are a part of the ebb and flow of your life. However, a festival friend is a special person; you share a love of music, and of the night, the campfire songs, and the bottle of good whiskey that you pass to each other. There is, in the night between you, a comprehension of your fellowship; the moment and the place have become fixed in your hearts and in your minds. Long after, when the snow lies deep upon the ground, and the wind howls in the black trees, you will remember the warmth of the campfire, and the sparks rising from the glowing logs, and the music, like the borders of a scroll, framing, and glorifying, your conversations. You will recall the faces of your friends, and the smiles that passed between you, and the laughter, and the warmth of it will remain with you; it is a treasure, to be cherished and remembered.

There were many different conversations in these settings, which took many turns; a discussion of classical guitar music might evolve into one of pie making, or auto-mechanics. Once, we had a discussion on gay rights and gay marriage, it was all very funny; the straight men thought it an excellent idea, until they realised their wives might have no one to take them shopping. Often, there would be a drinks table, with beer and whiskey; cigars might be passed around. My own *coronas* were in much demand, they had been hand-rolled for me; they were good, Dominican cigars made by a Cuban firm. The hula girls smoked tiny clove cigarettes, which are different from tobacco; the little, brown sticks have a strong, sweet smell. Conversations would often erupt into laughter, and there is much merriment amongst the pretty girls. There were always jokes to be told, or fanciful stories, legends of the forest, tales of northern Michigan. I heard of many things that went 'bump' in the night, and did not always believe them.

There was, as at all gatherings of good folk, a musician with a guitar, serenading us at the fire-pit. One of these, a very talented man, was Michael Rosteck; he became a good friend to me. I nicknamed him 'Guitar Mike', for that was how I met him; he was playing his guitar and singing; his songs were of his own composition. He once said to me, much later, that I was the only person who addressed him as 'Guitar Mike', and I was rather embarrassed, but he said it did not matter. He was an original artist, highly skilled with the guitar, the drums, and other instruments. He also showed me how to play the djembe, beating time with his hands on the taut goatskin. He had recorded many of his songs; he gave me a disk of them that I still have, and still enjoy. The music is soft and plaintive, and often very beautiful; he was a true artist, who shared his gifts with everyone.

My friends Wendy, Theresa, and Patty were at the festivals at the farm in July and August; I enjoyed seeing their laughing, friendly faces, and being embraced in the warmth and affection of their friendship. It was wonderful to sit with them around the campfire, sharing old jokes and inventing new ones. They were, and are, truly good, kindly people.

Wendy and I once shared a rather strange adventure, a rural version of Mr Toad's Wild Ride; I drove her down to the main stage one evening, in a golf-cart. The road, as it descended the hill, had been washed out by the rains; I had not seen it until we were on its pitted, gravelled surface and the golf-cart rocked dangerously from side to side. I was very alarmed, but I could not reverse the motor; Wendy was carrying a large, expensive guitar that did not belong to her, and I was certain it would be shattered to pieces upon the ground. As we crept down the long, rutted slope, our friends shouted encouragement, while I shouted at the golf-cart and Wendy clutched the guitar like a precious, gleaming trophy; we eventually came to the base of the slope, but it had been a hair-raising episode. When I asked Barton about it later, he told me that there was another, gentler slope with a smooth surface on the opposite side of the hill, and why did I not use that one?

"But you did not tell me, Barton," I said to him later, "I'd only just arrived, how on earth was I to know?"

"Didn't you see how bad the road was, Sanjay?"

"No, not until I was right on top of it, Barton. And then it was too late to go back, I could not reverse the engine."

"Well, you're the first one to get down that side of the hill this summer, so I suppose that is something."

"Yes, I think so," I agreed.

"Let's try it again, and see how you do," he suggested.

"No, I do not think so," I said.

Theresa and her husband organised the children's centre at the farm; they established many different activities, and their own children often joined in. Her son would often ask me to buy him a soda, when Theresa was not looking, but I would not do so; I did not wish to countermand her. One of her daughters was learning to drive, and once became lost on the road to the farm; it was a cause for some merriment when they finally arrived.

Theresa once asked me to join a tie-dye contest for the children, which was great fun; I donated a shirt to be dyed, but the effect of it was not as I had hoped. Perhaps I did not have the right colours, or was unused to the tie-dying technique, but the shirt, when completed, looked as though it had been trod upon by several different pairs of muddy boots, and not as though a rainbow had been fashioned upon it; I wore it to please the children, but then I gave it away. Theresa later told me that one of the older hippies at the festival, of some notoriety, had taken to wearing it at night, to frighten the young people, and I thought this a good finish.

Patty and her brother Pete came to the festivals each year; they set up their tents in the yard east of the farmhouse to enjoy the sunrise over the trees, and to have some privacy; in the camping fields and woods, there was a great crowd and it was very noisy at times. Pete was a quiet, soft-spoken, gentle man; he did not say much, but he always carried with him unique and wonderful gadgets that he would take from his pockets, and then he would demonstrate their utilities around the campfire. They were clever little items; I have often wondered where he procured them, but he would not tell me. I asked Patty about them, but she did not know.

They all greeted me with the same phrase; I had been expressing myself with a rather English exclamation that summer. It was not appropriate for polite conversation; it was a verbalisation of my being. The ladies enjoyed this very much; it became my signature for them, when they saw me coming across the fields, they would call, in unison, "*Bloody Hell!*"

My friend 'Italian Mike' also came to the August festival, and we shared many good stories and scotch together; he was very fond of a good single-malt, and I was delighted to share my appreciation. He was, in fact, of Italian descent; it was evident in his form and in his shape; he was very slender and very tall. His face was angular in profile, with high, sharp cheekbones; one might have cut one's finger upon them. His head was framed by a halo of thick, dark, curly hair, in the manner of a fine, bronze sculpture; he might have made an excellent subject for Verrocchio or a *mannequin du monde* for Davide Cenci. Nor would he have appeared out of place in a painting by Caravaggio, for his skin was the same, a clear, pale olive; he could wear any colour.

His girlfriend Dani was also a dear friend; we spent many hours discussing art, painting, and sculpture. Dani was a gifted ceramicist, and showed me many of her pieces; I enjoyed analyzing them and offering my criticisms, which she took very well. She gave me a perfectly round ceramic vase, glazed with green and bronze, which I still own; it is very pretty, and I keep copper roses in it, on my writing table.

Joe and his wife Linda were habitués at the August and September festivals; they were two of the kindest people I have met. They always welcomed me to their camp with something good to eat, or to drink; they enjoyed good coffee and made espresso in a well-used Italian coffeepot. When I produced my own Italian coffeepot one year, it marked the beginning of our friendship; Joe commented that it was the biggest he had ever seen, and the rollicking laughs that followed cemented our friendship further. He greatly enjoyed the espresso I made, and asked where I had purchased it; when I told him I had brought it with me from Paris, he was eager to procure some for himself.

Joe was a very good cook; his repertoire over a camp-stove was astonishing. One afternoon, he offered me a piece of pineapple upside-down cake, which he had mixed and baked himself; it was delicious. His *batterie de cuisine* consisted of very old cast-iron skillets and cast-iron Dutch ovens; they had seen much use; they were seasoned pieces. Since then, I have found the same equipment at tag sales, seasoned and heavy with age, and I have added them to my gear; they are the perfect appliance for meals to be prepared in the forest.

Joe was not afraid to express his thoughts on any topic; he had lived in many parts of the world; he had travelled across the country as a young man. Nor was he afraid to admit his own lack of knowledge on a topic; he possessed that strange quality of honesty and simplicity which is the heart of all genuine souls. Our friendship was further enhanced when we discovered we had been at the same concert in Ithaca, in the summer of 1981. The paths of our lives had converged briefly, for only a few hours, and after the passage of many years, they had joined again.

Some Like It Hot

My first festival experience was unusual for northern Michigan; I served as an interpreter for a French jazz band, touring across North America; their appearance at the farm was the finale to their long travels. I had not spoken real French in years, and was excited to do so; I was surrounded by it, I lived it, and breathed it in. The band members were not from Paris, but Rouen; their accents were not the same, but it did not matter; I was speaking French. They were not a very good band; they did not play real jazz or even blues, as one hears in Chicago, but it did not matter; I was speaking French.

Nonetheless, I took them shopping, and on tours of the farm; in the town, I was able to discuss my love of Paris with them; they asked me to visit them in Rouen, and I could not refuse. They stayed at the farm for several days, but on the morning of their departure, I prepared a little speech, thanking them for coming to Gaylord, and acknowledging my debt to them; I had been able to speak French, simple, glorious French, the language I loved.

The band members listened very politely, smiling and clapping as I spoke, and then one of them came up, and thanked me personally. *Monsieur, nous sommes reconnaissants que vous avez été ici, de parler pour nous,* he said, *Et je dois vous dire, nous avons tous parlé de votre français.*

Oh dear, I thought, here it comes.

Parmi toutes les personnes que nous avons rencontrés, he continued, *Votre française a été le meilleur. Vous ne parlez pas comme un Américain, vous n'avez pas d'accent. Vous parlez comme un Français, un Parisien. Où avez-vous appris à parler?*

I stammered some reply, but my mind was suddenly buoyant, and rose up over the green earth, racing towards Paris, alighting on the Seine River, near the Pont d'Iéna, and I was grateful; my French had been heard, received, and understood.

I had been a stranger in Paris, when I was a student and it was all new to me; I had spoken French there, and been heard. It had not been very good French; I was still learning the intricacies of the subjunctive tense, and the pronunciations were, at times, difficult for me; I could not disguise my American origins completely. Nevertheless, I had been told, by many Frenchmen and women, that I spoke it correctly, and beautifully; I did not speak like an American or even an Englishman; I spoke, as a Frenchman should do. I could not have imagined a higher compliment, to have been praised in such fashion, for the gesture of praise, in the speaking of a foreign language, is not an idle one.

The Lotus Eaters

There was another festival that summer, near the Mackinac Bridge, famous for its crowds, its wealth, and its stringent policies of trash collection. I had gone with my friend Peyton Marshall; we had not planned to stay very long. He had many friends there, and we chatted with the musicians and walked about the grounds; it was a perfectly sunny, hot day, a glorious summer weekend; there were crowds of people everywhere. I wondered if I might see anyone I knew there, and then, quite suddenly, I did.

The terms of friendship are not always rigid; they are not fixed like the stars upon the heavens, nor do they advance with them in the same arrangement. In northern Michigan, I had become friends with many persons, and had reached out to them after my arrival there; they had ignored me. Their behaviour was puzzling; I did not understand why they should do so; I had done nothing to them.

There was a woman, a housewife, from Indian River, with whom I thought I had begun a pleasing intimacy, for we had met on Beaver Island and had enjoyed many laughs together. I had made special dishes for her, which I did not prepare for very many people, and she had enjoyed them. She had been very kind, and visited me in Chicago, but when I called her, after I moved to Charlevoix, she had not returned my calls. I had visited her, and her husband, in their home on Burt Lake; it was very beautiful, but had suffered from a lack of clear direction and concept; however, that was not my fault, I had tried to help them.

Her husband John was another such person, with whom I had once thought a form of friendship had been reached, but he had also ignored me after I came to the north; I could not understand his disregard. He was an attorney of some distinction in the town; his name was well known and he had many clients. I had once asked him for a referral, to settle a small legal matter, but he did not know anyone, he said. When I later found a lawyer in Conway Bay and retained him, I asked him if he knew of John, and he said, yes, we play golf every Thursday.

There was another person I thought was my friend, an ageing, decrepit old hippie who pretended to an advanced intellect. He was neither intelligent nor clever, but grasping and audacious, in a manner that I had begun to find offensive. When I had first arrived in Charlevoix, he had offered to take me to dinner, but stipulated that I should pay for my own drinks, and that he did not plan to spend very much money, and so I should select some place that was cheap. We ate at a tourist café in town, where I ordered a black coffee with my meal and he ordered several large bottles of beer for himself.

I had once tried to discuss with him the history of the Celtic tribes; I had begun to study their history with some enthusiasm. I had hoped to engage him further on the topic, for he had spoken of them often, and claimed to be of Celtic descent. I was incorrect in my estimation; he possessed neither knowledge nor insight into the Celts, but limited his appreciation within his own, small sphere of comprehension. I spoke to him, of their migrations from north central Europe, across France and the Low Countries, and on to Britain, only to be fiercely rebuffed; he steadfastly denied their Germanic origins, to the point, I felt, of ridicule. The Celtic tribes could not possibly be Germanic, he said; that is incorrect. No, I answered, these findings are based on archaeological excavations, and are shared by most, if not all, historians; I told him of the Hallstatt and Urnfield cultures, followed by the La Tène. He refused to believe me; it was a splinter in the structure of our friendship, and I did not engage him in further discussions.

They were all together at the festival; Peyton and I saw them coming across the wide, sloping lawns. The sun was very hot; they were wearing sunglasses and floppy hats, carrying lawn chairs and coolers. They came towards us, and did not say hello, but glared fiercely at us.

Then, finally, one of them said, "What are you doing here?" The tone of his voice was almost an accusation, I thought. I was not accountable to them; it was a public festival; I had a right to be there, with anyone I chose.

"I'm attending the festival," I said. "With Peyton."

They said nothing but continued to glare; an escaped convict, apprehended by the local sheriff, might have appreciated my reception. The old hippie ignored me, and began speaking with Peyton, he invited him to a men's club dinner.

"We'd love for you to join us," the hippie said, urging Peyton to attend. "It would be great for everyone to see you."

"And what about me?" I asked; I could not help it. "Am I invited to this dinner, too?"

"Oh, Sanjay," he said, after a moment, his eyes red and glaring. "Of course, if you would *like* to come, you may."

I looked at him for a moment, and saw a fierce, burning anger flare up in his face.

"No, thank you," I said. "I will be away; I will not be here that weekend."

"How long are you planning to be here?"

"I do not know," I said, "We have not made any firm plans for the day."

"Peyton, you should come sit with us," said the attorney; his wife had said nothing to me at all, but stood glaring at me. "Sanjay, you should come, too."

"We do not have our lawn-chairs," I said, "I left them in the truck."

"Well, go fetch them, and come back. Peyton, you can stay here while Sanjay gets the chairs."

"I will need Peyton's help," I said. "Goodbye."

We walked away, and did not speak for some minutes.

Peyton looked up at me. "Sanjay, are you alright?"

"Of course, I'm alright," I said.

We continued walking.

"Of course, I'm not alright!" I exclaimed. "What the *hell* is wrong with those people?"

"I don't know," he said, "They were not happy to see you, and it showed."

"I was wondering if you'd noticed."

"I did."

We walked on for a few more minutes.

"Peyton…."

"Yes?"

"Have I done…or not done…something? *Anything*…?"

"What do you mean?"

"Well, there must be a reason for all this."

"You've done nothing, Sanjay."

"Then what just happened?"

"I think they were upset…because you were with me."

We walked back to the car, in silence.

The Walrus and the Carpenter

I camped one year at the farm next to a stranger, a man I had not met before. He told me he had not been to the festival for many seasons, but had been once before, long ago. It was a slow, rich, dark evening, the stars were dim overhead, and heavy, majestic clouds edged slowly down from Lake Superior. They appeared above us, coming over the trees, a rolling, rambling shape, grey-edged, with silver light; there was no moon.

Around his small fire, we shared a bottle of whiskey, and talked of many things, of shoes and ships, and sealing wax, of cabbages and kings. He had not heard the poem, but enjoyed it when I recited it for him; he thought it might be a blueprint of our conversation, for our discussions had taken many turns.

He told me stories of his youth, his marriage, and his divorce; he told me stories of his work as a prison guard and his experiences there. He had become used to traumatic wounds, he said, and showed me a scar along his left side, where a prisoner's knife had sliced through it. He lifted up his shirt to show me; it was a long, red slash, now healed, but still angry upon his bare skin. I asked him, how long had it been? He laughed and said, not long ago, my friend, not long ago. I did not think it possible that a big, heavy man like him could have been taken down, but he told me the prisoners could be very rough, if they were angry, and chose the right moment to strike.

"But what happened to the man who stabbed you?" I asked him, "Surely you are permitted to defend yourself."

"Oh, I did," he replied, looking into the fire, "I fought him off, and threw him down, and then I fed him to the wolves."

"I'm not sure I want to know what that means."

"No, I do not think that you do."

I noticed his hands in the firelight, knotted and roped, they were rough, large hands wielding great force. They trembled when he spoke of his prison work, or when he lifted the shining, clear bottle to my glass; they trembled upon my arm, when he brushed my sleeve.

He noticed my gaze, and asked, "Why do you look at my hands?"

"You have very big hands," I said.

"They are very strong, my friend," he said. "Try and push my palm back, if you dare."

"No," I replied. "I will not dare. I believe you; you do not need to prove it to me; I am sure you are very strong."

"Go ahead, try it," he said, again.

I pushed at his palm, clenching my own hand into a heavy fist; I could not move it. He laughed, and I laughed with him; his face changed, when he smiled at me.

"You don't want this coming at you," he said. "I've taken out much bigger men than you."

"That I believe," I said. "You are a very big man."

"You're a big fellow too, my friend," he said. "I think you have a strength that I cannot see."

"That may be," I answered, "But I think we all have hidden strengths that we may use, in time of need."

He took a long drink from his glass, and then looked at me for a moment, before he spoke. "I wonder if you would care to wrestle with me, in the morning. I haven't wrestled in a long time; it would be a good exercise for me."

"I have not wrestled in a *very* long time," I said, "Not since high school, in fact. I'm not certain I should be a good match for you."

"You have a good build," he said, "You look like a wrestler, or a linebacker. I could use the practise, to be honest."

"I didn't bring any clothes for wrestling, or any shoes."

"Just wear some shorts, or some trunks," he said, "You do not need a uniform."

"Why on earth do you want to wrestle?"

He smiled. "My boys are growing up fast, I need to keep them in line and make sure the old man is still on top. If you had sons, you would know."

"I think you will always be on top of things," I laughed. "How old are they, your sons?"

"Christopher is seventeen, Ryan is fifteen," he said. "They are fine boys. Would you like to see their picture?"

"Yes, please."

He drew out his wallet, worn and brown, bulging with slips of paper, receipts, bills, and cards.

"Here," he said, handing it to me.

"They look like very nice boys."

"Not like the old man, though."

"You are very handsome, Brian."

"Do you really think so?"

"Of course I do, who wouldn't? The ladies are certainly enjoying your company."

"I'm sorry about that; I didn't know she would be here."

"Brian, it's fine; I didn't hear a thing."

He stood up, and looked down at me. I could not see his face; it remained in the shadows, but his arms hung loosely at his sides, and I could see his hands, trembling again in the firelight.

"I want to show you something," he said.

"What is it?"

"Come with me."

I followed him to his tent; a single lantern gleamed dully beneath the canvas; it was a dark blue colour, like an underwater cave. He handed me another photograph from his pack.

"This is a very nice photograph, Brian."

"This is a very special thing to me, Sanjay. I don't show this to very many people."

"I see, Brian, thank you…who is this, with you?"

"Someone I used to work with."

"Is he here, at the festival?"

"No."

"Where is he?"

"He's dead."

"Oh Brian, I'm…I'm so sorry. I did not know."

He sat down roughly on the cot, and the shape of his body slumped, as though he were a wildly exhausted, hunted animal; I could not see his eyes.

"He was killed, in the knife-fight."

I stood there for a minute.

"Brian…*is that how you got your scar*?"

He did not answer me for a long time, and I thought he might have been drunk; he had had a lot of whiskey.

"Yes."

"Brian, I'm so sorry."

The lantern flared suddenly, and flickered out; in the darkness, I fumbled for the tent flap. I tripped and almost fell, he caught me with his hand; he looked at me in the light, and his eyes suddenly gleamed brightly.

"I want to tell you something," he said.

Under the Milky Way Tonight

There was another festival, on another farm, which I attended near Cadillac, but far out in the country. The land all around it was wide and flat, stretching to the horizon in all aspects, with only distant trees to form its boundaries. In the night, for there was no moon, the stars blazed brightly overhead, perhaps even more brilliantly than the stars over Beaver Island. One felt, in the perfection of the moment, that one might be able to count each one individually and name it, according to one's taste or fancies; it was a romantic sentiment, a piece of fine jeweled embroidery worked upon a length of deep, sable-coloured silk.

There was a night, a very late one, when I had wandered far afield, away from the brightly lit stages and the cooking-fires by the caravans, pondering the darkness and the stars. A friend approached me, as I stood there, whom I did not know well; his tent was next to mine, but we had not spent much time together.

"Are you enjoying the festival?" he asked.

"Yes," I told him. "I am enjoying it very much."

"What are you enjoying most?" he asked.

"The music," I said, "It is really very good this weekend, much better than I have heard at the other festivals."

"It is the last festival of the season," he agreed, "And so everyone is enjoying themselves, it is a last hurrah, if you will."

I did not answer him, but continued to walk through the field; during the day, it had been a wide, golden expanse of grasses, burnt by the sun; now, beneath the night, it was a dull ochre colour, faintly lit by the stars. At the edge of the pasture, the light stopped; beyond it was darkness. The stars came down from the sky at its border; there was no moon.

We both stood there for a long time, contemplating the night and the stars, glittering above us, and we did not speak.

I held him away from me, and looked at him; the night masked much of his face, but I could still see his eyes, shining in the glow of the stars.

"What are you thinking?" he asked me.

"I was thinking," I said, "That I could use a glass of very good Scotch right now, and a very good cigar."

Viens, mon amant, mon esprit
Pour danser dans la nuit étoilée
Car c'est dans la nature des choses
Que nous devons nous trouver
Et dans le vent sur les herbes
Est-ce que nous appelons à
Allez-vous répondre,
Irez-vous avec moi, avant le soleil ?

Where the Wild Things Are

I gave no concerted thought to the patterns of my abilities, or to the readings I performed for my friends; they were simply there, like kitchen or garden implements, to be picked up and utilised at will. My friends might telephone or send a message requesting my assistance, and I was happy to give what insight I could; my predictions and analyses were accurate in all their cases, to their great surprise, and to mine. It was not always clear to me how this gift was implemented, for those things, which I saw, were glimpses into another life, of which I knew nothing, and yet I spoke of it.

There are great moments of clarity, which occur when the structure of a thought or concept has been revealed to us; it is at times unexpected. Once, at a dinner in Humboldt Park, I arrived rather early; not wishing to weary my host, I went for a walk down the boulevard. It was a fine spring evening, I did not mark my promenade, and then suddenly, I stopped; before me was a lean, vertical sign. There was a house behind it, a small brick Arts & Crafts-style bungalow, charming and cozy.

The sign announced that this had once been the house of Frank Baum, where he had written *The Wonderful Wizard of Oz*. I looked at the house again, and thought to myself, *yes*. The story, the colours, and the construction of it were all there; they were a part of its walls and its roof, the art-glass windows and the painted trims; it was all visible, one saw it clearly, for the first time. Again I thought, *yes. Now, I see.* This is that birthplace, ennobled by its creator, he has made it real, and it is alive, we can go there, and it will be there, waiting; the lanterns will be burning above the door, and the lamps will be gleaming. The cool, evening breeze will gently lift the lace curtains, and the door will always be open. When we step through that doorway, we will find, not the fumed-oak interior of William Morris but another world, and another landscape, which we have heard of, but never seen. It is there, it is waiting for us; we have only to knock upon the polished door of deep, dark green, gleaming like an emerald.

And What Rough Beast...?

In the story of my friendship with Ginger Ballard, a singular episode cemented its mortar firmly; I gave a message to her. In terms of messages given or received, the wording of it was simple, yet its meaning had far-reaching consequences, which I did not foresee, and which became of great import. I have often wondered, had I thought differently of it, if I should have given her the message that I did; I had given the same message twice before to two other women, and in both of their situations, my messages had been accurate.

My friend Ginger was a very beautiful, very personable woman; we spent much time together, and she had many friends. Recently, she had been visiting her lover Branson, in New Orleans; I had spoken with him; he had been very friendly to me. Ginger loved him madly; he was a blessing to her, and a comfort after her painful divorce and custody battles with her former husband; we were all happy for her.

I remember the evening, for I had just arrived in Charlevoix, and taken up my life there; I was relaxing at home, and a thought came to me: *Ginger is pregnant.*

It was strong and insistent, as though someone was speaking to me in a megaphone, yet the room was silent. Ginger was in New Orleans; I could not call her.

I sent her a message, however, and wrote it out:

"*I know a secret....*"

The message was sent, and then soon forgotten; no one remarked on it. When Ginger asked me about it later, I invented some explanation; I could not tell her she was pregnant, I had no secure knowledge of it.

A few weeks later, however, Ginger telephoned very late one evening, and asked me pointedly, "What secret, Sanjay?"

"Pardon...?"

"*What secret do you know, Sanjay?*"

"I don't know what you're talking about, Ginger."

"Yes, you do, you sent me a message two weeks ago, do you remember? You said you knew a secret...."

"Oh...*that*...."

"Yes, *that*...."

"Ginger, I'm sure I was wrong. I couldn't have been correct on that one."

"Sanjay...you weren't wrong."

"What?"

"I'm pregnant."

"Oh, my God!"

"Sanjay...?"

"Yes...?"

"How did you know? *How did you know?*"

"I don't know; it just came to me, and I knew you were going to have a baby...."

The structure of that evening changed; I spoke with her mother and with her brother, and I cannot now remember which of them was the more excited. They remembered my message to her, and reminded me of another message I had given her, nearly a full year before, when I had not yet come to Michigan.

When Ginger and I had first met, she had asked me about Branson; I had seen many things when I looked at her.

"I see a little girl," I said, "She is your daughter, and Branson's also. She is very pretty; she is playing in the yard."

"Sanjay," replied Ginger, "You know this is a very difficult situation for me; I don't want another child."

"Perhaps I am wrong," I said, "But I am only telling you what I have seen."

Ginger reminded me of this later; I had forgotten it, as I usually did. When I gave readings, I did not always remember what I had said; the release of information was like a torrent, bursting forth from my mind, and I could not contain it. I sometimes wrote the messages down, on a piece of paper, to be handed on, and then forgotten; its recipient, however, would not forget the message, and would remind me of it, much later. The calls would come late at night, or in the afternoons; a breathless voice on the telephone would exclaim, with surprise, "How did you know, Sanjay? How did you know?" and I would not know how to answer them; I did not comprehend the power or the scope of my gift.

Ginger asked me, was it a girl? I told her *yes*, and Branson did not like my answer; he wanted a boy.

"Tell Sanjay to stop interfering," he demanded one weekend, "And tell him I want a boy."

I could not help it; the child was a girl, and I told him so. It was nothing to do with me; I had put no hand in it, nor could I have done. I could only tell him what I saw.

Ginger went for her ultrasound, and called me from the doctor's office. "Sanjay," she said, "It's a girl."

"Yes," I said. "I know."

I was very happy for Ginger, but I did not know what to do with Branson; he might have other things to say to me, and I really did not wish to interfere. In the event, he was very happy, and I finally met him, at the hospital.

The night before her delivery, I went to Ginger's house; Branson was with her, his parents had arrived from Metairie. She was in the nursery when I found her; she was shaking back and forth, sitting in the white-painted chair I had found for her.

"Ginger, honey, what's wrong?"

"I'm so worried about this baby."

"She will be alright, Ginger, she will be a healthy, happy baby, please don't worry."

"Are you sure?"

"Yes, I'm sure."

"Would you," she hesitated, "Do a reading for me?"

I took her hands in mine.

"Your child will never know fear, or hatred, or anger, only love, Ginger. She was conceived in love, and she will be surrounded with love, every day of her life."

Ginger was comforted by those words, and she slept a little, after I left her; her daughter was born the next day, and she was very beautiful, like her mother. There had been another message in the reading I did for her, and other words that came to me. I could not say them in the night; I cannot say them now.

The Obelisk

The manifestation of my gift often created amusing episodes, particularly when I was not present to witness their effect; the distance, however, only served to amplify its truth. I would offer insights based on what I had seen, which would later be confirmed, very often by others. It was as a photograph developed in a darkroom, sometimes very dim and at other times quite clear. The image would slowly materialise, from the darkness; I did not always comprehend my visions. I shared my sight, and allowed my friends the benefit of their own interpretation; I could offer none.

A friend in Petoskey called me very late one night, reporting disturbances in his house.

"There have been some very strange noises," he told me. "I don't know what to do."

"What kind of noises?" I asked him.

"There is a terrific banging," he said. "As though a heavy box has fallen on the floor. In the front hallway, there is a sound like someone kicking the door, with heavy boots."

"How long has this been happening?"

"For a few days, now."

I closed my eyes, and I saw something very strange, which I did not understand.

"Have you re-arranged the furniture in your office?"

"No, but I moved some things upstairs, why?"

"Something is out of place there."

"What do you see?"

I closed my eyes again.

"There is a piece of crystal, shaped like an obelisk. It is a beautiful deep purple colour, like an amethyst. Perhaps it is a piece of lavender quartz."

He did not say anything.

"Do you have a piece of lavender quartz?"

"*Yes*...."

"Is it shaped like an obelisk?"

"*Yes*...."

"Did you remove it from the office?"

"*Yes*...."

"Perhaps you'd better put it back."

The Long Way Home

I attended a festival one weekend outside Gaylord; the drive there was beautiful beneath the high, blue skies of the Michigan summer. I had not been able to camp; my schedule was full, and the time away ill afforded. Still, I made the trip, and returned to Charlevoix very late; it was a long drive, after dark.

As I drove home, heading out of Elmira, I thought of taking the East Jordan Road, running west from M131; it is open country and sparsely settled; I should have returned to Charlevoix through Boyne Falls, as I usually did. I thought the East Jordan Road might be faster, but I had not driven it at night.

As I turned off the highway, I slowed Jane, almost to a stop. I could see nothing ahead of me; the darkness swallowed up the road as it rose over the hill, and then disappeared altogether. I might have been driving off a cliff.

A message came to me, suddenly: *You are not welcome here.* I kept driving; there was no place to turn around.

Then, another message came: *You have been warned.*

The nights in the northern country are very dark; there is a solidity to them that presses up against you, when there is no moon and the stars are hidden behind a cloud. You creep blindly forward, hoping for some sight of the road ahead, a curve to the left or the right, a mailbox or a fence; there is nothing. The road vanishes before you, just beyond the glow of your lamps; beyond the light, there is nothing. You are alone in the night; there is only the sound of your breath, rapid and hurried, and the truck is silent, it is waiting, and watching, for anything may happen.

That night the air was heavy and dark, intensely charged with a strong current; I felt the strength of it running through me, as the hot bolt fired from a pistol. I drove as fast as I dared; I have no idea how far, but I must reach East Jordan. Once in the town, I would know my way home, but I was now in a strange land; I felt, all the time, that I was trespassing upon the property of something I did not know, or comprehend.

The road flattened out and curved gently through wide farmlands; there were houses and lights; I felt a relief as it turned back north, and I came into East Jordan. Like a warrior in battle, I had run a gauntlet; it had not harmed me; I had been badly shaken, but I had only won the first round.

I returned to the festival some days later, and again had to drive back to Charlevoix very late; the weather was dark and cloudy, there was again no moon. My experience of that road should have governed my behaviour, but I turned west again; I thought I might confirm the quality of my experience.

I felt strangely apprehensive, however; a police cruiser followed me from M131, and turned west with me; he stayed behind me for much of the way.

Again, the message came: *You are not welcome here*; it came again as I crested the hill: *You have been warned*. The police cruiser was directly behind me; his lamps shone into the truck, and illuminated it as I drove.

The cruiser swung out upon the road and swept past, it disappeared over a ridge; his lights faded into the darkness almost instantly. When I crested the ridge a few moments later, I was surprised to see nothing ahead; I was alone, I was not alone. Strange things moved upon it; shadows reached out from the ditches and the culverts; they stood by the mailboxes; they spoke to me.

There were headlamps moving again behind me; they came closer, and I pulled to the right. It was the same police cruiser; I recalled the numbering. It sped past me again, and disappeared around a curve, but when I arrived, it was gone.

I came, suddenly, upon a man as I rounded the curve, walking along the road; he was leading a bicycle. He had no lantern or flashlight, and I thought him very foolish; it was very dark. No one would see him, coming around the curve. He had dark hair, and a blue plaid shirt, with dark jeans; he did not look at me, but stared straight ahead, as I drove past.

There were headlamps approaching; another car came around the curve and its beams swept brightly across the road. The man and his bicycle were illuminated; I caught a glimpse of his profile. The car sped past; the night was black once more. I glanced behind me; the man was gone.

The man walking along the road with his bicycle returned to my thoughts in the following days; I often wondered about him. I thought it very odd, and was grateful I had not struck him; anyone might have done so. At various times of the day, the image would return to me, walking in the darkness along the road, and I wondered why he did so; I did not know him, yet his presence remained with me, and I pondered its regularity, and its effect.

Several weeks later, I was dining with friends, and I mentioned the East Jordan Road.

"Has anyone," I asked, "Ever travelled on the East Jordan Road, out of Elmira; has anything happened there?"

"Yes, of course," my friends answered. "There is the phantom cyclist; have you seen him?"

"The...*phantom* cyclist?"

"Yes, the phantom cyclist. He walks along the road at night, with his bicycle. A car comes along, and then he vanishes."

"Have you seen him there, before now?"

"Everyone has seen him, at one time or another. He was walking home one night, with his bicycle, and a car came around the curve; the driver was drunk, and struck him. He was killed, instantly."

"Oh, that's dreadful; his poor family. Did they ever find the driver?"

"No, they never did. It happened years ago."

"But…?"

"Yes; his ghost still walks along that road, late at night, when there is no moon."

I did not say anything.

"Sanjay…?"

I did not answer.

"You've seen him, haven't you?"

My Bodyguard

My friend Perry owned a beautiful white Irish wolfhound; he called her Wiggle. Her real name was Puddleglum, inspired by the water-folk of Narnia, but this had proven too long for every-day use. She was a very large dog, who could place her paws on my shoulders with no effort. Perry, much shorter than I, was overwhelmed by her; she could, and did, often knock him to the floor. Once, she pushed him into the pool, fully clothed and holding a fresh drink, I do not know which upset him more: the loss of his dignity, or that of his cocktail.

Wiggle presented a strange reaction to me at our first meeting: she barked incessantly. In time, she grew quiet, but for many weeks, Perry would have to shut her in the garage when I would visit; she would bark long, and loudly, at me. When I telephoned, she would bark, whenever Perry spoke my name; we thought it a good joke that she knew I was on the line.

When I first stayed with Perry, he gave me the downstairs guest-room; it was very comfortable. We then noticed Wiggle would come down with me; she would sit outside the door, and remain there through the weekend. I found this amusing, as did Perry; we felt her self-appointed mission was to keep a guard upon me, at all times.

Perry once told me, after I left, "Wiggle is still sleeping downstairs. The guest-room is empty, I do not know why."

"Maybe she likes sleeping on the bed?" I asked him.

"No, she is sitting outside the door."

"How very odd," I agreed. "Why is she doing this?"

"Don't you know?" he asked me.

"No, I do not."

"Is there…." He hesitated, "Is there…*something in the guest room*?"

I thought for a moment.

"No, Perry, I have not felt, or seen anything."

At the end of another visit with Perry, I was packing up my bags; Wiggle came to the door and stood there. I welcomed her, rather surprised, and she walked slowly into the room. She ignored me, however, and settled down at the foot of the bed, where she watched the open door intently.

Her attitude was unusual; she was guarding the bedroom, watching the open door closely; she did not take her eyes from it.

I continued to pack, and glanced up as I did so; a brief flicker of movement, like a wisp of smoke, hovered in the hallway beyond; it vanished almost immediately.

I dropped my bag; I did not believe it.

It came again, a wisp of something white, like a puff of smoke, moving through the hallway. I raced upstairs to speak with Perry; we were both immensely excited.

"What do you think it is?" he asked me, "I have never felt anything there. What is it?"

"I do not know," I said. "But Wiggle has seen it; she keeps an eye on it."

"But is it friendly, or not?"

"I do not know," I said. "Wiggle is watching it; now we know why she is there."

Perry reported to me later that Wiggle was still in the guest-room; she remained there, guarding the door. What walked there, I did not know; it remained in the house but disturbed no one, not while Wiggle was watching.

Service with a Smile

There is an old bar in Petoskey where Hemingway once drank, perhaps more than once; I have certainly done so, alone and with friends. This advertisement is not surprising; bars all over Paris share this history, and I have drunk in them as well. In northern Michigan, however, the memory of it becomes a seal of approval, a legitimacy of history in the taverns along Mitchell and Park Streets. We were here first, they say, we have been patronised by Literature and Art; we are now rewarded for our efforts; therefore you may approach, and be served.

It is a fine old bar, with dark wooden carvings and a tin ceiling; there are several large dining rooms, which are rumoured to be haunted. There is a persistent tale that a man had once hanged himself in the basement; his ghost roamed about the building and appeared, at times, to the patrons. It had been observed that children would play 'hangman' in the ballroom, at wedding banquets, at the table where his death took place. There is a special beer sold in northern Michigan, named for the unfortunate man and the manner of his death; it was very popular and many of my friends enjoyed it.

I usually seated myself at the bar; the dining room was always crowded, and I did not like the ballroom. I could not dispel the feeling I was not alone; I would see shadows in the corners;

other shapes and figures came and went; they were not patrons or employees.

I met a friend for drinks one evening, and by some small fortune, we were seated at a table near the tall windows, which overlook Park Street, towards the bay. It was a delightful day; the light was a clear, strong blue, and the candles had just been lit. Our conversation turned to ghosts, and their impact on the patrons; some might be sensitive about such things. I told my friend, were she to see it with my eyes, she might find the atmosphere disturbing.

"Do you believe there are ghosts here?" She asked me, with her eyes wide. "I have never seen one."

"Yes, I do," I answered. "I have seen them."

"Where?"

"In the ballroom, and here, in the bar."

"Here?"

"Yes, here." I smiled. "Don't worry, they won't hurt you; they are quite harmless."

The candle went out, a leaping flame that vanished in a rush of air. We jumped from our chairs; our napkins had been pulled from our laps, and thrown to the floor. The windows were shut; the doors had not been opened; there was no breeze. The candle was cased in a tall, glass cylinder; it should not have gone out.

"What just happened?"

"I don't know. It all happened at once."

I looked up and saw a woman standing at the table. She had bushy, dark hair, streaked with grey, and wore a dark green apron over her starched, white blouse and black skirt; she carried a towel and glasses in her large, firm hands. She smiled at us and then she disappeared, fading into the light, and as I watched, the candle on the table flickered back to life.

The Christian Brother

My friend Kristina lived near my house; she was very small and very pretty, and practised different forms of pre-Christian spirituality; we had many conversations. Some might have labelled her a pagan; she herself did not. She was not a witch, but dwelt in her cottage with the gentle spirits of the field, and the flowers; she walked among them, and danced in showers of golden petals at the harvest.

She was a lively, bubbling creature; the life within her body flowed easily, and she had many friends. In the mornings, we would spend much time talking and laughing together; her other male friends would look strangely at us, they did not share our confidences, and gave me many hard looks. When she would introduce me, they were rigid and formal; they did not comprehend our choice of topics, nor did they approve of them. When I would see them later, in the town, they would say hello, but they would not waste any time about it.

Kristina came often to my house; we had many adventures there, for she did not come alone. The air would change when she entered; it expanded and shone with a clear, sparkling light; other figures came into the room. She saw them, as did I, but there was one to whom she offered no introduction; I saw him, and he spoke to me; she did not anticipate our meeting.

He appeared in my sitting room one winter afternoon; Kristina and I were seated on the long sofa, engaged in our conversation; he might have been there some time. I became aware of him slowly, but steadily, as though a pitcher were being drawn from a deep well; I felt his presence. He was standing there watching us; I had not seen him before.

"Kristina," I said, "I don't mean to alarm you, but there is someone else here, in the room with us."

She did not turn around, as she might have done; she smiled very prettily, and asked, "Who is it, Sanjay?"

"Well, to be perfectly honest, it's a monk."

"A...*what*?"

"A monk. A Dominican, or a Greyfriar, I think."

"Does he look like anyone you know?

"Well, this is all very strange. He looks *quite* familiar, but I don't remember seeing him before."

"What on *earth* do you mean?"

"He's rather plump, and he has a tonsured head. He is wearing a brown habit, tied with a cord. He seems very happy to be here, I think. Does he know you?"

"What else do you see?"

I looked at him again; his nose and cheeks were a bright red colour; he was grinning broadly, and swaying slightly.

"Well, to be perfectly honest, he likes to *drink*."

The Michigan Dog-Man

The Michigan Dog-man is a strange creature, raising fear in all who have heard of him in the remote farms and villages, deep in the country. There are tales of him throughout the north, of a large wolf-like dog that runs on all fours, but with blue, human eyes; when confronted, the dog stands up on two legs, and strides off into the woods like a man. He is not to be trifled with; he is dangerous.

The Dog-man has been reported in Wisconsin and in Michigan; he is part of the folklore, the legends, and the history of those places; he is a thing that goes 'bump' in the night. One much-reported incident took place on a deserted road in Wisconsin; the Dog-man was seen stealing a deer carcass from the flatbed of an open truck; the driver, shaking, only repeated what he had told the police: *it was not a bear*. Much has been made of the Dog-man's proximity to the ancient burial grounds of the Ojibwe and the Menominee peoples; I myself have wondered if he was a type of tomb guardian or spirit.

There was a weekend in January when Barton came to stay with me; the women were gathered at the farm. The night was wild with heavy snows and blowing winds; I did not think we would get out in the morning. Around the table, after dinner, I became aware of a presence; it was outside the house, but it was looking in the window.

Barton did not see it; his mind turns to things mechanical, defined and programmed in logical, progressive order; he suggested I might go outside and speak to it. While I sat there, I had a powerful vision of its appearance; it was very tall and hairy, in the shape of a large, wild dog or wolf. Its fur was white, with grey and brown patches; I can still see it, clearly and distinctly, as it waited for me. It was standing on the snow-covered lawn outside my bedroom, standing on two legs, which bent forward as a dog's might, but it stood upright like a man. Its head was large and wide, with an impressive row of teeth, and a wide, red tongue; its eyes gleamed in the light from the porch; I did not dare open the door.

I felt it calling me; it wished me to come to him. He had many things to show me, he said; we would run together.

He called to me, he spoke to me; he waited while the snow fell, for me to respond. I am grateful I did not go out to him; the familiarity of the wild creatures was still new to me. I had been approached by a very wild creature before, at my brother's house in Dana Point, and the attraction had been very strong; I still remembered it, and thought of it again, that night, while I sat at the table, and the winds howled outside.

I have not regretted my decision, nor have I wished for it to be presented again to me, although I have encountered him again, and then again, and not far from Charlevoix; the paths of our journeys together have not yet been sundered.

I encountered him for the first time at a house in Harbour Springs, where I attended a party one summer evening. The house itself lay in a sheltered, wooded dale at the base of a long, sloping hill, surrounded by wide, flat lawns. Beyond were heavy woods of white pine, hemlock, and hickory; they were very old, and nearly impenetrable.

A friend had invited me, and we had driven up together from Petoskey. As we approached the house, coming down the hill, I felt a presence there, on both sides of the road; I had passed through a gate, into a different world. I thought of ancient, stone gargoyles, mounted on tall pillars, but these did not have wings. I asked my friend about it.

"Yes," he said, "There are many things in these woods."

Later that evening, I stood outside on the lawn; the air was damp and cool, and I felt very strange. The stars were very low, and the night air was soft and comfortable, a blanket of ebony silk chiffon.

I laid down on the grass, and rested there silently, looking up at the sky, seeing nothing, hearing nothing; the air swayed above my head; I closed my eyes, and hoped I might not be ill.

I heard a noise like a dog, but not a dog, louder, with a high, foreign pitch. It was coming from the woods, not far from the house; it grew louder as it approached. My friend came out and spoke to me; I was still lying on the grass.

"There is something coming; it is walking up through the woods," he said, "To tell you the truth, I'm a bit nervous."

The words that came to me then, I did not understand and I still do not pretend; they were nothing I should have said. Yet they appeared upon my lips, and the purpose of that evening was revealed; it was a strange gift, but it was not meant for me.

"There is nothing to worry about," I said. "He cannot hurt us; I will not allow him near the house."

"He...?"

"He...or it."

"How do you know it is a male?"

I knew, and the creature approaching knew; he had called out to me, in the night.

"It's getting closer," he said. "He has been here before."

"Yes, I know," I said. "But, I will not let him enter."

"How will you stop him?"

"I will put a Light around the house," I said. "And he will not pass through it."

It was coming closer, it walked upon the gravelled path in the woods; I could hear its footsteps as it came, left, right, left, right. The dogs whimpered, and cowered at the door; the other guests returned to the house; it was coming closer.

With some difficulty, for I was now very ill, I sent out the Light, and it formed a wall around us; it could not be penetrated. It took no small effort to do so, but intense concentration of thought and direction; the Light spread its high, golden walls about us, flowing like a high water in the spring, through which nothing could pass.

The footsteps stopped, and the howling rose from the woods, and I felt, then saw him, like a chilling, cold wind, and standing inside the trees. He appeared in the shadows, and he paced back and forth, but he could not come near. His dark, matted fur gave no reflection, but his eyes gleamed like gold in the night, and his jaws hung open; his tongue lapped furiously upon his sharp teeth, but he could not come near the house; I would not allow it.

The Stone Garden

There was a clearing in the woods near the farm; a smooth, circular area bordered with many small red and blue granite stones; it had been laid out by one of the itinerant farm workers. It was deep in the trees, hidden from the land, a secluded, guarded place, where only a few might go. I had been invited to enter it, and consequently spent much time there; it was very a quiet space, removed from the noise and commotion of the festival. In the afternoons, the trees shaded it from the sun, and the light was soft and clear, a grey colour, like a dull silk, in a setting of pale green leaves.

A high wall had been thrown up around it, of wind-fallen branches and tree limbs, like a pile of refuse; they screened the garden, and enclosed it further. In the centre, there was a sawn-off stump, wide and flat; there were candles and lanterns set out, that one might burn in the evenings. In the night, when I would come there, the lanterns would form a circle around me, and I would remain, alone and perfectly silent. The forest would be still, there would be no sound, until, to the west, a step would be heard, and then another; there was a shadow passing, but it did not linger.

The full moon in August is a round, glowing disc of pure, gleaming silver; it is very bright, with a clear, steady radiance; it passes swiftly in the southern counties. In the north, however, it rises very late, and rides slowly upon the sky; one can see by its light, and navigate easily through the forest.

The stone garden was illuminated by the full moon; the light was silver upon it, flooding through the trees like an enormous beacon. The moon passed behind a wisp of cloud and the light faded; there was an opening in the branches, and she poured out her radiance. The silver leaved fluttered softly; I heard soft music, of violins, rising upon the air, and I looked upon the leaves, gleaming in the night.

I felt the light upon me; I was bathed in a silver essence, as though I were being washed in its rays. The beam pierced the trees, and took on a familiar shape and form; the figure of a woman seemed to appear before me; she whispered, *all will be well*, and smiled. She was beautiful, and gracious; her silver-grey robes were gathered around her, seated upon a silver lotus; in her hands, she carried a silver lily, and her hair was graceful in its sable chignon. I bowed low to her, and remained, until the light passed over the trees, and I was in darkness once more.

The Angel of the Lord

It is difficult, for me, to write of the Angels, for they are beings of Light, bent to the Divine Will, focussing solely upon God; they do not resemble Man in this aspect, we are easily distracted.

The Angels who have come into my house have done so quietly, unannounced, with no fanfare of trumpets or crashing of cymbals; they have simply appeared, and I have always known they were there. They take on the form of men when they call, for their essence is Light, and Fire, and Air, but not of Earth. The visage of God burns in their faces; they have seen Him; they speak with Him, they bow down before Him. I have often wished to ask them many questions about God, but I have been intimidated; it is a knowledge unfit for my ears, and they have not answered.

They appear as men, ageless but sometimes younger or older; their faces are smooth; their hair a mass of thick, golden curls. Their robes are a single piece of shimmering golden cloth, as one with the light, wrapped at the waist with a golden cord; they are usually barefoot. If I were to name a true representation, then perhaps those of the Renaissance painters are the most like unto them; it is a highly ornate portrait.

Their wings are beautiful; high, reaching pennants of feathers that gleam about them; I have seen them with two, four, and even six wings; they are splendid. Sometimes the wings will be proportionate; others have had very large wings, which spread the width of the room; they are very powerful, and can lift themselves effortlessly into the air.

When the Angels have appeared, they have always directed me to my Bible; they bring messages from God, and He chooses His words well. I never knew what I might read, for the words would not always appear to me on the page; once, the Angel directed me, with his outstretched finger, to a chapter and a verse in Isaiah. I read the words set there, and understood their message, when I looked up again, the Angel had gone, and I was alone in my room, as I had been before.

For what we are about to receive
Let us give thanks unto the Lord.

Et la Pomme Lui Dit, Merci

Nobility of gesture, and of faith, is an acknowledgement of humility in the face of a kindness, a favour extended; it is the form of gratitude, and its foundation, which is grace. Like the apple, which famously thanked Picasso, there was an aspect of my life in northern Michigan where I was blessed sufficiently to give thanks, and in similar fashion.

North Central Michigan College in Petoskey enabled my first exposure to academic life, it was a world in which I became very comfortable; I should not mind entering it again. I am grateful to them, for they accepted my presence as an unknown element, and offered me a class for aspiring architecture students; it was a perfect start for the autumn semester.

I had not taught before, excepting the assistances I had performed at university; here, I was teaching the concepts of architecture, of form, space, and order, to freshmen who might have no recognition of it otherwise.

It is a strange task to be blessed with knowledge, which one must then transmit to others. What is to be handed out freely, and what is to be retained for the future? From the great storehouse of my brain, where much learning had accumulated itself, what must be gleaned from it, that it should now be handed on to those who came to hear me? Had all the years of my education led me to this moment, where I might pass on the gift, the discipline, and the training?

It was strange, also, to select the text for my course, it was one I had first read as a freshman in Chicago; the book was still current, and in its third edition; it had been revised, and expanded, with new drawings and figures. Much of it was familiar to me; much had remained. Yet there were new drawings, new buildings, which I had not seen before, and which presented new examples of design, pattern and reflection; they were exciting to see; another vista presented itself.

I did not expect my students to love the subject, for it maintains its own esoteric. I entertained no rose-coloured perspective; it should be enough that they retained some appreciation. Much cannot be taught in a single semester; the study of architecture can consume one's career. Yet here I was, breaking down the elements of architecture into succinct, defined terms, of point, line and plane, volume, mass and form.

Before term, I inspected the room assigned for my class. I strolled about; it was a large square space, with desks and chairs; there was a lectern with equipment. The technical department guided me through the projectors and controls, so that I was familiar with them; it was a rehearsal, for the performance to come. The moment of that visit, when I first stood at the doorway, is emblazoned upon my memory, even now. I see it clearly; I am standing there, walking slowly through the room, touching the smooth surfaces of the desktops, feeling the backs of the hard plastic chairs, testing the lights, and lowering the blinds to gauge the shade, when I should have the projectors running.

I shall never forget my first day, when I entered my classroom with my books and papers, dressed in comfortable tweeds, as I felt a real professor might be. The eyes of my students were focussed upon me, I realised they would remain so for the semester; I was being watched; I was being observed. By my actions, I might influence them; I was now become an example, a standard of behaviour, which I might not comprehend, yet to which I must now be held accountable.

I worked hard to prepare for my classes, that I might have all my materials ready each session; there was much to learn, and then to teach. I assigned short essays on architecture, and the history of a place and its spatial analysis. However, beyond the pedantry, I wanted to hear their voice, their thoughts, their feelings of a building, and its history.

"Tell me what *you* think of this structure," I said, "Do you like it, or do you not? Tell me what you *think*; I do not want to read something copied from someone else's book."

They responded in full measure; it was a delight to read their papers. I could *hear* their voices in them; they were well formed, and developed. They had analysed the buildings assigned and had delivered their verdicts; they had not allowed other declarations to influence their thought.

I remember one student very well. There were others whom I remember also, but his presence has left its mark. I enjoyed teaching him very much; he participated fully, and had much to say; he presented an eager mind; always, he seemed, to be seeking to expand his knowledge. It was always a pleasant experience to speak with him; he asked thoughtful, insightful questions; his mind did not run along the same track as the other. His paper, however, was foreign to me; the writing was rich and formal, it was the voice of another.

With some trepidation, I looked up his words, and found them in other articles, other publications; they had been lifted whole and complete, without acknowledgement or credit, a compilation of others' work. The suspicion of it had made me ill;

the confirmation of it sent my head spinning. I could not focus, I could not think; I could not imagine such an action.

A difficult task lay before me; I had to speak to my dean, and then to my student; even now, I recall our conversation. He made no excuse, he made no apology; he merely stood there while I spoke, and presented the evidence against him. I did not shout, or raise my voice; I spoke to him calmly, yet inside I raged, and my body shuddered beneath its tweed covering; I had not thought it so simple, to be so severe. I asked him what remedy he should suggest and he offered to write the paper again, in his own words, to earn a passing grade. I thought this a good course and outlined the terms of it, which he accepted. He did not do it; the deadline came and went; he ended the term by failing, and I was sorry, for I had only wanted him to succeed.

It did not occur to me, in the dull, throbbing sickness that swept through me, that the student had failed. I myself had failed; I had not done my job. That the student had failed me, as he had failed the course, I did not comprehend fully; only later, when I reviewed the work of my other students, did I realise it, and welcome its revelation.

My other students, however, did very well; they responded to my questions, they took extensive notes; they were prepared for the exams. Their papers were well written; they showed appreciation. At the end of the semester, when the class was finished and the grades posted, they sent me little notes of gratitude, and I have kept them, printed out on good paper, stored in my scrapbook; I like to look at them sometimes, and I smile to myself, when I do. I sometimes think of them, and wonder what they are doing, if their careers have continued in architecture, or if they have begun to explore other facets of their life. I do not know; I have not seen them; the pebbles, dropped into the still water, have disappeared from my view.

One does not always know or guess what influence we may have, when we present our truths, coloured by our own lens; they are but words to us; to another person they are gospel, sacrosanct and immutable; they may not be altered. The actions of our behaviour and the conduct of our lives may be of a second nature to us; we have always lived in this fashion. Seen by another, however, it is something new and altogether different; it is another world. Someone has emerged from the sawdust and the glitter, and presented himself for our inspection. He is a figment, a creature of our will and our thought, but he is standing here now, and he has many things to say.

In a film, when a favourite character has stepped out from the written page and become visually real, a tangible presence printed upon celluloid, it is become a fulfillment of what we have envisioned, and perhaps we have captured that delight God must have felt, as the animals issued forth from His hands. As they were created by His divine will, so are these other creatures, borne of another's mind, reflecting on earth that which is in Heaven. We rejoice in the imitation, not because we have reached so high, but in grasping to comprehend the mind of God, we have touched that part of the Divine, which dwells within each of us.

It is a strange blessing to see a character realised, with which one has walked, laughed, and cried; one has known him as a friend, or an enemy. The book has been lost; we cannot find it, but the character remains with us, even as we have loved him, we have created him, and he is real to us; he is not a fantasy, a collection of words on paper. We return to the first, precious moment of our acquaintance; the journey of a thousand miles is rewarded. Do we remember the child, and in that moment, the journey we have now completed?

And Round That Early-Laurelled Head

My friend Michael and I would race across a suspension bridge to our studios, in our college days; sometimes Michael would win. The lasting benefit of our sport was the sustenance of our friendship, which has now lasted many years, not only did we compete on foot, but, more importantly, on drawing-paper.

I often ran through the fields on our farm in South Dakota, laughing and looking behind if I was being pursued. I remember the warmth of the summer light in the cornfields, and the flaming sunflowers near the high fences; they are forgotten, now. There were twining, bright green leaves upon the old wooden railings; they had pale lavender flowers, but I did not know their names. Once, I fell, and lay laughing on the grass; I lay perfectly still and buried my face within the trembling, green spears. A small garter snake came up to me; its head hovered a few inches from my own, its mouth was a row of black, jagged teeth, and I jumped screaming to my feet, and ran away.

The laurelled garland and the burnished cup are the reward of the victor, but what of the race itself, and the others who ran with us, laughing, along the rainy beach in our bare feet; where are they? Is it enough that we have won, or is it of greater worth, that we have run with our equals?

Aftermath: The Poems for Jane

In the autumn of 2009, my first book was published: *Aftermath: the Poems for Jane*. I was very proud of it; the circumstance of the accident had been exorcised, dispelled onto the blank page, purging them from my mind. There was a book-signing party in October, I had many friends in attendance, and it was a night of celebration for me, a milestone of my career.

Later, my friend Mike Rosteck purchased a copy, which I signed for him; I was delighted he should have it. The pleasure of sharing my work with my friends was enhanced by his enjoyment of it; he read it carefully, and studied its pace and its rhythm. Inspired by my story, he set many of the poems to music of his own composition, and recorded them. This was a magical gift, it added dimension and colour to my words. Many of the songs are very good, haunting in their spell, and in their embrace of the story. They took on a new form, which was unfamiliar to me; a strange, smoke-filled cloud that rose from the page and presented itself to me; it was not my creation, for I had written only the words; the music fashioned a new dimension upon it. I have the recordings here; I often listen to them as I write, the memory has dimmed, but remained clear.

The gift of telling a story is like the weaving of a spell; the listener is held captive under a magician's wand. The story encompasses you; you are carried to distant gardens, fragrant with blossom, or to a path in the forest, moving beneath the trees. Figures walk beside you, you are part of the tale and become one with it. Arachne, at her warp-weighted loom, has imprisoned you, and the click of the spindle is like a clock; with each pass over the glowing threads, you are transported further away. The story becomes heavy with embroidery, it is the weighting of the cloth and its decoration, which gives it the hand and the movement; when you hold it and it is become your own fabrication.

  The story is shared with friends and their joy enriches it, the threads are as burnished gold. It speaks with its own voice; it is no longer your own, it is shared by many; the stars fill the sky as you float silently in the quiet pool, and all around you, you hear the music of the eternal spheres of heaven.

Upon a distant road,
A traveller came walking
Under the golden leaves
He chanced upon her, the forest-maiden
They have gone on, together.

The Itinerant Traveller

Growing accustomed to the smooth, wide highways of northern Michigan, it was, nonetheless, necessary for me to make frequent drives to Chicago, to meet with clients, for I still had work there. I always left Charlevoix very early, so that I might arrive in good time; my days in Chicago were always full, and I could not spare any moments for trifles. Always, always, I was hurrying back and forth, to be done with the tasks at hand, and then to be gone again. Chicago was no longer my home; I had no place there, and the northern roads called to me; I could not help but to follow.

On these journeys, I would leave while it was still dark; the sun would not be up, and the eastern sky would still be very, very black. In the winters, the dawn comes late; you have only the stars to guide you, and their patterns and forms become familiar to you; you set your course by them. I began to comprehend why the great caravans would site their charts to the stars' movements; it was a measured, orderly progression. It was comforting, for me, to see the great figure of Orion rising up into the night sky over the pine trees, as I drove towards Cadillac. He would appear on the road beyond Kalkaska, shimmering in the night, the dawn was approaching. His glittering belt rose up; I would see his long, striding legs and his raised shield; he was marching forward; we travelled in the same direction.

It was a pleasant conceit that Orion was my travelling companion, for do not the stars bow to us? Here I am, a tiny speck crawling upon the great earth, scurrying like a beetle, yet all creation looks upon me, and is therefore humbled. I am the greater, for I have a soul; I am seated at the right hand of God. What is this blue planet, turning through the void, that it should house such fantastic creatures?

The drive to Chicago is neither short nor long; it is exactly six hours. It is the same length returning to Charlevoix, but only in the summers, in the winter it can be a terribly long voyage. It is a pleasant journey if one is travelling at one's leisure, but an endless, winding expanse of road when one is anxious to be home. The miles stretch out before you; there is no end to them; the road seems to wind away forever as you come up from Grand Rapids to Cadillac. Each turn of the grey pavement presents another hill, another valley; it is beautiful in its austerity and its colouring, but there are still many miles to go. When you come to Cadillac, the road begins to fall, into the Manistee National Forest, and becomes a pleasant drive; it winds gently through the river bottoms and wide, flat fields until you come to Kalkaska, and beyond that, Antrim and Mancelona. From there, one can take the Petoskey Road or the East Jordan Road; they offer pleasing vistas, in the daylight.

It was always good to walk into my house after a long journey, and find it there, silent and warm. It was a comfort, like my old, heavy jacket with the fleece lining; I felt at peace there; I was safe. The house would be perfectly quiet; there was no sound. My footsteps would echo upon the wide, oak floors as I walked down the hallway, and I felt its embrace about me once again; I had come home; I had returned.

There was one night in November, however, when the house seemed different; I had been gone nearly a week. It was very dark, and the streetlights did not pass through the windows. There was a strange, restless movement inside; I heard, as I entered, the sound of a door shutting; was someone in the house?

I fumbled in the dark closet for my old cricket bat, and called out, but received no answer, and again heard another door opening, and then shutting; the sound of it came clearly through the still air. Gripping my cricket bat tightly, I entered the hallway.

To my surprise, the kitchen light was burning, and I recalled that I had turned it off, before I left.

All the doors were open; none was shut. As I stood there, my heart racing, I heard the unmistakable sound of another door opening. Turning, I saw the laundry room door slowly swinging out, into the hallway. A chill raced through me; I gripped the bat tightly, but there was no one there.

You've Got to Be Carefully Taught

The failure of Christianity in northern Michigan is due to its bigotry and prejudice, as practised by its followers; it is a blind hatred of difference and variation in class and structure. I had been warned of it, but I did not experience it but once, at a department store in Holland.

I had stopped for a few sundry items; I was visiting friends in Muskegon that evening, a pleasant stop along my journey home. I noticed strange looks as I stepped from my truck, which puzzled me and drew my attention. One man in particular, whose face I cannot erase, stood staring intently at me, as I crossed the carpark; his gaze was wary, and strangely loathsome. I posed no threat; I passed him by, and went inside.

As I found my purchases, I watched a family, Latino by their colouring and manner, go about their weekend shopping; they comprised a father, a mother and two small children. The children were remarkably well behaved, and the family went about their business quietly. As I watched them, passing slowly down the aisle, my gaze was interrupted by the store clerks.

All the clerks, and there were many, had fixed upon the family a look of utter hatred; a glare of great anger and disgust filled their faces, as though some vicious crime were being committed. The family was not creating a disturbance; the children were quiet and stayed with their parents; they did not speak, and were helping their mother.

I was filled with my own anger and disgust; the family was minding their own affairs, tending to their own needs; they had offended no one, save for the colour of their skin.

The features of racism are ugly; they exist solely within the constructs of the stupid, the ignorant, and the unintelligent. Had these persons created a disturbance, as children are wont to do, such a reaction might have been justified, and perhaps a manager might have spoken to them. They were simply doing their shopping, in a store where the colour of their skin was not welcomed, but the colour of their money was still green, and thus accepted.

The Winter's Tale

One February, as I was returning from Chicago, the snows came heavily on the roads, north of Grand Rapids I could not see the highway; the landscape was pure white. I shall never forget that drive; I was a fool to attempt it. In the dark, black night of the Michigan winter, there was no illumination, save the pale beams from my headlamps upon the snow. Drifting across the highway, the drifting, blowing flurries took on the appearance of strange, elongated faces, leering old men with long beards, grimacing horribly as I passed over them. There was no end to them, they formed a long, extended procession; their faces were stretched and distorted; they were not of this earth.

It was a night of fear, a great fear that I might spin off the road, as I had already done that winter, or wreck my truck, as I had done the winter before. I did not drive fast, and began to slow my pace; my speed crept slowly down to fifty-five, then fifty, then forty, then thirty-five. Other cars sped past; trucks, campers, vans, and buses with all their flying colours. I was appallingly tired, and could not lift my hands from the wheel; my fingers were clenched tightly about it. I longed for a drink, but dared not stop; I had come to the long stretch of road from Cadillac, past Manton, which leads, eventually, to Kalkaska and then to home; it was the last leg of my journey; I had been driving for hours.

I can still see, quite clearly, the wide, yellow signs north of Manton, and their flashing, amber lights as the road curved west, and the lanes merged into one path. There were cars behind me, which passed, and others that followed; I was grateful for those, their headlamps added dimension and clarity to my vision. I had prayed for light upon my road, and always, one truck had stayed behind me. He had not passed me; his headlamps brightened the road.

I crossed the Manistee River; the road was a broad sheet of white; I could not see the edges, only the dark pine forests on both sides. The land began to rise again, coming up from the river bottoms, and flattened as I drove to Kalkaska.

The northern counties do not plough; they are infamous for their inaction. Wexford County roads are horrifying in the winter; that night, they had cleared only one narrow lane; Kalkaska County was only slightly better. Antrim County was worse; there was no appearance of ploughing across its breadth, and I still had to cross Charlevoix County. I could not be certain of the East Jordan Road; in the darkness and the hurling snows, there would be no one to come to my aid. I elected, with some trepidation, to hurry along the Mackinac Trail Road north to Elmira, and to turn off at Boyne Falls; at least there were places along the way where I might stop, if needed.

I had forgotten that the road descends, north of Elmira, in a long, sweeping slope towards the flatlands; in the night, it was a broad sheet of ice. I crept blindly down; I do not remember whether my foot remained on the gas or the brake; it was all ice, and the road seemed to fall forever.

I saw the lights of Boyne Mountain ahead of me; the slopes were still active. I longed to pull into the lodge and ask for a room; I had come this far, I could go no farther. I did not do so; I was nearly home, and I turned off at Boyne Falls, where the road runs straight and smooth, into Boyne City. It had been ploughed, but was still covered with snow, but my grip upon its surface was easier, and assured.

I came into Boyne City, quiet and pale beneath the night, and the streets were white; they had also been ploughed. I turned onto the Boyne City Road, and headed for home; I had only sixteen miles to go; I was closer, closer.

No tales I had heard, of the Boyne City Road in winter, were fabrications; they were an appalling fact. The road had not been ploughed outside the city limits; ahead were only two narrow lines in the deep snow.

The truck behind me followed closely; it stayed there as I pushed forward. My exhaustion began to take hold of me; I could see nothing but the endless expanse of white, I saw no other feature. The truck behind me did not pass; it stayed close, and when I would swerve, it would tap its horn softly; I would tap mine in return, to thank him.

The road curved, sloped, and rose again; the sweeping lanes that I roared down in the summer had vanished, to become horrifying crevasses and mountains, which I must somehow negotiate. Other cars came up; they passed me easily in the night, and their lights, ahead of mine, were my only guide in the darkness. All was black; the snow had begun to fall again, thickly and heavily, and I could not see the road, only an expanse of white broken by tyre marks. The truck remained behind me; he did not move from his position, and I thought it strange he did not pass me, when others had done so.

I came into Charlevoix at last, the road turned north and the land spread out before me; I was home, home safely. The truck passed, and the driver waved to me, a friendly greeting, and I tapped my horn softly. I turned onto Petoskey Avenue; the road had been ploughed, it was still wet, but it was clear. Ahead of me, the truck pulled into the gas station, I pulled in behind him.

The truck was parked beneath the canopy, dull green and black beneath the fluorescent lights; the driver was standing outside. He wore a blue mechanic's suit and a dark cap; I could not see his hair; his hands were scarred, and stained with oil. He looked at me, he smiled warmly, and I spoke to him.

"I hope I didn't slow you down," I said. "I really appreciated having your lights behind me; it's really hard to see, out there on the road."

"No problem," he said, "I wanted you home safely."

"Thank you," I said. "My house is just down the road."

He smiled, and a sudden thought came to me.

"Wait, just a minute… *how long have you been following me?*" I asked him.

He did not answer, and then he smiled again.

"Long enough, to make sure you got home."

I turned to Jane, the tank had filled, and when I turned back around, he was gone; I was alone beneath the lights.

We do not always realise, when we pray, that we are being heard; it is enough to have called upon the Lord. He has heard us, and He has sent His Angels to protect us, we should not be dashed against the rocks, in His hands, we have reached our destination.

A View from the Bridge

The towers of North Michigan Avenue, viewed from the Fullerton Avenue Bridge, are at their finest in the morning, when the light is palest silver, and the last wisps of night are washed away by the sunrise. As one comes up over the bridge, hurtling south towards North Avenue, they are revealed in their splendour as if new, for the first time.

After September 11, it was startling to see the Sears Tower silhouetted in the morning sky as I drove into the city. I would look for its vertical, stepped profile rising above the Loop, and like a beacon, it would be standing proudly.

One morning I came down Lake Shore Drive, and the sunlight was blurred through a fine mist. The water, sparkling with silver, diffused into many twinkling points; it merged imperceptibly into the horizon where the sky rose up, close enough to touch. It was not a day for speed, but for leisure, with the top down and my arm outstretched to feel the soft, cool breeze. The towers of the city dissolved into the mist, gently shaded blocks of grey and taupe. The lawns of Lincoln Park seemed newly green, of a deep, vivid emerald, and I remembered that morning for a long, long time.

The Evening Star

The air in California is very dry; it is the aridity of the desert, tempered by the humidity of the ocean. It is drier than Michigan, and certainly more so than Illinois. The stars are clearer and lower in the sky; they hang at a different angle to the earth. From the terrace of my mother's house, I felt I might reach out to them; Orion himself should take my hand, and assist me upon his carpet, to journey with him through the night.

The skies in California are different from Michigan in winter; they are the clear, dark blue found in the heart of a violet, which itself is barely seen, but adds subtlety and depth to its colouring. In the morning, they brighten to a vibrant azure, which the Virgin herself may have worn; it is the same colour of her robes, seen in Renaissance paintings and altarpieces.

The daylight in California is white, a vermeil gleam that does not soften or flatten, but outlines all shapes and forms with crisp, defined shadows. The rough, sand-coloured adobe walls and fired red clay tiles of the Spanish missions look their best in this climate, for it is native to them and their origins.

In the evening, the California sky deepens to a radiant, shimmering blue, which I have not found elsewhere. It is difficult to describe this colour; it is beyond the depth of the sea, or a woman's eyes. It is a dark colour, yet glows brightly, as though a veil of cobalt-blue silk were being lighted by a single, silver lamp.

Venus, the evening star, shines brightly against this glowing backdrop. I have often thought of her, not as a celestial orb, but as a single, perfect diamond, radiant and bright, in the ear of a blue-skinned maiden with dark hair, or perhaps held at the throat on a fine silver chain.

Perhaps there really are alien beings, or perhaps it has been too long since I looked at a woman properly. It is appropriate for a goddess, I think, to bear the colour blue, for it is but a reflection of the heavens, and the deepening of the shade is but an enhancement of her beauty. Shakti, the great Earth Mother, is often depicted with blue colouring, as is Kali; Vishnu, in his aspect of the Narayana, is a blue-skinned god.

If I were to compare the evening skies over California to a woman, I should exploit my prejudice for the women of India, for they truly belong to that colour of luminous blue. It was designed for them, it colours their golden-hued skin, and balances it, the warmth, and the coolness. Only the colour of rose pink is its equal, when matched to the skin of a beautiful Indian woman; therein appears the truth of the statement, and equally, by its inversion, "Navy blue is the pink of India."

The Voice

It is a source of great pleasure to me, at the end of the year, to contemplate the night. The sky is sparkling clean, washed by the autumn rains, and the stars have a hard, cold brilliance that is apparent only after the solstice. I have often wondered if the sky appeared this way on that Night, to the shepherds in their fields. How it must have blazed with light and music, of the angels rejoicing in the birth of the Holy Infant. Perhaps it is this representation of the heavens, which we find in the season, in the dark, green-needled spruces and firs, glittering with many tiny, white lights; it is a cosmos in miniature.

When I have considered the possibilities of time-travel, it is to this Night I have always wished to direct my course. Who would not desire to witness such event, which, in all its simplicity, changed the course of our own history?

I have not made the stable my priority, however; it is the shepherds, watching over their flocks by night, which have retained my attention. The life of a shepherd is hard, wearying work, with ceaseless guard against wolves and other predators. One is exposed to the elements, there is little comfort or riches to be found; one is very poor. Nor is their lot to be envied in the social orders and calendars of the world. It is a reminder to us, that the presence, and the worship of God is not to be confined to the glittering splendours of the Church, but to carried forth, that His message is given to all who wish to hear it.

     Yet to these humble folk, the glorious multitude appeared, lighting the heavens with their chorus. How they must have sounded, the great choirs of Heaven, rejoicing with God in the birth of His Son. Whenever I have heard a mighty choir singing, I have imagined we are being afforded a glimpse of it.

     I have heard it elsewhere, in the crashing of mighty waves, on the northern beaches of Hawaii. There is no equal to the sound of it in the world; it is the great, powerful voice of Nature, a concert of water, and earth, and air. It is in the pounding surf, the furious wind, and the air whips past you and bends the trees. It is the Voice of God; it defines the world and your place within it. The earth moves beneath your feet, there is the booming of the reef and the tilt of the waves over the coral; you are being moved, you are carried away, and you are powerless in the face of God's creation. The waves lift you up; you are borne aloft in a strange, weightless embrace, the grip of the storm; yet within the maelstrom, one finds the centre, the refuge that is the Hand of the Lord, and His ways are mighty to behold.

     The power of the human voice raised in song can be considered an approach to the divine music. How much more beautiful is the voice of an angel, raised in glorious song, to honour our Lord, and the fruition of His divine Will.

The Nativity

There has been much discussion on the origins of mankind, and whether they lie in the stars or, more crudely, from some long-vanished cavern; it is one's own profession of faith.

In a secular perspective, the Nativity may be interpreted as impregnation of a human woman by an alien god. We have heard these stories; Zeus, in the Greek pantheon, fathered several children on human women, as did Apollo; the Bible speaks of gods coming to the earth, and loving human women, in Genesis.

In the Christian faith, however, the Nativity is the entire foundation of one's belief in God, it defines and directs our progress; it is the belief to which I adhere. It is not possible from our remote position to comprehend or explain these parallels.

Is Jesus, truly, the Son of God?

I can only answer this question truthfully, because I believe Him to be the only begotten Son of God, born of the Virgin. That is my belief; it is an article of my faith, and my celebration of it. Were I to gain a greater understanding, I might have a different answer, encompassing a broader knowledge of His purpose, but that day has not come, and I do not anticipate it with any impatience; it is enough, that it shall come to pass. This should require a super-human effort, which I am not certain I possess. "Blessed are they who have not seen, and yet have believed."

The Nativity: A Poem

And now the light at blushing dawn,
In eastern sky aflame,
Upon the dome of starry night,
At last we hear His name,
Where angels sang in throng-ed host,
Above the silent field,
Returning there the shepherds come,
Their silent thoughts to wield,
And in a stable dark and cold,
There sleeps a little child,
The greatest gift the world has known,
The Lamb, so meek and mild,
Still watching Him, his mother smiles,
In gratitude to God,
From virgin womb the child is born,
To take up sceptr'd rod,
For just this moment, as the light,
Is still, and cold, and grey,
Rejoice ye men, and merry make,
For this is Christmas Day.

The Hummingbird

One must find strength within oneself, it can neither be imagined nor fancied; should it not exist, it cannot be created. It is a force of the mind, a victory of the self, in its lonely dispute and its daily conflicts, which one must overcome. The refusal to surrender to one's daemons takes many forms; there are many skirmishes and raids, but the battle can also be lost.

A life inhabited alone demands a certain *froideur* in the face of others, who might judge it of lesser value and whose own influence may govern one's direction. They do not hold one's solitude equal if they are married or in partnership; their sole desire, in their friendship, is to encourage the acquaintance of someone they think will be suitable. It is not easy to refuse when these gestures are borne of kindness; your friends only seek to share their own happiness; in their minds, it is lacking in your own, and they will not subscribe to your protestations.

There is a benefit to a solitary existence, useful at social events: the ability to hover like a hummingbird, to stay or to leave at one's own choosing. One can stop effortlessly in mid-air, sip at the nectar, and then take one's leave; your wings beat furiously, they are invisible, but they are supporting you, and what mechanic has fastened these faint, shimmering feathers upon your shoulders? There is an unspoken query on the lips of your friends, at your departure: What will happen when the currents of the air, upon which you are floating, sweep you out the door, and into the evening?

I do not doubt that the next day's report, served up hot with the bacon and eggs, and poured out with the coffee, expands, and enlivens itself in the accounting; Dr Frankenstein himself might have been pleased to witness such vitality injected into such dead flesh. My friends have often told me of their imaginings, that I should be engaged in an adventure of certain anonymity. The evening's outcome would not be in doubt, yet the identity of its participants should remain unknown. I once said, to be humourous, that my solitary evenings were a safari; I knew not what I might shoot, but that I was well armed for it.

This appliance has served me well when I have had need to depart a dull soirée; the fantasies of the most stolid of persons will outweigh the reality of my wanderings, for I would invariably find my way to a favourite café, to get a good dinner, very late. They imagine me moving purposefully down the street, and they will smile, for their minds are moving along the same, darkened path, passing through shadows; I have followed those paths before, and the results have not always been worthy of recognition, or indeed of repetition. I have found it best to leave such a reputation unchallenged, for the truth would surprise them, if they chose to believe it at all.

Et In Arcadia Ego

I have imagined a solitary hunter deep in the African night, and I think, somehow, we would have much to say to each other. The great hunters have learned the enviable art of remaining motionless, like a leaf clinging to an unadorned branch, while the world passes before them; there is much to be gained from their perspective, for it is a trait known by the mystic and the seer.

An artist wielding his brush possesses this talent, as the canvas stretches before him, and the brightly coloured oils await the strokes of his vision; he does not see anything else, only the white square before him; all else is forgotten. When I lived in northern Michigan I had friends who hunted; I would often follow them into the woods, to study their movements and their arrests in the face of the entwining green, impenetrable. It was easy for them, with their experience, to become one with the trees; it is not a trait found in the urban jungle; on the streets, there is no place to hide. While they waited, I would sketch furiously upon my pad; they were the perfect subjects, for they remained motionless, and I was able to complete several rough portraits. They made excellent gifts; my friends appreciated them, and took them as a form of gratitude, for their sufferance in permitting me to join them in the early morning.

What strength one finds in oneself is a great undertaking, requiring many hours of preparation and planning, as if one were going on a great journey. It is not an easy task, for it requires much thought, much reflection, and much foresight. The action of it, when it arrives, is almost anti-climactic; you have laid out your course for miles ahead. That you cannot foresee its end is but the law of God, for He alone knows its outcome, its twisting and turning, its rising and its falling; all else is darkness.

It is a last safari to the rim of the world, where, in the first glow of dawn, the animals materialise slowly out of the dark mist to find you waiting for them. You are not there to shoot them, you have no weapon; you stand rigidly silent and await their presence. You are an audience of one; the whole world passes before your eyes, and you neither applaud nor rise; the spectacle is not for you. The animals are not come to be received, but to receive; it is the supplication of the servant to the master, silent and terrible.

The night is drawing back its curtains; there is a hush, great things are stirring upon the plain. The mist is the colour of charcoal, tinged with gold, the sun is rising far to the east; the shadow is ebbing slowly away. The world has tilted itself, and the borders of night have slipped back, like water falling from the shore-lined rocks, to the time that is forgotten.

Here come the first signs of life, the world has been renewed; there is a sudden ripple upon the still water; the sun takes its first slow, rising steps upon the sky. The giraffe are first out of the trees, like giant, speckled orchids, walking stiffly through the wet morning. They frolic in their strange, ambling gait through the grasses of the plains, and one can imagine an alien group of insects with strange appendages; their legs moving in that strange rhythm peculiar to them alone. Where their heads poke above the trees, one can imagine a row of flowers on long, slender stalks, nodding to each other in the morning breezes. There are zebras, passing slowly back and forth in front of each other, like striped fish in a glass tank. They are the prey of the lion, the cheetah, and the other great predators of the night; they are the hunted, the sustenance of the wild beasts. Their numbers do not change, however; they are there in great multitude, a shifting pattern of chocolate-brown and cream-coloured stripes, passing back and forth, before you.

There is a dull, distant noise, a strange, slow rumbling, a heavy weight moves upon the earth, and suddenly the mists are broken. Here passes the great elephant, swinging his mighty tusks, cleaving the air before him. He sees nothing, including you, but he will smell you, and he will recall that smell, when it suits him. The very earth has risen up, high into space, and become his great flanks; they are solid, like the walls of a fortress. The mahouts know this, and respect it, when they ride upon their backs, singing songs to Colonel Haathi. There is nothing so terrible and as splendid as the elephant, only the great Himalayas are equal to his majesty. They say the same thing to you and me: Look upon us and be humbled, we were here at the first and shall be here at the last, when you are gone from this place. The elephants can remember; they do not forgive; they are old memories with long shadows that reach from the past to take hold of us. One must take care not to offend, they are a very old people, and their manners are very formal, even in the face of the spitting rifle, and the long, iron-tipped spear.

Here one finds the brink, the edge of nothing, before or past. There is only the cliff, and the pure, sweet air rushing up from the valley plains below. One puts out one's foot, and ~

The Morning Star

It is a pleasure unique to my travels that I have seen the sun rising over Lake Michigan, as I set forth from Chicago. The skies would be a deep, velvet colour like sable fur, dotted with stars; the lights of Chicago at night blur all but the most brilliant, in a red glare. Overhead, a long line of planes was suspended over the lake; they waited their turn to land at O'Hare, a string of sparkling brooches, set with rubies and emeralds.

On the horizon, now faintly lit, there would be a glow, a whisper; the first, pale light of dawn, dusky and blue, like the edge of a lace collar, ruffling in the gleam of a red flame. As the light mounted, I would be on the Drive heading south, and the scattered clouds would reveal themselves, slowly and cautiously, shy, timid creatures of the forest emerging onto the plains. Their colours were dark and mysterious; their shapes were rounded and full; I could count them as I drove southeast, around the curve of Lake Michigan, where the road hurries through the steel-towns of Indiana.

As the road widened, and turned east once more, the light would mount high, high upon the sky, and all the world would be cast in a warm, rosy pink, like the colour of a fine rosé champagne, blushing with gold. On certain days, the wine might be a non-vintage blend, but the light was still welcome, and admired from my truck; when the light was *saignée*, I would pull to the roadside, and exclaim at its beauty. The clouds would change and their undersides would glow a deep crimson, their crests would shimmer with gold as the sun raised its head far, far to the east. The clouds would move slowly, passing over the road as I drove; they were not rain-clouds; I did not fear them.

As the road turned north, past Michigan City and La Porte, the sun would lift up suddenly, and the light would spill across the high, green cuttings, piercing through the pine forests, falling upon the asphalt; the day had come. As one topped the hill, the light would be green and gold, full of the promise of the day, I would see ahead of me the signs for Michigan, I had come home, again.

The clouds of Michigan, as one is driving up, are unlike any I have seen elsewhere; it is the bend of the sky and the fashion of the earth, it is unique to the northern country. The clouds are not rounded, like the colossal puffballs of cotton wool I admired in South Dakota, nor like the wide, spreading swaths of tulle common to the North Shore; they are piled high, upon a flat, horizontal base, like a very large scoop of white, vanilla-flavoured ice cream upon a glass table.

The clouds remain at a fixed height; they do not vary from it. One is aware of their position; when the road rises up, one feels close enough to touch them; they are directly overhead. The clouds remain, and create a ceiling, a dimension to the sky, tangible, and real; it is a demarcation of light and colour upon a blue canvas.

There is one effect in Michigan I have always observed, whether I have gone south to Chicago, or north to Charlevoix. The weather and its patterns have changed, usually for the better, as I have passed through Grand Rapids; it is the middle dimension of my drive in both directions. I have been told there is a change to the land, an uprising of the hills, which creates an escarpment, a broad, wide buffer against the prevailing winds; the weather is thus affected, and is manifested.

There have been many journeys north under cloudy, rainy skies, which I did not enjoy; I do not like the rain. Yet as I drove through the early morning of palest grey, a faint, lavender gleam would rise, as the road passed Benton Harbour, up through South Haven and Saugatuck; it was the promise of sunlight, and the clouds would drift away. When I rounded the great, sweeping curves that fall down, down into the Grand River Valley, the city would spread before me, and the sun would be invisible in the golden mist. I could not stop, I could not linger; Charlevoix called to me, and I hurried past; the skies were clear, and the light was full, the long miles lay ahead of me. I was on my way, and the metre ticked steadily; I was going home.

Holy Mary, Mother of God
Pray for us sinners,
Now, and at the hour of our death.

A Death in the Family

However we may choose, the will of God moves us in ways we do not understand; the track goes running away before us; in the light of our own faith, we can neither see its end nor comprehend its turning. At times, there are those paths that will join it, however briefly, and this is purposeful, there are blessings to be shared by both parties. In these moments, one realises the blessing of one's own presence; it has been bestowed upon another, and has been blessed; we have been moved by the hands of God. A gift like this is received hungrily; it is a spiritual manna. Yet we, whose presence is that heavenly gift, are unaware, we are focussed solely upon our friends, not ourselves.

In Aslan's Country

When I first read *The Chronicles of Narnia* by CS Lewis, I was nine or ten years old; my parents presented me with a handsome boxed set for my birthday. I still have the set; the box has vanished. The book covers are a hallmark of Pop Art graphic design; the four Pevensie children, in their rich fur coats, display a striking resemblance to the Beatles, on the cover of *Yellow Submarine*.

Others have listed *The Lord of the Rings* as their favourite mediaeval fantasy, and I read these later, when I was eleven or twelve; I began with *The Hobbit* and never looked back. The world of Middle-Earth as imagined by Tolkien was rich and fully realised, bursting with characters, songs, voices, and languages in a dramatically complex setting. It presented its own mythologies, legends, and histories; it was complete, a realm unto itself. It has been suggested that Tolkien envisioned Middle-Earth as a version of English pre-history, a time lost to us; his gift for languages reveals much of his knowledge.

Narnia, however, as conceived by CS Lewis, was different; a lighter offering that rose higher in the pan; it is full of the air and the light and the morning breezes on the wooded hills; it is a realm of the mind, not of the earth. I have often wondered why Lewis' other fictions failed to resound; he did not lack talent. The realms of *The Space Trilogy* were heavy and cumbersome, difficult to navigate, dark and foreboding; I felt the story too rigid, immutable, to be enlivened with perception. The world of Narnia moves among us, it is not a permanent, fixed place. We may go there, or attempt to do so, but from it, we may not necessarily return. Were I to receive an invitation, I should accept immediately. I should not think over it, I should not regret my decision; I should not look back.

The geography of Narnia is vague and unfinished; there are only brief descriptions and no maps. This is a valuable omission; most writers of fiction are meticulous about these details. They arrange wide, complex charts of rivers and mountains, valleys and plains, with their own names. It is not so in Narnia; the landscape is simply defined, with only a few geographies to learn. I myself could draw it up in an instant; it is as clear to me now as in my youth.

The peoples of Narnia are neither wholly good nor bad; they are not perfect; they make their own mistakes and must pay for them. Some of them are misunderstood, but not evil, and all are afforded redemption; this is a tenet of the Christian faith, upon which all interpretation of Lewis' work must depend. There are those characters that are truly evil; one may consider the trousered Ape, Shift, in *The Last Battle*. I will not dwell on his symbolism; that is not my purpose. Yet even in this book, there are those who are saved at the final moment, who have come to Aslan of their own will, seeking for truth. One of these is a young Calormene soldier, seeking the knowledge of good and evil. His name is Emeth; it is the Hebrew word for *truth*. I like him very much; I have found in his character many similarities to my own.

In many of the books, we are afforded a glimpse into the world that is Aslan's Country; it is removed from the plane of the Narnian realm, and not everyone has seen it. All have heard of it; in *The Silver Chair*, Eustace Scrubb and Jill Pole travel through its gardens. It is a beautiful place, an enchanted, tranquil paradise, everything is perfect, and no darkness mars any feature. One can easily imagine it as the proverbial garden from which we have all been exiled, and to which we will all return. Perhaps it is some feature of that original garden we seek to capture within our own inventions, for we are all gardeners; we are those creators of a world in which perfection is bound.

The Silver Chair features one of my favourite characters, King Caspian, properly styled Caspian X, King of Narnia, Lord of Cair Paravel, and Emperor of the Lone Islands. His death at the end of the book is a sad event, much has happened during his reign, and we have met him in many stories.

However, Caspian does not remain dead; he reappears in the enchanted garden of Aslan's Country. There, his body and his spirit are renewed in the waters of a clear, swiftly flowing stream, tinctured by a drop of Aslan's blood. He awakens, and is taken into Paradise with Aslan; he has been restored to his youth and his vigour, and is afforded a glimpse of our world, at his request. However, he does not stay in it for very long; his spirit departs from it, and he has gone beyond the wall from us; he has remained in that garden, from which we have been exiled.

Landscape, With Figures

When one reads a story, and is captured by it, one walks through its landscape with the characters: we hear their voices, we read their thoughts, and we comprehend their actions. We fashion ourselves into eavesdroppers, stalking upon the page.

The characters do not recognise us, their stories occur outside our existence, yet we know them intimately and consider them friends; they are realities that breathe, speak, and think, sentient beings possessed of voices, bodies, and souls. No matter how many times we read of their adventures, they are never the same, they grow as we grow; they live as we live.

When we die, we are mourned, yet the world does not stop; the motions of our lives propel us, and we continue to grow, to think, and to expand. We remember the person who has gone, and we are saddened. We will see him again, but that day is far in the distance.

A fictional character, however, is possessed of his own life and his own permanence. He cannot be easily turned aside; he is there on the page. We carry our eyes to the next word, we look for the rest of the story; we are impressed into his fabric.

I cannot give a definitive answer, how the death of a fictional character should affect me. I do not think it a matter of ego, other issues may present themselves; I am not the character, despite any correspondence of the self. I am saddened; the effect of it has captured my thought. How strange it is that a work of fiction should resound within our psyche, that we should feel emptiness at its passing? It is only a collection of words on a paper, bound up in leather, a gift for the mind.

    I have sometimes wondered how I should die, and leave this earth, for each day is numbered and we cannot predict its termination. In the Christian faith, this is a moment of rejoicing, for we shall then be announced to God. Will I awaken in a place like Aslan's Country, lush and fertile, high on the great mountain of the world? Will God greet me personally, as He is, or will I recognise Him in some other costume? It may be a rare blessing to see God as the Lion of Judah, for this is a Christian allegory; yet in the end, it will have been enough, to see Him.

Frei lebt wer sterben Kann

I had friends near Charlevoix, two men who had been together for many years. They were older, caring, considerate persons, whom I often visited. We would often go out to paint and draw in the rolling fields and woodlands outside their home; there were wide, sweeping views to the west, over Lake Charlevoix. Jeffrey, the older and therefore the more serious, cared for his mother in the house; she was very ill. He told me she might go at any moment, and he had determined her last days should be comfortable. With Francis, his partner, they often invited me to join them at painting, to capture the landscape, *en plein air*. He painted with watercolours, which I could not abide; I only used oils, as I had been trained, in Paris.

"What is the difference?" he asked me.

"Watercolours are for art students in Italy," I said. "Oils are for serious painters, who do things properly."

"I am not a serious painter."

"But, I am."

"I thought you were an architect."

"I am also a serious painter."

We had a mutual friend, Paul, who pretended to use acrylics, which I found abominable. He would present his canvasses to me, heavily covered with paint, lacking in form, structure, or technique. There was no depth, no transparency, the colours masked, instead of enhanced. I could not see into his paintings, they were flat, like the walls of a badly constructed house. Paul would not listen; he was, and remained, strictly an amateur. Francis, however, maintained some rudiments of technique, and his watercolours presented small, careful glimpses into his mind. I did not care for his art, but I respected him; he was an honest painter.

Jeffrey's mother was dying, propped up in a vast bed, looking out towards the lawns and the gardens, with the trees beyond. I wonder if she was aware, when she was brought there, and while she remained, that she must die there, tended carefully and attentively, with the long, drawn-out days, waiting for the end. Did the trails of her thought abandon her, or had she already departed, her body remaining in mute witness?

I wonder at the human fear of death, if it is truly a thing to be feared. The ancients did not fear it, nor do many cultures around the world; to them it is a doorway, a passage from one existence to the other. According to their beliefs, when one dies from this world, one is born into another. Do we then die from another world, when we are born into this one? In our rejoicings upon the birth of a child, is there another plane of existence, where its loss is mourned?

I do not think it foolish to fear a horrible death, who should depart in this manner? There are those who die in horrible accidents, their bodies torn and bloodied, or from wasting illnesses; I should not wish to have done like this. I prefer to go peacefully in my sleep, smiling, but if not, then to go quickly, painlessly, without knowledge of it, until I should open my eyes to the Light, when I stand before the presence of God. Yet we cannot know when this miracle should occur; we are not appointed the hour of our passage, and the boatman's fee has not yet been purchased, but must still be redeemed.

Nor can we know what force, in the face of death, impels others to gather around us. They do not know why they have been called, or for what purpose, but they are there. Within the comfort of their presence, we are able to leave, and at the last, to say goodbye.

Jeffrey and Francis had desired for some time to host a dinner-party before the end of summer. One difficulty or another had arisen, but now we were gathering, as the days began to shorten and the leaves were turning gold. Their cottage in Bay Shore commanded a view across the water towards Harbour Springs, high on the bluffs. It sat squarely beneath the towering old trees, mainly white pines and hemlocks, part of the old forests left by the logging crews. There are wooden steps down to the beach; mostly shingle, tumbled about with larger boulders; many birds nest here, and one may find old fish-bones in the brackish pools.

As the Saturday approached, Francis rang up. "Jeffrey's mother is very ill," he said, "And she may go at any moment."

"Oh dear," I said, "I am so sorry. Perhaps it would be best to reschedule our dinner?"

"Oh no," he said, "Jeffrey's looking forward to seeing you, Paul, and Dickie; he's been planning this all week."

Dickie was Paul's life-partner.

"Well, then I will see you on Saturday," I said, ringing off. "Is there anything I can bring?"

"Oh no," he said. "We will have everything ready."

I set out a bottle of wine nonetheless, and wrapped it in a pretty cloth; it was not appropriate for hamburgers and hot dogs, but I did not drink beer.

Saturday morning, Paul rang up while I was having my coffee. "Are you going to Bay Shore tonight?" he asked me. "I do not feel I should go, with Jeffrey's mother being so ill."

"I know," I said. "I do not feel like going either, but I feel we must, that we should be there."

"Yes," he said. "I feel I should be there, but I don't want to be there."

"This is all very strange," I said, "I don't want to go, out of respect for Mrs Gardner, but I feel I must, out of respect for Jeffrey."

"Have you had any word?" he asked me.

"No," I said, "I will ring up Francis and ask him."

Jeffrey answered the telephone.

"Yes," he said, "We are still on for tonight. We are looking forward to having you."

"Oh, Jeffrey," I said, "Are you certain? I do not wish to intrude on your privacy, not now. How is your mother?"

"She is as well as can be expected, I have made her comfortable. But it will be any moment now."

"Jeffrey, we can reschedule, I don't want to take you away from your mother at this time."

"Sanjay," he said, "It would be good for us to get away, and to be with our friends; we've waited all summer to have you to the cottage, and I will manage."

"Very well," I said, "Then I will see you this evening."

When I rang Paul, he was surprised, but told me, "Yes, then we will be there, I'll see you tonight."

Just before I left the house, another friend called and asked; could I help her? I could not refuse, it was not in me; I went to her house. I was delayed, and delayed again, while I looked at my wristwatch around the corner, I could not leave.

I could not ring Paul; I was frantic to get away; I could not reach Jeffrey or Francis.

Finally, I left my friend's house, south of the Castle, and roared my truck north, praying I should gain the bridge. If there were boats coming in, I might be delayed; the summer was over, but the ferryboats were still running.

There were no boats that evening, I crossed without incident, and called Paul from my truck. "I'm running horribly late," I said, "Where are you?"

"We are late, too," he said, "We are just now leaving."

"Oh, God," I said, "Have you spoken with Jeffrey or Francis? They aren't answering the telephone."

The road was busy; I drove behind someone cruising below the limit. I could not pass him; there were oncoming cars. I could not go faster; I was very late.

Even as I drove, swearing loudly, a message came to me, that this was all of a purpose; this was intended. The fashion of the evening had begun to take its shape before me; the curtain had been lifted upon the stage, and the lights now gleamed upon the wooden boards. The movements of six different persons had been plotted; the pieces were moving; the *scène* was in motion and we all had our parts to perform.

I pulled up to the cottage; Paul, Dickie, Jeffrey, and Francis were waiting; they had waited dinner. The moon was rising and the early stars winked over Bay Harbour. The wind was down; there was no breeze. The air was cold; I shivered, and reached for my sweater.

Jeffrey was thrilled, he came to my truck to welcome me, "I'm so glad you're here, it's so wonderful to see you."

Jeffrey and Francis had a small dog, a black terrier that was normally well behaved; he was running to the car, scrabbling at the doors, and then returning to the cottage. His manner was frantic, hurried, and impatient. Jeffrey was very puzzled, "He's never acted like that before; he was running in and out of my mother's room all day today."

The coals would not ignite; there was no starter fluid. Paul and I drove into town to get some; the evening was unreal, it was intangible; we could not grasp its meaning. We sat in the truck as she moved slowly down the lane; the light was grey around us, and we could not find words to speak. I looked at Paul, and asked, "Is this really happening?"

"Yes," he said, "It is really happening."

"But…*what*…is happening? *Why are we here?*"

"I don't know," he said. "I think you are right, that we are meant to be here, this has all been planned."

We watched the other customers engaging in loud conversations, with their tattoos, their beer, and their cigarettes; it was not real, it did not exist, it was not a part of our world; we did not know them.

The meat sizzled and sputtered on the grille, and we all gathered, none of us had eaten, and we all commented upon it.

We looked at each other's faces; we were waiting, the movements of the evening carried us forward, a *tableau vivant* around a charcoal fire; we continued our conversations and we had no other thoughts. The bell had not sounded; class was not yet dismissed, and we waited for the signal to come.

When the food was ready, we carried it to the table, covered in its gay, red-chequered cloth; there were houseflies suddenly, swarming everywhere. The table was black with them, they covered the lanterns like Spanish lace from a very old mantilla; they could not be brushed away.

Paul leaned in close, and whispered, "I don't like this."

"We can't leave now, Paul."

"No, I meant the flies."

"What do you mean?"

"The last time I saw flies like this, it was the night my father died."

"Keep your voice down…!"

Jeffrey and Francis came to the table, with platters of hot food; the steam rose into the air; as they seated themselves, the telephone suddenly rang. I looked at Paul; we knew that Mrs Gardner had died with the sound of the telephone, and its harsh ringing was a pull upon the brake, jerking us into another world. The train had stopped; we had been jolted awake, but the evening was not over, we had not yet reached the station.

Jeffrey and Francis left; they had driven over in separate cars. The three of us stayed: Paul, Dickie, and myself; we ate our cold dinners in the empty room. Jeffrey begged us to stay and to eat something, saying, "We'll be back later, please, eat something, have a few drinks, we will be back."

I did not think they would return, but I could not leave; the current continued to buffet me against the invisible rocks, and the shoals veered beneath us as we steered through the mist.

In the bare, empty dining room, we found napkin rings, which Francis had created himself; they each bore our names, painted in bright, gay colours and spelled correctly. There was a cake under a glass dome, which we did not touch, and coffee, which we drank, hot and black. We ate silently and quickly, not speaking; Dickie washed up. I badly needed a drink, but could not find any brandy, or even sherry, in the house.

We were locking the front door, with keys in our hands, when headlights crept down the street, and Francis appeared out of the darkness, very pale and very tired; he looked like an old man, I thought, and we helped him to his chair.

He offered us some cake; he had baked it that morning for our party; we could not refuse. Jeffrey was doing well, he said, as well as might be expected; he was making arrangements, and he had called his son in Memphis. There would be no service; our presence was not needed beyond the evening. In the gleam of the lanterns, his face was pale and drained of colour; he looked very tired. After Paul and Dickie left, I remained there sitting with him; after several long minutes, he began to weep silently, the tears running down his tired, grey face, and he continued to eat his slice of cake, that he had baked that morning, for our party. I handed him a napkin, and he unwound it from its painted, wooden ring, and looked at it closely.

"You know," he said to me, "I painted a set of these for Mrs Gardner, for her birthday, after I met Jeffrey."

"That was very kind of you," I said, "I'm sure she appreciated it, very much."

"We've been together for nearly twenty years," he said, "And he has always been the strong one."

"No," I said, "I do not think that is true."

He looked at me closely.

"Yes," he said, finally, "I think you are right."

Out flung the web, and floated wide,
The mirror crack'd from side to side,
The curse is come upon me, cried
The Lady of Shalott.

      Alfred, Lord Tennyson

THE LADY OF SHALOTT

A face, looked upon for the last time, does not always present a visage that one should remember. One is aware of a door shutting, in the silence between you; it is a terrible, final sound. Do we see the face as it was, in that final moment, or do we see it as we have loved or imagined it, as it once might have been?

I once looked upon such a face, a woman's, which I had once known but did not now recognise. The stone had been inverted, and the creeping things swarmed out, a hundred spitting vipers coiling about her head. Like a warrior before the Gorgon, I was paralysed; I could not speak, or move, but only stare in horror. Its lips moved and its mouth spoke words, dripping with venom; they were hateful and angry; I did not comprehend them; they were a scythe decimating the tall grasses, uncaring of the budding stalks.

The Moments of Happiness

A detachment takes hold of us, in moments of joy or sorrow. In joyfulness, we are carried along, swept by a great wave of feeling, lifting us up from the earth. Where it shall crest, we do not know, we have lost our direction and do not look down. We take hold of the moment, grasping at it firmly, so we may remember the feeling; we have been blessed.

There are moments I do not remember; there are others, which remain. One of these was the afternoon when I received the official notice of my licensure; I was finally a true architect, with the paper to prove it. I do not remember what I said, if I wept or cheered, but I do remember marching briskly around my sitting room, while Elgar's *Pomp and Circumstance* played at full volume on my stereo. My neighbours flooded the apartment, and we drank a toast to my achievement; they had monitored my anxiety for weeks, and my long nights of study for the exam; they were all delighted and happy in my achievement. Later, when they had all left, I drank another, and the bottle remained in its silver bucket, as the pale liquid foamed gently in the glass; I drank more champagne, ate some strawberries, and held the paper in my hand; I looked at it for a long time.

I remember another, paralysing happiness, on Sheridan Road in Lake Forest; I was coming up from a client's house, and turned off to Lansdowne. I did not understand what I felt, only that I was entering into another world, in which I might make an impression of beauty and composition, to be remembered someday, when I was much older, and perhaps wiser.

There was yet another moment, when I had left Chicago; I was on the road to Michigan, and Palmer rang up on my mobile.

"Where are you?" he asked. "Are you on your way?"

"I am in the truck," I told him, "I am still in Indiana."

"How are things going?"

"One delay after another," I told him, "It has been a very long day, and I am very tired."

"Still," he said, "You are on your way."

The road, which had been running flat for several miles, emerged out of the trees, passing between steep, green cuttings and under a bridge; it began to slope upwards. At the top of the rise, I saw a bright blue placard with a large letter 'M'.

"Don't hang up," I said, "I want…."

"What do you want?" he asked me.

I passed under the sign, and was in Michigan; I was home, and the journey of that day, with many long, tiring miles to go, was behind me; I was in Michigan.

"I've just crossed the state line, into Michigan," I said. "I'm coming home."

Leave Right Now

I have often asked myself, how I did not see the end coming, until the strength of it was full wrought and wielded against me; it came suddenly, and the beginning of it preceded the end by only a few weeks. For a passenger waiting on a platform in the early morning, the lights of the approaching train give no substance to its mass; there is only the light, gleaming through the dark mist. It holds you fast, you stare into its beam, it is beautiful, but it will sweep you away in its grip, and you will be taken with it, removed from the plane of the earth to land in another time, and another place. When the train pulls into the grey station, in the morning that is still dark, you awaken; you find yourself surrounded by persons you do not know.

The people who ended my life in Michigan did not speak to me directly of their purpose; they moved among the shadows of the trees; they whispered strange words to others, and took a careful account of my presence in their calculations. The tiniest stone can make a great rumbling, a gathering of stones sliding down the mountain. The rolling hordes devour all as they gather force and momentum; the avalanche cannot be stopped. When the great cloud has lifted, the damage may be assessed; there is death and destruction, beneath the splintered rocks. I did not heed the warning signs; they had been visible, but I had not seen them. The clues were there, the fractures beneath the smiles, and the anger and hatred simmered beneath our morning coffees. I should have watched, listened, and learned, but I continued to dance, like a wild, possessed creature; my revels in the woods took hold of me, and I could not be gainsaid.

The piper's tune could not be mastered; I had not learned all its intricate steps, even though I had performed many. There were many more movements within the dance, with different partners; I did not know them all. The tune had changed, and a different air hastened its breath within the embouchure. The currents tremble beneath the surface, in the dark places where daylight does not penetrate. In the gloomy depths, strange creatures come forth; they are silent, stalking their prey with great patience; they know the moment to strike will come, and they will not hesitate. Their jaws close upon their victim, floating happily upon the surface, and he is swallowed up by them; they return with their prey to the depths, and begin to feed.

Trio in E-Flat Major

It is a difficult task, to become, and to remain, an intimate friendship with a man, especially if that man has a lover. It becomes even more difficult when that lover moves to ensure the downfall of your intimacy; he is threatened by your presence, and his jealous and his anger will find ways to draw blood. You yourself have done nothing; you have only been a friend to him, yet he will put forth an extraordinary effort to poison the hearts and minds of those around you.

I did not appreciate the lover's movements until our last meeting, when I looked into his eyes across the kitchen table. There was a cold, steady glare, void but of a burning anger, and I knew he hated me. He hated me with every fibre of his being; he had hated me from the first day of our friendship; he had hated me from the time of my arrival; he hated me now.

The warning bell had sounded; his hand had moved upon the board, and he now rejoiced in the destruction he had wrought; the pieces flew about the room. The shadows that had passed behind me in the night and the currents of blackness that filled our conversations, all became clear to me then; he had engineered them; he had moved them around me, so that I might not see his hand in those actions.

It had not occurred to me that such emotions could be aroused with such fury, or what I might have done to avoid them.

They were not of my making; I did not create them. Yet, my presence had been the spark to the tinder, and the blazing anger, which had once simmered beneath the black logs, now blazed fiercely, and consumed all in its path.

The marriage of two men is secured only by their agreement; there is no legal statute to hold them. Palmer's marriage was not secure; it was an arrangement, like many others, and thus it was not held fast to any form or shape. I had not contributed to their marriage, nor had I sought to dissolve it; my friend was not my lover, nor had I desired him to be.

Tony, his lover, would not have agreed; he despised my presence, and hated it; he spoke pleasantly enough to me in his house, but when I left it, his voice changed. Palmer would tell me of his conversations with Tony after our evenings together, and his words troubled me, but I did not comprehend their purpose or their intention.

He had moved stealthily, silently, through the trees like a sly creature seeking his prey, who danced with his lover on the moonbeams. That we might have been only dancing did not occur to him; the Achilles heel was bared, and he struck. The blade of his knife flashed swiftly, the blood stained the white petals; they lay dying upon the leaves. Palmer often discussed our friendship; he compared it to his marriage, and spoke of it as a union, which I did not like. He once asked me, during a weekend trip to Grand Rapids, "Sanjay, I think we would make a good marriage."

"No, Palmer, I do not think so."

"Why not?"

"Well, for one thing, you're married to someone else."

"But...." He paused. "What if I were not married?"

"I do not think we should be good partners."

"Why not?"

"I'm not in love with you, to begin with."

"But you love me, don't you?"

"Of course I love you, as a friend. A very dear friend, I might add, whom I love very much."

"But since we are such good friends, it might be a good thing for us to be together."

"No, I do not think so."

It may be supposed I felt some empathy with him, for who would not do so, if their own marriage were threatened? I understood the possession of his partner; I had felt the same emotions, when other men had spoken to my husband, and I had clenched my fists, in anger, when they had done so. I held myself, however, blameless in the pattern of Palmer's marriage; I had done nothing; I knew my position within his household; I had made no sign, nor had I spoken any word, which should have indicated to him that my motives were selfish.

Palmer might have done something, but he did not. He let the voices of others speak, and guide all his decisions; he did nothing to stop them, but let them turn where they might, and take what they desired. He allowed it, and did not stop; he did not consult with me, nor consider our friendship, but agreed to all that was determined; it came upon me, like a thief in the night, and I was powerless against its fury and its strength.

I recall our last interview, in his house on Mitchell Street; he was living there alone. Tony was not there; I would not have entered, had he been present. He said words to me, which I do not now remember, and which I cannot forget; they were the words of blind jealousy and hatred, filtered through the mouthpiece of another human; they were not his words. The persons who had placed them in his mouth were nowhere to be seen; as in all their operations, they receded into the background, and the pale green walls of his sitting room were like the walls of a cavern of ice, a cold, bare fortress of solitude, in which he dwelt, and from which he did not depart.

I looked at my friend, at a person I had once thought was my friend, and I saw not a man, but a child. A child, dressed in his father's clothes, is still a child; he wore pyjamas with feet on them. It was an appropriate costume; he could not wear a man's suit of clothes. He behaved like a child, he thought like a child, he spake like a child, and the time for him to put away childish things

371

had not yet come. Like a child, he discarded his toys when they no longer pleased him; the house was littered with his refuse; there were rejected articles throughout, purchased but never used.

He said to me that we should still be friends, but my life in Michigan was over, and with it our friendship; I did not think something so easily discarded might be picked up again. I did not know what to say to him; the suddenness and finality of it weighed heavily upon me, and our last conversation was only a few days before I departed; he did not come to say goodbye, or to assist me in my packing.

Our friendship had been bought at a price, which I had not questioned, I knew its value; I had only been grateful for the purchase. It had now been sold and the value refunded; the balance sheet, however, was negligible; it was not worth the cost of its printing.

Adjö Min Vän

On the last night, as I sat alone on the bare, empty porch, the red fox came, and then returned east; I did not see him again. In the twilight, his red fur had darkened to the colour of dried blood, and it was not easily discernible.

In the morning, the sky was grey and there was no sun; the clouds remained over the town and a light rain fell. It was a cold, damp drizzle, common to late April, which shivered the bones; I reached for a sweater, and put it on, under my jacket. I could not find my scarves, and remembered I had packed them; my gloves were all packed, too.

My truck was loaded; I carried out my bags and my case, and the last bits of trash, and swept up the floor one last time. I walked through the silent, echoing rooms; the doors were all open, and the closed blinds cast a grey light; all was silent and waiting. The house had retreated; it had removed itself from my life; it was no longer mine.

I sat for a moment, in the big room with its white walls and its white furniture, and said goodbye to my friends there; they were not coming with me. The bowl of leaves and grasses, the gifts of the Elder Children, I left on the mantelpiece; it did not belong anywhere else; it remained. Paul and George looked at me from the kitchen, and I could not return their gaze; I was leaving them to keep the house in order. I will send for you, I told them, when I shall once more have a house of my own, and I shall need your assistance; they said nothing, but bowed their heads; I saw their tears, but could not offer them any comfort.

I stood at the door, and looked to the eastern sky; the clouds were gathering in dark masses, promising more rain. There was still no sun and the clouds did not part; no sudden ray of light shone upon me; I was alone.

Adjö min vän, I said, goodbye my friend, who is not my friend. I am releasing you, I am casting you into the air like an unfettered hawk, and I will not see you again. The words arched themselves skywards, carrying their message; I saw them fall to the earth in a dark clearing over a red door.

Adjö min vän, I said again, goodbye my friend. What is done is done, and what is unfinished cannot now be completed. The tracks of our lives have run together for many miles, but now we are parting. In the green grass, the woods draw up before us, and each path must go on alone, to the left or to the right. The leaves under the trees are golden, and the shadows are green and dark, but the track is clear.

Adjö min vän, I release you, my friend, and there is no anger, for I have not failed. There is no sadness, for nothing has been lost, you have thrown it away with your own hands.

I turned up the drive, and headed out to the street; I stopped my truck, there was something lying on the asphalt. I got down for a moment, then sat on the running board.

The red fox was dead; he had been struck by a vehicle in the night, and flung into the gutter; his body was flattened in the centre, there were tyre marks upon his fur. His mouth was drawn back in a terrible smile, but his eyes were closed, and I was thankful he could not see me.

I wondered if he had been killed instantly, or had crawled, in terrible pain, to the side of the road where he had died. Did he choose to die in the night, so I might see him before I left? Did the currents of his mind suggest that this was, after all, a better ending, than what I might have imagined?

I looked at him for a long time, and thought this must now be our ending; our travels had brought us here. I wondered if I should feel pity for him, or jealousy, he had gone to another place, where the light was golden upon the meadow grasses. Sinté-Hla, my Brother, I am calling you; we will play together in the fields of the Lord. Come, take my hand, that I might be glad of thy strength; thy rod and thy staff, they comfort me. Yea, though I walk through the valley of the shadow of death, I shall fear no evil, for though art with me. I climbed back into my truck, and drove away through the town.

When I reached Cadillac, the skies cleared, and the sun shone brightly; a light wind came up from the west. I reached for my telephone to call my friend, as I had always done, but I could not do so now; I set it back in its cradle, and continued.

THE END

AFTERWORD

Love is a strange concept; it an emotion at once reviled, enthused, pursued and invoked. In the many conversations about my life in Charlevoix, the word was used, and often: I loved northern Michigan.

It is not always easy to outline, and thus define, the feelings that enrapture one's heart and one's mind; the contemplation of a sunrise over Round Lake, or the mist, rising along the Kalkaska Road early in the morning. There are starlings, swooping and whirling in a great cloud over the fields, and white-tailed deer, standing in the trees, lifting their heads to look at you.

There is heat, and there is cold; there is darkness, and there is light. When I look back across the pages of this book, and the passages of my life, I see many things; I close my eyes, and those days report to me again, as they once were.

I think of it even now, although I am far away, and in the winter, my thoughts return to the north country, for it was very beautiful beneath its white mantle. The cold, silent air hisses in your breath, and the fog rises around your throat; you reach for your scarf, wrap it around your neck, and pull on your heavy gloves. There is a sudden glint of light in the corner; you turn your head, and a ray of sunlight pierces the gloom; the morning has come.

The skies are clearing; they are a brilliant, luminous blue, and the shadows recede beneath the advancing day; the world is a strange, abstracted piece of Chinese porcelain, and I am driving north, in Jane, to the ski-hills. The truck is warm and comfortable; there is piping-hot chocolate in my thermos, and the floor mats are wet and muddy; it does not matter. It is a fine day in northern Michigan, I am going to ski, and when I have finished, I shall have come home.

NOTES

INTRODUCTION

1. *"For those whom I have not met...."* An excerpt from my forthcoming book *Exodus: The Collected Poems*.
2. *"But that the dread of something after death...."* William Shakespeare; *Hamlet*, Act III, Scene 1.
3. *"Where I shall find thee...."* An excerpt from my forthcoming book *Exodus: The Collected Poems*.
4. The Fates, or Moirai, in Greek mythology, were three beings, incarnated as old women, who determined the course of one's life: one spun the thread of life on her spindle, one measured the length of it, and one cut it with her shears.
5. *The Land of Counterpane*; Robert Louis Stevenson; *A Child's Garden of Verses*; 1885; publisher unknown.

820 PETOSKEY AVENUE

6. *"Look, before you*
   There are petals, on the white linen
   Hold them, in your hands
   For their beauty, which has fallen
   And their perfume, like a veil
   Still lingers in the air
   You cannot hold it
   Yet there they float, and the scent remains." An excerpt from my forthcoming book *Exodus: The Collected Poems*.
7. The chapter title is taken from the street address of my house in Charlevoix; it remains one of my favourite residences.
8. *Centrum mundi*, in Latin, means "The Centre of the World."
9. In the legendarium of Middle-Earth, *Lothlórien* is the realm of Celeborn and Galadriel; *The Lord of the Rings*; JRR Tolkien; 1954; George Allen & Unwin; London.
10. *Laurelindórenan* is another name for Lothlórien; *Unfinished Tales*; JRR Tolkien; 1980; George Allen & Unwin; London.
11. Goldilocks, in case you really needed to know.
12. Josiah Wedgwood, 1730-1795. Potter and founder of the Wedgwood Company, and grandfather to Charles Darwin. Famous for his reproduction of the Portland Vase in 1780, and for his Queen's Ware, produced for Queen Charlotte.
13. The Portland Vase is a famous example of Roman cameo glass artistry, and the inspiration for the Wedgwood corporate logo; dating to approximately AD 25, it is presently on display at the British Museum in London.
14. The Neptune Vase by Baccarat is famous for its pure, ovoid form and contemporary design; notably, it led the way for other modern crystal designs, and propelled others to follow their example.
15. Baccarat Crystal was founded in 1734 by Louis XV of France, and continues its operations to the present day; they are known worldwide for the quality and beauty of their crystal.

16. Browns Lane, Coventry was the main assembly plant for Jaguar Cars from 1951 to 2005; since relocated to Castle Bromwich, Birmingham.
17. Marc, the French name for pomace brandy, is a spirit distilled from the skins, seeds, and stems of wine grapes, after they have been pressed for their juices. *Amazing.*
18. *The Lady and the Unicorn* is a series of six tapestries from the Middle Ages, first popularised by the novelist George Sand; they are considered one of the greatest works of art of the period, and are presently on display at the Musée de Cluny.
19. Ryoan-ji is a Buddhist temple outside Kyoto, Japan; the garden is considered one of the finest examples of *kare-sensui*, or dry landscape gardening. It once featured a *shakkei*, or 'borrowed view' of Mount Hiei.
20. Petoskey Stones are small rocks, about the size and shape of a large egg, composed of fossilised coral; they are usually found in northern Michigan around Little Traverse Bay.
21. *Cursum Perficio*, in Latin, means "I have completed my course; I have run the race." Famously, Marilyn Monroe's home in California had these words over the front door.
22. *Tarva* and *Alambil* are planets in the legendarium of Narnia; *Prince Caspian*; CS Lewis; 1951; Geoffrey Bles; London.
23. *A la meunière* refers to a preparation sautéed in flour and butter; the literal translation is "the miller's wife."
24. Chenin Blanc is a white wine from the Loire Valley; Vouvray and Saumur are its most famous appellations. One of my favourites, and well worth seeking out.
25. Edward VII, 1841-1910; King of England 1901-1910. Eldest son of Queen Victoria; father of King George V. His appetite and zest for life inspired the king-sized bed.
26. Georges Auguste Escoffier, 1846-1935. French chef extraordinaire; considered by many to be the father of modern *haute cuisine*. Dude. *Sweet.*

27. Château d'Yquem, a *Premier Cru Superiéur* from the Sauternes; one of the most famous Bordeaux in the world, and a personal inspiration.
28. In Greek mythology, the chimaera was a strange animal with the body of a lioness, a tail with a snake's head, and a goat's head rising from the centre of its spine.
29. Originally named Sweet Jane, when I replaced her after the accident; however, this was soon shortened to Jane.
30. François-Marie Arouet de Voltaire, 1694-1778. French writer, historian, and philosopher; scourge of Louis XV, confidant of Madame de Pompadour, close friend of Frederick the Great.
31. Sissinghurst Castle, Cranbrook, Kent. Famous for its gardens.
32. Vita Sackville-West, 1892-1962 and her husband, Harold Nicholson, 1886-1968. They purchased Sissinghurst in 1930 and transformed it into one of the premier gardens in England.
33. Ludwig Mies van der Rohe, 1886 – 1969: the Master. Born in Germany, he immigrated to Chicago in 1937. Proponent of the International Style, and founder of the Second Chicago School of Architecture. My hero.
34. Frank Lloyd Wright, 1867-1959: the Rebel. Self-taught, and self-inventing American architect, proponent of the Prairie Style; his influence on modern-day residential architecture cannot be underestimated. An *astonishing* career, and oeuvre.
35. Charles Rennie Mackintosh, 1868 – 1928: the Craftsman. Scottish architect, designer, writer, and artist. His interpretations of the Art Nouveau point the way to Art Moderne, and to the Zen aesthetic. And yes, I am on a first-name basis with each of these men.
36. Nancy Lancaster, 1897 – 1994. American-born English designer, creator of the "English Country House" look. Business partner of John Fowler. Her rooms have inspired much of my own design work.
37. Ditchley Park, Nancy Lancaster's famous house, near Charlbury, during her marriage to Ronnie Tree.

38. Oxfordshire is a county in south-central England, bordering Wiltshire and Gloucestershire; famous for its university, and for its country houses and estates.
39. The Bauhaus School was founded in Weimar in 1919, and remained there until 1925, when it moved to Dessau.
40. The Barcelona Pavilion, 1929, by Ludwig Mies van der Rohe. My favourite building, anywhere.
41. Venetian Festival in Charlevoix is usually held during the third week in July.
42. *The Overture in E-Flat Major*, Opus 49 by Tchaikovsky, is more commonly known as *The 1812 Overture*.
43. "She is charming, distinguished, and elegant." Spoken by The Queen of Transylvania, as portrayed by the Baroness Rothschild. *My Fair Lady*; directed by George Cukor; Warner Brothers; 1964. Really.
44. *The 1812 Overture* is played during Notre Dame football games, during which the students salute the head coach, unless he's doing a very poor job. Believe me, I've been there.
45. *"They have prepared a net for my steps; my soul is bowed down: they have digged a pit before me, into the midst whereof they are fallen themselves."* The Book of Psalms; Chapter 57, Verse 6; King James Bible (Cambridge Edition).
46. In the Greek pantheon, Hephaestus was the blacksmith of Olympus, who forged the thunderbolts for Zeus.
47. In Greek mythology, Antaeus was a demi-god, the son of Poseidon and Gaia, who regained his strength each time his feet touched the earth.

LIGHT, DANCING ON WATER

48. "*Should I be queried....*" Poem fragment by the author.
49. Newton's Laws of Motion; *Philosophiae Naturalis Principia Mathematica*; Sir Isaac Newton; 1687.
50. Carnevale is an annual festival held in Venice every winter, before the start of Lent, and is famous for its elaborate costumes and masks worn during the celebration.
51. "*Un bal masqué où tout cacher....*" Ralph Waldo Emerson, 1803-1882, American essayist and poet.
52. The Piazza San Marco in Venice is heralded as the city's most famous outdoor space, where people come to see, and be seen.
53. The Herberts are a notable Anglo-Welsh family, first knighted in 1461, whose members have held the earldoms of Pembroke, Caernarvon, and Powis for generations.
54. Wilton House, near Salisbury in Wiltshire, is the seat of the Earls of Pembroke, granted to the first Earl in 1544.
55. Highclere Castle, in Hampshire, is the seat of the Earls of Caernarvon, built in 1830.
56. Kundalini, in Hindu philosophy, is often described as a dormant, potential spiritual force residing within the body.
57. *A Moveable Feast*; Ernest Hemingway; 1964; Scribner's; New York.
58. In Greek mythology, the beautiful maiden Psyche spilled a drop of hot oil upon the cheek of the sleeping Eros, which awakened him; he awakened, and, angrily, flew away and banished her from his palace; later, however, he forgave her. This legend became the basis of *Beauty and the Beast*.
59. In the early Christian church, the butterfly was considered symbolic of the rebirth of the soul, in its emergence from its chrysalis in a new form.
60. Savoie is a French *département* in the Rhône-Alpes region in the French Alps; I first learned to ski there.

6101 NORTH SHERIDAN ROAD

61. *"What is real, or is imagined...."* Poem fragment by the author.
62. Again, the chapter title is taken from my last address in Chicago, before my move to Charlevoix.
63. *Sorrow Rides a Fast Horse*; Dorothy Gilman (writing as Dorothy Gilman Butters); 1962; The Ladies Home Journal.
64. *Dispatches from the Edge*; Anderson Cooper; 2006; Harper Collins Publishers; New York.
65. *Istali mashi, kwar mashi, inshallah*, in Arabic, means "May you never be tired; may you never be poor; God willing." A traditional greeting in much of the Muslim world.
66. *"But his wife looked back from behind him, and she became a pillar of salt."* The Book of Genesis; Chapter 19, Verse 26; King James Bible (Cambridge Edition).
67. *"....and, behold, the mountain was full of horses and chariots of fire round about Elisha."* The Second Book of the Kings; Chapter 6, Verse 17; King James Bible (Cambridge Edition).
68. Anne of Cleves, 1515–1557, fourth wife of Henry VIII of England.
69. *The Land That Time Forgot*; Edgar Rice Burroughs; 1924; AC McClurg; Chicago.
70. In July 1540, after the annulment of her marriage to Henry VIII, Anne of Cleves returned her wedding ring to him, with a letter requesting that it be destroyed, as it an object of which she knew "no force or value."
71. In Imperial China, the use of the colour yellow was strictly reserved for the Emperor's robes.
72. *"And as he journeyed, he came near Damascus: and suddenly there shined round about him a light from heaven."* The Acts of the Apostles; Chapter 9, Verse 3; King James Bible (Cambridge Edition).
73. King Henry VIII of England, 1491-1547.
74. Richmond Palace, Thameside, built 1501, demolished 1649.
75. Bletchingley Place House, Surrey.

76. Catherine Howard, 1521-1542, fifth wife of Henry VIII.
77. *Les Quatre Cent Coups*; directed by François Truffaut; Les Film du Carosse; 1959.
78. Patsy Cline, 1932-1963; American country music singer and one of the most acclaimed vocalists of the 20th century.
79. *Crazy*; Willie Nelson; 1961. Famously recorded by Patsy Cline, whose version remains my favourite.
80. *"The sharp edge of a razor is difficult to pass over; thus the wise say the path to Salvation is hard." Katha-Upanishad.*
81. *"That struts and frets his hour upon the stage...."* William Shakespeare; *MacBeth*, Act V, Scene V; 1606.
82. Cassoulet is a rich, slow-cooked casserole originating in Provence, usually containing some combination of pork, goose and duck meat, and white haricot beans.
83. *Vivit Post Funera Virtus*, in Latin, means "Virtue lives beyond the grave." The motto of the Robbins family.
84. *"And he said, Let me go, for the day breaketh. And he said, I will not let thee go, except thou bless me."* The Book of Genesis; Chapter 32, Verse 26; King James Bible (Cambridge Edition).
85. *Send Me An Angel*, performed by Real Life; *Heartland*; 1983; Curb Records.
86. *The Book of Genesis*; Chapter 19, Verses 1-22; King James Bible (Cambridge Edition).
87. *The Gift of the Magi*; O Henry; 1906; New York.
88. *"And after the earthquake a fire; but the LORD was not in the fire: and after the fire a still small voice."* The First Book of the Kings; Chapter 19, Verse 12; King James Bible (Cambridge Edition).
89. The Hill of Tara in County Meath, Ireland, is considered the seat of the High Kings of Ireland.
90. The River Shannon is the longest river in Ireland, running (roughly) north-south from Cuilcagh Mountain to the Limerick estuary.

91. "*Between the pear and the cheese.*" In traditional French luncheons, the appropriate time to discuss business.

THE BEAVER ISLAND BOAT FERRY

92. *"Come, my love, my lover, dance…."* Poem fragment by the author.
93. Charon, in Greek mythology, ferried the dead to the underworld in his boat, for which passage coins were placed upon the closed eyes of the corpse.
94. The River Styx, in Greek mythology, formed the boundary between the earth and the underworld; an oath sworn on its waters could not be broken, even by the gods.
95. *"In Rama was there a voice heard, lamentation, and weeping, and great mourning, Rachel weeping for her children, and would not be comforted, because they are not."* The Gospel of Matthew; Chapter 2, Verse 18; King James Bible (Cambridge Edition).
96. The sword of Damocles, as related by Cicero, is an illustration of power and the dangers inherent in its possession. Damocles, seated on the throne of Dionysus II, looked up to see a sharp sword suspended above him.
97. Lúthien Tinúviel, Elf-Princess of the Elven kingdom of Doriath; *The Silmarillion*; JRR Tolkien; 1977; George Allen & Unwin; London.
98. Beren Erchamion, Man of the House of Bëor, in Dorthonion; *The Silmarillion*; JRR Tolkien; 1977; George Allen & Unwin; London.
99. *Esgalduin* is a river in Doriath; in the legendarium of Middle-Earth, one of the Elven realms of the First Age.
100. The Field of the Cloth of Gold takes its name from the meeting in 1520 near Calais, when Henry VIII of England met Francis I of France; their tents and pavilions were woven of an enormous quantity of gold cloth.
101. *The Secret Garden*; Frances Hodgson Burnett; Frederick A Stokes; 1911.

102. *Mouvement* is a false cognate; in this context, it means a sense of motion, not motion itself. The eye wanders, and does not remain still, nor does the observer stand in one place, but walks around the room.
103. *Ode an die Freude*; Friedrich Schiller; 1785.
104. The Aragon Ballroom in Chicago, was built in 1926 on Lawrence Avenue, features a vaguely Moorish interior. In its heyday, it was a very popular, very beautiful venue, but it has declined since the 1950s.
105. *The Mishomis Book: The Voice of the Ojibway*; Edward Benton-Banai; Red School House; 1988; Minneapolis.
106. A wild man, half-daemon, half-human, imprisoned by the magician Prospero, he is nonetheless freed by him at the end of the play. *The Tempest*; William Shakespeare; 1610-11.
107. *La Belle au Bois Dormant* is the French name for Sleeping Beauty, and is associated with the Chateau de Rigny-Ussé in the Loire Valley; I have been there, often.
108. Brighid is the Celtic Goddess of inspiration and healing; later associated with Saint Bridget of Ireland.
109. *"Make haste, my beloved, and be thou like to a roe or to a young hart upon the mountains of spices."* The Song of Solomon; Chapter 8, Verse 14; King James Bible (Cambridge Edition).
110. The Blue Grotto, on Capri, is famous for its intense, blue-lit waters; the colour is impossible to describe with any degree of accuracy. It is very, very beautiful.
111. Tiberius Julius Caesar Augustus, 42BC-37AD. Second Emperor of the Roman Empire.
112. *The Way of All Flesh*; Samuel Butler; 1903; Grant Richards.
113. *Negotium est factum*, in Latin, means "My work is finished."

GHOSTS OF BOYNE CITY

114. *"In that realm, between heaven and earth...."* Poem fragment by the author.
115. The Great Chicago Fire of 1871 is commemorated by the second star in the city's flag.
116. *All About Eve*; directed by Joseph L Mankiewicz; 20th Century Fox; 1950.
117. *The Night Watch* is one of Rembrandt's most famous paintings, presently housed in the Rijksmuseum, Amsterdam.
118. *La Règle du Jeu*; directed by Jean Renoir; Janus Films; 1939.
119. *"And this is good old Boston,*
    The home of the bean and the cod,
    Where the Lowells speak only to Cabots,
    And the Cabots speak only to God." JC Bossidy.
120. Gianni Versace, 1946-1997. Italian fashion designer to the stars, known for his flamboyantly coloured and patterned clothing.

BARTON BRILEY AND THE NEW MOON

121. "*When the summer rises....*" Poem fragment by the author.
122. *The Hundred-Acre Wood* is a forest in the world inhabited by Winnie-the-Pooh and his friends, as imagined by AA Milne.
123. Stanley Smolak, 1887–1968; founder and builder of the Legs Inn Restaurant in Cross Village.
124. The Tunnel of Trees extends along State Road M119, famous for its groves of second-growth forest, and breathtaking views of Lake Michigan.
125. *When the Moon was High: Memoirs of Peace and War 1897-1942*; Ronald Tree; 1975; MacMillan.
126. An ouroboros is an ancient symbol first known in Egypt, and used in Greece and the Middle Ages, of a dragon or serpent, eating its own tail, and thus creating a unity of past & present.
127. The Haute-Saône is a department of Franche-Comté, in the northeast of France.
128. *Where the Wild Things Are*; Maurice Sendak; 1963; Harper & Row; New York.

A BLOODY GOOD TIME AT THE BAR

129. "*I should like a very dry martini....*" Spoken at the Ritz Bar, Paris. No, I am not going to tell you who was with me.
130. "*Only wise men know the art of eating....*" Jean-Anthelme Brillat-Savarin, 1755-1826. Considered by many to be the father of modern gastronomy.
131. M Henry is a restaurant in the Andersonville neighbourhood of Chicago, famed for its breakfast.
132. Ann Sather's Restaurant in Lakeview is famed for its Swedish style cooking and its cinnamon rolls.
133. Stoke-on-Trent; Staffordshire, England; locally known as 'The Potteries' for the quality of its ceramics; home to Wedgwood, Spode, Minton, Royal Doulton, et al.
134. Pewabic Pottery, founded in 1903 in Detroit, is one example of the revitalisation of traditional Ojibwe ceramics; their pottery is displayed at the Musée du Louvre.
135. Maria Montoya Martinez; 1887-1980; renowned potter from the San Ildefonso Pueblo in New Mexico; she and her husband Julian revitalised the production of black-on-black indigenous pottery.
136. *A Farewell to Arms*; Ernest Hemingway; 1929; Charles Scribner's Sons; New York.
137. *The Old Man and the Sea*; Ernest Hemingway; 1952; Charles Scribner's Sons; New York. Considered by many to be his finest literary work, including myself. In a word: flawless.
138. *For Whom the Bell Tolls*; Ernest Hemingway; 1940; Charles Scribner's Sons; New York. All of the tragedy of the Spanish Civil War is captured in this poignant, painful story.
139. Nancy "Slim" Keith, Lady Keith; 1917-1990. American socialite and fashion icon; former friend of Truman Capote and a close friend of Ernest Hemingway.

140. The Villa d'Este is the former summer villa of the Este family, outside Rome; built 1550-1572; famous for its extensive water gardens and sculptural features. I was once photographed on the terrace, rather scandalously clad in fuchsia & turquoise Capri pants.
141. The Twisted Spoke in Chicago is a famed biker's hangout, known for their *incredible* Bloody Mary cocktails and weekend breakfast menu.
142. *"He who speaks to you of others, will speak to others of you."*
143. Château Greysac Médoc is a Bordeaux wine from the region of the same name; Château Greysac was reintroduced in the early 1970s through the efforts of Baron de Gunzburg.
144. The Villa Rotonda is also known as Villa Almerico or Villa Capra; Vicenza; 1565; Andrea Palladio, architect.
145. The boys, of course, are Young George and Big George
146. The WPA, or Works Progress Administration, was responsible for employing millions of people during the Great Depression, and, as a result, completed many building projects across the country, much of which is still extant.
147. Art Moderne was a stylistic movement in the arts and architecture which emerged in the late 1930s from Art Deco, characterised by long, horizontal lines and curving forms.
148. The Art Deco style in the visual arts emerged in Paris in the 1920s, characterised by bold, geometric shapes, lavish ornamentation, and rich colouring. Sometimes referred to as the Machine Age, in certain areas.
149. The Merchandise Mart was designed in 1930 by Graham, Anderson, Probst &White, on the north bank of the Chicago River. Its lobby murals were created by artist Jules Guérin.

150. Mounted for the wedding of the Dauphin Louis Auguste to Marie-Antoinette, these *feux d'artifice* are generally acknowledged to have been the finest display of fireworks ever to be presented at Versailles, or in the whole of Europe. The country was bankrupt, and the King had merely signed letters of credit for the festivities. At the time of the French Revolution, they had still not been paid for, hence the courtier's prescient remark (see below).
151. The Palace of Versailles, southwest of Paris, was the seat of the French kings from 1664 to 1789; its splendour and magnificence continue to astonish and impress.
152. The Galerie des Glaces, or Hall of Mirrors, is perhaps the most famous room in Versailles, featuring seventeen tall mirrors balanced by windows looking over the gardens.
153. The Water Parterre, or Parterre d'Eau, is a large, paved terrace on the west side of the Palace of Versailles, set with two large reflecting pools lined with bronze statues.
154. The Basin of Apollo at Versailles is the focal point of the palace and gardens; it features a large, oval basin from which the god arises in his chariot, drawn by horses and flanked by dolphins and other sea creatures.
155. Louis XV asked a courtier what he thought of the display. The courtier replied, "Sire, I think they are…*priceless!*"

UNDER THE MILKY WAY TONIGHT

156. "*What fumbling hand....*" Poem fragment by the author.
157. Dominique Francon is the female protagonist of *The Fountainhead*; Ayn Rand; 1943; Bobbs Merrill; New York.
158. *Sic transit gloria mundi*, in Latin, means "Thus passes the glory of the world."
159. *Batterie de cuisine* is a French term, which refers to the equipment in one's kitchen; the American equivalent would be "pots and pans."
160. *Au poivre* is a French culinary term, indicating that the dish has been prepared with a great amount of black pepper.
161. Côtes du Rhône is an AOC in southern France, along the Rhône River, dominated by Grenache and Grenache Blanc.
162. Côtes du Rhône Villages is an appellation in the same region, wherein certain villages may add their name to the label; a famous example would be Châteauneuf du Pape AOC.
163. In the Roman Catholic faith (and others), the Virgin Mary is sometimes addressed as Mary, the Mother of God.
164. Isis was a goddess in ancient Egypt, worshipped as the ideal mother and wife, and patroness of nature and magic; she is acknowledged today by adherents of pre-Christian faiths.
165. Ishtar is the Babylonian goddess of fertility, war, love, and sex, which usually turn out to be the same thing, in the end.
166. Krishna is a Hindu deity, the incarnation of Lord Vishnu; he is manifested, and worshipped, in many forms.
167. Diana is a Roman goddess, the equivalent of the Greek Artemis, presiding over the hunt, the moon, and childbirth (but not necessarily in that order).
168. Hecate is an ancient Greek goddess, often depicted in tripartite form. In modern Wiccan practises, she is considered the patroness of witches.
169. *Mere Christianity*; CS Lewis; 1952; Geoffrey Bles; London.

170. Lincoln Park is a neighbourhood on the north side of Chicago, bordering Lake Michigan and extending, approximately, from North Avenue to Belmont Avenue.
171. Wrigleyville is a neighourhood in Chicago, north of the city, centred around Wrigley Field and its environs. Sometimes confused with Boystown, adjacent to it to the east.
172. *The Nightingale*; Hans Christian Andersen; 1843; CA Reitzel; Copenhagen.
173. Interlochen Centre for the Arts is a performing & dramatic arts school in northern Michigan, located near Traverse City; I have many friends who have studied there.
174. Oberlin Conservatory of Music is the oldest such institution in America; it was also the first to admit female students.
175. In the legendarium of Middle-Earth, the Sun is always referred to as "She." *The Silmarillion*; JRR Tolkien; 1977; George Allen & Unwin; London.
176. "....*Consider the lilies of the field, how they grow; they toil not, neither do they spin.*" *The Gospel of Matthew*; Chapter 6, Verse 28; King James Bible (Cambridge Edition).
177. *Café au lait* is a soft, beige colour, derived from the French coffee preparation of the same name.
178. The Labours of Hercules were twelve tasks, possibly allegorical, which the hero performed as penance for the murder of his children.
179. *"Many a rose-lipped maiden; many a lightfoot lad...."* *A Shropshire Lad*; AE Housman; 1896.
180. Mr Toad's Wild Ride is an attraction at Disneyland Park in Anaheim, California, inspired by the novel *The Wind in the Willows*, adapted by Disney Studios in 1949.
181. Andrea Del Verrocchio, 1435-1488. Italian sculptor, goldsmith and painter; mentor to Leonardo da Vinci.
182. A *mannequin du monde* is a non-professional model, either male or female, who wears couture on the street, as a form of advertising for the *maison*.

183. Davide Cenci is an Italian clothier of exquisitely fashioned yet conservative attire; beautiful, beautiful fabrics and colours. I should consider him the Italian version of Brooks Brothers.
184. Michelangelo Merisi da Caravaggio, 1571-1610, Italian painter noted for his dramatic use of lighting, and his influence upon the Baroque style.
185. The Grateful Dead performed at Cornell University in the summer of 1981; both Joe and I had attended the show.
186. *Some Like It Hot*; directed by Billy Wilder; 1959; United Artists.
187. The Pont d'Iena is the bridge which connects the Eiffel Tower to the Trocadéro and the Chaillot Palace across the Seine river.
188. *The Lotus Eaters*; Alfred, Lord Tennyson; 1832.
189. The Celts were an ethno-linguistic group of societies in Iron Age Europe, surviving into the Mediaeval period, who spoke Celtic languages and shared a similar culture.
190. The Hallstatt culture was the predominant Early Iron Age group in Central Europe from the 8th to 6th centuries BC, commonly linked to Proto-Celtic and Celtic populations to the west.
191. The Urnfield culture preceded the Hallstatt, and is considered the last Bronze Age culture of Europe.
192. The La Tène culture succeeded the Hallstatt in approximately 450 BC and survived until the Roman conquest; it spread throughout much of France, Great Britain, and Ireland.
193. *The Walrus and the Carpenter*; Lewis Carroll; *Through the Looking-Glass*; 1871; Macmillan; London.
194. *Under the Milky Way*, performed by The Church; *Starfish*; 1988; Mushroom Records.

WHERE THE WILD THINGS ARE

195. *"Come, my lover, my spirit*
   To dance in the starry night
   For it is in the nature of things
   That we must find ourselves
   And in the wind, on the grasses
   Which calls to us
   Will you answer?
   Will you come with me, before the sunrise?" An excerpt from my forthcoming book *Exodus: The Collected Poems*.
196. Humboldt Park is a neighbourhood on the northwest side of Chicago; there are many fine houses there, and a large park.
197. The Arts & Crafts Style in Chicago, although it originated in England, flourished in its residential neighbourhoods via the bungalow, a long, low type of house with a pronounced roof, brick walls, and art-glass windows. In many ways, it is a precursor to the Prairie Style as developed by Wright.
198. Frank Baum's house has since been demolished.
199. William Morris, 1834-1896, was one of the earliest proponents of the Arts & Crafts movement in England; many of his textile patterns are still available today.
200. *The Second Coming*; William Butler Yeats; *Michael Robartes and the Dancer*; 1921; publisher unknown.
201. In northern Michigan, roads are usually named by their destination; the East Jordan Road thus applies to both M66 and M32, depending on one's origin of travel.
202. *My Bodyguard*; directed by Tony Bill; 1980; 20th Century Fox.
203. Puddleglum the Marshwiggle is a central character in *The Silver Chair*; CS Lewis; 1953; Geoffrey Bles; London.
204. *Service with a Smile*; PG Wodehouse; 1961; Simon & Schuster; New York.
205. Short's Brewing Company in Bellaire sells 'Hangin' Frank' pale ale, named after Frank Fochtman, who hanged himself in the basement.

206. The Dominican Order, or Order of Preachers, is sometimes referred to, in England, as the Blackfriars, because of their black cloaks worn over their white habits.
207. The Order of Conventual Franciscan Friars of Great Britain and Ireland, so named for their grey habits.
208. The Dogman has been reported numerous times in Michigan and Wisconsin; he is a creature not to be trifled with.
209. The deer carcass incident was reported in *Greater Milwaukee Today* in November 2006.
210. While on holiday in Dana Point, California, I was approached by a Great White Shark, who invited me to enter the water and travel with him; I refused. Still one of the most hair-raising shamanic experiences I have had.
211. The Buddhist Goddess of Mercy is sometimes addressed as Kwan-Yin, spellings variant.

ET LA POMME LUI DIT, MERCI

212. Traditional mealtime prayer.
213. *La Promenade de Picasso*; Jacques Prévert; 1949. The artist goes for a walk, and meets an apple he cannot refuse. *Bite me.*
214. North Central Michigan College is the state's twelfth community college, founded in 1958 in Petoskey.
215. *Architecture: Form, Space and Order*; Francis DK Ching; 1975; John Wiley & Sons; New York.
216. *To an Athlete Dying Young*; AE Housman; *A Shropshire Lad*; 1896.
217. *Aftermath: The Poems for Jane*; Sanjay R Singhal; 2009; Amazon; New York.
218. In Greek mythology, the maiden Arachne was punished by the goddess Athena, not for her skill as a weaver, but for setting herself equal to her, thus becoming the world's first spider.

THE ITINERANT TRAVELLER

219. *"Upon a distant road...."* Poem fragment by the author.
220. *You've Got to be Carefully Taught*; Richard Rodgers & Oscar Hammerstein II; *South Pacific*; 1949.
221. *The Winter's Tale*; William Shakespeare; 1623.
222. *A View from the Bridge*; Arthur Miller; 1955.
223. Shakti, in the Hindu pantheon, is the Great Divine Mother, the personification of the divine feminine, in its aspect of creativity.
224. Kali is the Hindu goddess of time, and change.
225. Vishnu the Preserver is the supreme god of the Hindu pantheon. He is one of the Trimurti, along with Brahma the Creator and Shiva the Destroyer.
226. Narayana is an incarnation of Krishna, as an avatar of Vishnu.
227. Diana Vreeland once famously said "Pink is the navy blue of India." She probably said it several times, to be honest.
228. In Greek mythology, Zeus fathered the heroes Hercules and Perseus, as well as many others.
229. *"That the sons of God saw the daughters of men that they were fair; and they took them wives of all which they chose. And the LORD said, My spirit shall not always strive with man, for that he also is flesh: yet his days shall be an hundred and twenty years. There were giants in the earth in those days; and also after that, when the sons of God came in unto the daughters of men, and they bare children to them, the same became mighty men which were of old, men of renown."* The Book of Genesis; Chapter 6, Verses 2-4; King James Bible (Cambridge Edition).
230. *"Blessed are they who have not seen, and have yet believed." The Book of John*; Chapter 20, Verse 29; King James Bible (Cambridge Edition).
231. *The Nativity: A Poem* is excerpted from my forthcoming book *Exodus: the Collected Poems*.

232. *Frankenstein; or The Modern Prometheus*; Mary Shelley; 1818; Lackington, Hughes, Harding, Mavor & Jones; London.

233. *Et in Arcadia Ego*, in Latin, is often translated as "Even in Arcadia, I am here," an oblique reference to mortality.
234. Colonel Haathi is a character from *The Jungle Book*; Rudyard Kipling; 1894; Macmillan; London.
235. Haathi is the Hindu word for elephant.
236. *Saignée* is a method of making rosé champagne, commonly used in France; the pink juices are removed from the grapes after the first pressing, and used for champagne.

A DEATH IN THE FAMILY

237. *Hail Mary Full of Grace*; RC prayer; fragment.
238. Pop Art emerged in Britain in the mid-1950s, utilising images from popular culture, hence the name.
239. *The Chronicles of Narnia*; CS Lewis; 1953; Geoffrey Bles; London.
240. *Yellow Submarine*; The Beatles; Apple Records; 1969.
241. *The Lord of the Rings*; JRR Tolkien; 1954-55; George Allen & Unwin; London.
242. *The Hobbit*; JRR Tolkien; 1937; George Allen & Unwin; London.
243. *The Space Trilogy*; CS Lewis; 1938-45; The Bodley Head; London.
244. *The Last Battle*; CS Lewis; 1956; The Bodley Head; London.
245. *En Plein Air* in French, means "In the open air"; a term used to denote paintings done out of doors, Claude Monet being a notable example.
246. *Frei lebt wer sterben kann,* in German, means "Freely lives those who may yet die"; a famous line of verse from the former Swiss national anthem.

THE LADY OF SHALOTT

247. *"Out flung the web...." The Lady of Shalott*; Alfred, Lord Tennyson; 1833; publisher unknown.
248. In Greek mythology, Medusa, one of the Gorgons, had snakes for hair; the sight of her would turn one to stone.
249. *The Moments of Happiness* from *Four Quartets*; TS Eliot; 1943; Harcourt; New York.
250. *Pomp and Circumstance, Opus 39*; Sir Edward Elgar; 1901.
251. Lansdowne Estate in Lake Bluff, Illinois was designed by noted Chicago architect Benjamin Marshall in 1911.
252. *Leave Right Now*, performed by Will Young; *Friday's Child*; 2003; BMG Records.
253. An embouchure is the term used for the mouthpiece of a flute, or another similar instrument.
254. *Trio Number Two in E-Flat Major for Piano, Violin, and Violoncello, D929*; Franz Schubert; 1827. Commonly known as the *Trio in E-Flat Major*; used in the film *The Hunger*.
255. In Greek mythology, the heel of Achilles was the only vulnerable part of his body, dipped in the River Styx by his mother, the sea-nymph Thetis. She held him by the heel, thus forming the one area where he could be injured or, as it turned out, struck by an arrow.
256. The Fortress of Solitude, in the legendarium of Metropolis, is the arctic retreat of Superman, used as a place of refuge, and known only to himself and a few, close friends.
257. *"When I was a child, I spake as a child, I understood as a child, I thought as a child: but when I became a man, I put away childish things."* The First Letter of Saint Paul to the Corinthians; Chapter 13, Verse 11. King James Bible (Cambridge Edition).
258. *Adjö Means Goodbye*; Carrie A Young; 1966; publisher unknown.

Made in the USA
Lexington, KY
19 January 2016